Microsoft 365 Word Tips and Tricks

Discover top features and expert techniques for creating, editing, customizing, and troubleshooting documents

Heather Ackmann

Bill Kulterman

BIRMINGHAM—MUMBAI

Microsoft 365 Word Tips and Tricks

Copyright © 2021 Packt Publishing

Associate Group Product Manager: Rohit Rajkumar
Publishing Product Manager: Rohit Rajkumar
Senior Editor: Sofi Rogers
Content Development Editor: Rakhi Patel
Technical Editor: Joseph Aloocaran
Copy Editor: Safis Editing
Project Coordinator: Manthan Patel
Proofreader: Safis Editing
Indexer: Hemangini Bari
Production Designer: Roshan Kawale

First published: November 2021

Production reference: 3171121

Published by Packt Publishing Ltd.

Livery Place
35 Livery Street
Birmingham
B3 2PB, UK.

ISBN 978-1-80056-543-2

www.packt.com

To my husband, Alan Ackmann, for your never-ending love and support. And to my mother, who will buy this book and never read it, thank you.

– Heather Ackmann

To my wife, Marilee Kulterman, thanks you for all your love and support, and putting up with me for all these years. I could never have done it without you.

– Bill Kulterman

Foreword

The only thing that's constant when it comes to technology is that people's expectations of technology keep rising with time and as advancements happen. Numerous entertainment surveys have concluded that an average viewer today expects no less than full-color HD content on streaming platforms such as Netflix. As we all know, there's an emerging trend to colorize classic black and white movies and make more and more corrections during post-production. When it comes to new shows and movies, the likes of "Emily in Paris" are shot in 4K UHD from the get-go. If we take a parallel in the context of documents, the world today is similar. People have come to expect documents that are appropriately formatted, collaboration-ready, accessible in various ways, free of spelling and grammatical errors, and that maintain high fidelity across platforms and devices. Be it a resume, an assignment, a technical draft, an e-book, a script, or any kind of professional document, the skilled versus unskilled use of Microsoft Word could have a huge impact on how the content and the author are perceived. Back as an undergraduate student, I once handed a copy of my resume to a recent-grad investment banker friend for proofreading. Within a second, he commented, "you will be rejected." I said, "at least read a few lines before you conclude that." He noted, "I don't need to, all the bullets here are misaligned." Then, he went on to explain how my resume reflected that I don't have an eye for detail, and how it was visible that the points in the resume have no structure or formatting. It was eye-opening for me how the entire conversation revolved around the formatting of the resume and the actual content, that is, my accomplishments, got completely sidelined. This may have been a one-off judgment and there is also no denying that certain industries and sets of people are more serious about this stuff than others, but I got the basic principle – *there is no getting around Microsoft Word skills*. This was true then, and is truer now, with a massive increase in online collaboration over the last few years. The comforting thing though is that Word itself has become much more powerful with time and tons of good news keeps emerging from Microsoft, especially around the Microsoft 365 version of Word. Unlike the perpetual versions, with Microsoft 365 Word, updates are available every month. More important to note is the nature of advancements within these updates. Microsoft is increasingly harnessing advancements in artificial intelligence and machine learning to build complex scenarios and help authors in ways never possible before. The innovation shows conspicuously in features such as Editor and Accessibility Checker, where Word doesn't just act as an authoring tool but assumes the role of an assistant figuring out problems with document content and providing meaningful suggestions to improve it. There are also major advancements to note in collaboration and coauthoring, cloud storage, online templates, and numerous other areas that allow for much faster and richer formatting and exponentially better collaboration than was possible in the past.

In this book, Heather and William have done an incredible job of covering the basic tips and tricks of Word that are relevant for any Word version and have also gone into the relevant details of the latest features and scenarios that Microsoft 365 Word enables. There is a lot going on with Word and it's hard to decide where to start and where to finish when talking about it. In that regard, it's great to see that instead of just creating a feature guide, Heather and William have focused sharply on the must-know things and attacked some very real-life problems that authors face with Word. I really hope that you all will find the content of this book extremely useful in your day-to-day use of Word. For me, as I reviewed chapters of this book, I just wished I had access to it earlier. Maybe I would have made a better first impression on my friend and had an alternate life on Wall Street. Just kidding!

Ramit Arora

Senior PM

Office Experience Organization

Microsoft Corp

Contributors

About the authors

Heather Ackmann is an author, Microsoft Certified Trainer Alumnus, and Microsoft MVP. Since 2006, she has designed, authored, and narrated over 300 hours of video-based training for a variety of public and private entities. In 2016, she cofounded AHA Learning Solutions to provide high-quality custom learning materials to educational institutions and businesses nationally. She is an active member of the presentation community and a proud member of the Presentation Guild. You may find her sharing advice and Microsoft Office news on Twitter (@heatherackmann). When she is not teaching, she is herself a student and is currently finishing an MS degree in human computer interaction at DePaul University.

> *I want to thank my friends at the Presentation Guild (Echo Swinford, Stephy Hogan, Nolan Haims, Chantal Bossé, Sheila Robinson, Julie Terberg, Glenna Shaw, Sandy Johnson, Rick Altman, and so many others), and my fellow Microsoft MVPs for their help and guidance over the years, especially Ed Liberman, Dan Rey, Doug Spindler, and Beth Melton. I especially want to thank Bill Kulterman for saying yes and for being so easy to work with, and to thank the greatest CEO I've ever had the privilege to work with: Scott Skinger. My career would not be what it is today without your support, encouragement, and constant never-ending improvement.*

Bill Kulterman is an e-learning content author who has been involved with software education for many years. Focusing mainly on the Microsoft ecosystem, the last several years, he has spent most of his efforts on creating video training for SharePoint and the Power Platform. Recently, Bill has turned his attention to HR training, starting a UK-based training company specializing in generational and gender bias training, but MS Office will always be dear to his heart. When not teaching, Bill can be found either making cheese or relaxing beside his koi pond.

I would like to thank Ben "Coach" Culbertson. I would never have become an educator without his help and mentoring. I would also like to thank Scott Skinger for giving me an opportunity and launching my career in E-Learning. Big thanks also to Heather Ackmann, J. Peter Bruzzese, Tim Duggan, Aaron Quigley, Steven Fanizza, Georgia Delis, and all the people who never thought I would amount to anything. Lastly, thanks to Graham Parkinson, RIP brother.

About the reviewers

Ramit Arora is a senior product manager for Microsoft 365 Consumer Growth at Microsoft. He holds a BS in computer science from the University of Illinois, Urbana-Champaign, and has worked on various areas of Microsoft 365 Word, Excel, and PowerPoint applications. Ramit has driven initiatives in many important Office areas, such as Licensing and Activation, VB, Fonts, Office Collab, and so on, and is best known for his work on Office for Mac and mobile applications. You can find Ramit on Twitter and other forums interacting with customers about Microsoft 365. Ramit advises various start-ups on growth hacking, digital distribution, and App Store optimization and co-teaches an Intro PM course on Udemy with Dean Slawson, ex-Director of PM, MSR.

Stephy Hogan is two parts designer, two parts developer, three parts perfectionist, and one part impatient mother. She's a founding board member of the Presentation Guild, works on a UX team by day, runs the Accessible Design Lab and Maker Science Lab channels on YouTube, teaches how to design accessibly to anyone who will listen, and loves glitter. Once, she drove through a tire fire on a golf cart because it was part of her job as a chemist. Now she enjoys making typically mundane experiences a lot more fun – like sitting through an 80-slide benefits presentation, dealing with that really crappy website, or reading this bio.

Table of Contents

Section 2: Making Sense of Formatting Short and Long Documents

8
Saving Time and Ensuring Consistency with Styles

9
Working Faster with Automation

10

Working with Illustrations, Charts, and Tables

11

Writing for Everyone – Understanding Document Accessibility

Section 3: Help! Word Is Being Strange! Troubleshooting Common Problems

12
Formatting Problems – Too Much Space

13
Transforming Annoying Automation

14

Fixing Frustrating Numbers and Bullet Lists

15

Stuck Like Glue – Word's Deceptively Simple Paste Options

Other Books You May Enjoy

Index

Preface

Microsoft Word is a popular word processing program for document creation, editing, formatting, printing, and online collaboration. Business professionals use Microsoft Word to create, edit, format, read, print, and collaborate on short and long documents at home, at work, and while on the go. Business professionals working with Microsoft Word will be able to put their knowledge to work with this practical guide. The book provides a simple problem and solution-based approach to implementation and associated methodologies that will have you up and running and productive in no time.

Who this book is for

This book was written for business professionals who use Microsoft 365 Word on Windows 10. Many screenshots, therefore, reflect the options and actions available for Microsoft 365 subscription Word users on Windows rather than on Mac or mobile devices. We do, however, provide notes and alternate directions if steps vary greatly or are missing on Mac versions. You can find some tips for using Word on mobile devices in *Chapter 1, There Is No One Word*.

What this book covers

Chapter 1, There Is No One Word, covers the difference between versions of Word for Windows, Mac, and mobile, and how these versions impact certain collaboration and sharing features and the basic look and feel of the user interface.

Chapter 2, Working with Others Remotely, explains how to share and collaborate, both locally and remotely, and how to save and recover files.

Chapter 3, Reviewing Documents Remotely, explains how to collaborate better by tracking changes, commenting, replying, and mentioning team members. You will also learn how to best view, compare, and combine changes.

Chapter 4, Concentrating Better with Microsoft Word, contains tips and tricks for using features of Microsoft 365 Word, such as the Immersive Reader, Dictate, and the Focus View, to help you focus your attention while reading and writing documents.

Chapter 5, Working with Short Documents, covers essentials and tips for writing short everyday kinds of documents faster with Office templates and Quick Parts.

Chapter 6, Lists and Characters, explains how to effectively use lists and custom list styles, as well as special and hidden characters, such as paragraph marks.

Chapter 7, Structuring Long Documents for Better Organization, covers how to better organize a long document by creating different kinds of breaks, sections, page orientations, and custom headers and footers so your readers will be able to locate the information they are looking for within the document more quickly.

Chapter 8, Saving Time and Ensuring Consistency with Styles, explains what styles are, which features of Word uses them, how to apply quick styles, and how to create custom styles.

Chapter 9, Working Faster with Automation, makes you rethink automation by using some of Word's built-in features for automating common processes, corrections, procedures, and sequences of commands.

Chapter 10, Working with Illustrations, Charts, and Tables, explains how to add illustrations, how to wrap text around them, and how to anchor them in place.

Chapter 11, Writing for Everyone – Understanding Document Accessibility, explains how to write for the most diverse audience possible by learning to design for document accessibility, how to use the new Accessibility Checker, how to type with your voice, and how to transcribe audio files.

Chapter 12, Formatting Problems – Too Much Space, explains how to troubleshoot common issues that may arise when someone sends you a document that contains unwanted and additional "white" or "blank" space.

Chapter 13, Transforming Annoying Automation, covers how to stop Word from automatically doing, changing, or suggesting things, such as automatically suggesting you should "correct" your name.

Chapter 14, Fixing Frustrating Numbers and Bullet Lists, explores ways to get lists to work the way they were intended to work.

Chapter 15, Stuck Like Glue – Word's Deceptively Simple Paste Options, discusses copying and pasting text, which sounds like it should be simple. Sometimes it is not. This chapter makes it simple again.

To get the most out of this book

To get the most out of this book, you should have some familiarity with Microsoft Word already. In other words, this book is not intended for total beginners but for people looking to fill the gaps or expand their skills in word processing using Microsoft Word.

Software/hardware covered in the book	Operating system requirements
Microsoft 365 Word (subscription to Microsoft 365)	Windows 10

If you are using the digital version of this book, we advise you to type the code yourself or access the code from the book's GitHub repository (a link is available in the next section). Doing so will help you avoid any potential errors related to the copying and pasting of code.

Download the color images

We also provide a PDF file that has color images of the screenshots and diagrams used in this book. You can download it here: `https://static.packt-cdn.com/downloads/9781800565432_ColorImages.pdf`.

Conventions used

There are a number of text conventions used throughout this book.

`Code in text`: Indicates code words in text, database table names, folder names, filenames, file extensions, pathnames, dummy URLs, user input, and Twitter handles. Here is an example: "If you would like to practice and recreate the preceding example yourself, just open a blank Microsoft Word document and type `=random()`."

Bold: Indicates a new term, an important word, or words that you see onscreen. For instance, words in menus or dialog boxes appear in **bold**. Here is an example: "In the **Show group**, click on the **Navigation Pane check box** to open the **Navigation Pane**."

> **Tips or important notes**
> Appear like this.

Get in touch

Feedback from our readers is always welcome.

General feedback: If you have questions about any aspect of this book, email us at customercare@packtpub.com and mention the book title in the subject of your message.

Errata: Although we have taken every care to ensure the accuracy of our content, mistakes do happen. If you have found a mistake in this book, we would be grateful if you would report this to us. Please visit www.packtpub.com/support/errata and fill in the form.

Piracy: If you come across any illegal copies of our works in any form on the internet, we would be grateful if you would provide us with the location address or website name. Please contact us at copyright@packt.com with a link to the material.

If you are interested in becoming an author: If there is a topic that you have expertise in and you are interested in either writing or contributing to a book, please visit authors.packtpub.com.

Share Your Thoughts

Once you've read *Microsoft 365 Word Tips and Tricks*, we'd love to hear your thoughts! Scan the QR code below to go straight to the Amazon review page for this book and share your feedback.

https://packt.link/r/1800565437

Your review is important to us and the tech community and will help us make sure we're delivering excellent quality content.

Section 1: Working More Efficiently, Together or Alone with Word

In this section, you will learn how to share and collaborate, track changes, and comment, both locally and remotely, as well as how to use Word's navigation and view features to improve concentration and productivity.

This section comprises the following chapters:

1
There Is No One Word

Whether you've been using Microsoft Word every day for years or only occasionally, I can promise you that you haven't seen all that Word can do. Microsoft gives users a variety of choices in how to experience Microsoft Word from a variety of devices and operating systems. Often, with Word, your experience with the app will change based on which version you are using, the operating system, and the device. This chapter is meant to clarify the differences between the many possible options.

This chapter will cover the following main topics:

- How to check your version
- The different versions of Word
- Word for different devices
- Word on different operating systems
- About this book

Before we start learning how to become more proficient in Microsoft Word, we need to figure out which version of Word we are using. There are several options available, and they are all slightly different from each other.

How to check your version

To check which version of Word you are using, open Microsoft Word.

On a PC

Follow these steps to check your Word version on a PC:

1. From the Word **Home** screen, click **Account** in the bottom-left corner of the window.
2. Under the **Product Information** area, in the **About Word** section, you'll find the version and build number.

On a Mac

Follow these steps to check your Word version on a Mac:

1. From the Word **Home** screen, open the **Word** menu.
2. Click on **About Microsoft Word**.

There, you will find the version number and other license information.

Why is this useful? You might be looking for a specific feature or tool that you have heard about from a friend or colleague and discover it doesn't seem to be part of your version of Word. Different versions of Word may have different features. It is important to understand that the subscription and online versions of Word receive product updates sooner than the Classic Word 2019 version. If you are missing something, you might need to update your version, or it simply may not have the latest updates available yet. The following screenshot is an example of the **Product Information** area within Microsoft 365 Word:

Figure 1.1 – Microsoft Word 365 version information

The following screenshot is an example of the **Product Information** area within Word 2019 perpetual version (that is, "Classic Word"):

Figure 1.2 – Classic Word 2019 version information

To look up the update history for your supported version, the best place to go is Microsoft's documentation on the web:

- **Update history (by date)**:

    ```
    https://docs.microsoft.com/en-us/officeupdates/update-
    history-microsoft365-apps-by-date
    ```

- **Office for Mac**:

    ```
    https://docs.microsoft.com/en-us/officeupdates/update-
    history-office-for-mac?redirectSourcePath=%252fen-
    us%252farticle%252fUpdate-history-for-Office-2016-for-Mac-
    700cab62-0d67-4f23-947b-3686cb1a8eb7
    ```

On these Microsoft web pages, you will find the most up-to-date information for changes and releases as they are rolled out. But to help you understand what is on these pages, you need to know a little about the various versions of Word out there.

The different versions of Word

In the next few sections, we'll take a look at the various versions of Word that you may or may not have used, starting with Microsoft 365 Word.

Microsoft 365 Word

Microsoft 365 is a subscription-based service that includes the Microsoft Office suite of apps, which Word is a part of. There are several different subscription packages available, but all of them include some version of Word. There are subscription packages that are geared toward business, education, and home users.

Click-to-Run

The Click-to-Run version of Office installs Word locally on your computer. This allows you to use Word at any time, regardless of whether you are on the internet. The Click-to-Run version is available with all Microsoft 365 subscription packages, except for the Microsoft 365 Business Basic package. The Microsoft 365 Business Basic package only comes with the web and mobile versions of the Office apps.

If paying monthly or annually for a software package that continually updates is not something you want or need, you might want to consider the latest perpetual version of Word.

Word 2019

Word 2019 is the latest classic or perpetual version of the Word app. For those of you who have been using Microsoft Word for many years, this will be the purchase option you are most familiar with. You buy the software once, license it for a computer or device, and then can keep using it so long as that software is supported – in other words, perpetually. You don't need to purchase both a Microsoft 365 subscription for Office apps and the perpetual Office apps; you just need one version to use Office.

Do keep in mind, however, that the perpetual apps do not come with the same features or perks that the Microsoft subscription apps get. For example, the Word 2019 perpetual version will occasionally get security updates, but not get any new feature updates. Those on a Microsoft 365 subscription will get new features as they are released. Also, Word 2019 perpetual users do not have access to features that require Microsoft **artificial intelligence** (**AI**), such as the LinkedIn Resume Assistant and the new Editor in Word. Those advanced features are only available with a subscription since they require access to Microsoft AI services and ongoing updates. For many users, however, the Word 2019 perpetual version is more than enough. It is familiar and offers all the word processing power they require.

Older versions

There are many prior versions of Word that are still popular and in use; however, not all of them may be supported. Microsoft ended support for Office 2010 on October 12, 2020. These applications will still work, but they no longer receive any security updates. So, if users continue to use these outdated applications, they potentially expose themselves to security vulnerabilities. Using these outdated applications is incredibly risky, and we advise you to update to a supported version immediately.

Word for different devices

Word travels with you on a variety of mobile devices, which means Word has to adapt to a variety of different screen sizes and situations, as well as connectivity scenarios.

Word for the Web and mobile

All Microsoft 365 subscription packages come with the web and mobile versions of the Office suite, which includes Microsoft Word. Word for the Web is an online-only version of Word that is not as full-featured as the Click-to-Run version, while the Word mobile app can be installed on Android and iOS mobile devices.

Word for the Web

Word for the Web is a free, browser-based version of the app, and you must have a working internet connection to use it. You do not need a Microsoft 365 subscription to access Word for the Web, but you do need a free Microsoft account to log in. Word for the Web receives the latest product updates automatically, so you can be assured that you will be using the latest version. This is different from Word 2019, which receives updates much less frequently.

Word Mobile

Microsoft Word is currently available for download through the Apple App Store and Google Play Store, as well as several Android stores. Even though the app is free to use, signing in with a Microsoft account or a subscription account will allow you to store files in the cloud and access files on your desktop. With a Microsoft 365 subscription, the mobile app will have more features available, such as **Track Changes**, as well as the ability to add and edit chart elements, edit headers and footers, insert section and page breaks, and more. So, if you plan on editing documents from your mobile device or tablet, having a Microsoft 365 subscription is an advantage. The following screenshot shows what Microsoft Word looks like on an iOS device:

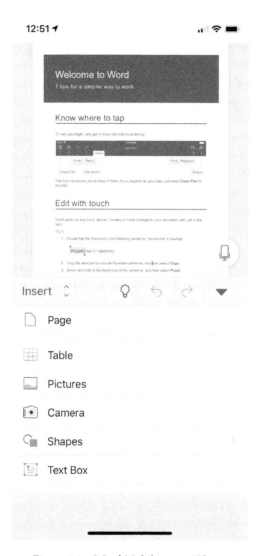

Figure 1.3 – Word Mobile on an iPhone

Now, compare this to Word Mobile on an Android phone:

Figure 1.4 – Word Mobile on an Android phone

Word Mobile is not limited to phones. You can also run Word Mobile on tablet devices. The following screenshot shows Word Mobile on an Android tablet:

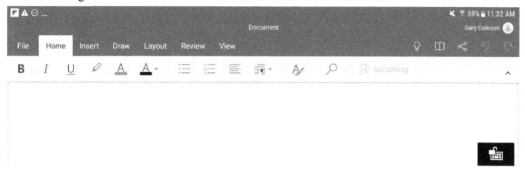

Figure 1.5 – Word Mobile on an Android tablet

Upon comparing these Android devices, even though both are running on the same operating system, we can see that the device sizes determine the look and layout of the interface. On a phone, all the buttons and commands appear at the bottom of the screen, making it easier to tap commands with your thumbs, while on a tablet, all the commands and buttons appear at the top of the screen, making it easier to tap with your index finger.

Word on different operating systems

In addition to Word changing its appearance with new updates and features being added every year, Word will also look different depending on what operating system you are using. Working on a Windows device or a Mac will have a subtle impact on how Word looks and behaves.

Word on a Mac

In addition to the different purchasing options for Office, you can also download either a Windows-based version of Office or Office for Mac. If you have a Microsoft 365 subscription, you get access to both Mac and PC versions of Office. Word, for either PC or Mac, is essentially the same, though it will look and act slightly differently, depending on its host operating system. If you buy a perpetual version of Word, you can choose whether to buy a PC version or a Mac version, so be careful which version you choose.

Differences in user interfaces

Take a look at the following screenshots of Microsoft Word. They are using the same subscription but on different operating systems – one has been taken of Word for Mac, while another has been taken of Word on a Windows PC. The first screenshot shown is of the Mac version of Word:

Figure 1.6 – Word for Mac user interface

Notice the ribbon, menu, and title bar at the top of the screen and compare this screen to the Windows version of Word:

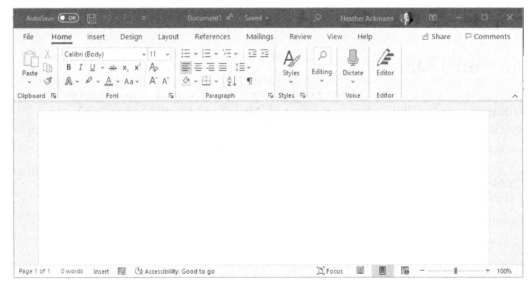

Figure 1.7 – Microsoft 365 Word on Windows 10

On the PC version of Word, you will not have any of those menus at the top. Instead, you will find a **File** menu in the top left-hand corner of the screen that will open a kind of backstage view. In this view, you will find options and controls for both your document and your copy of Word:

Figure 1.8 – The backstage view

On the **Account** tab, you'll find all your account information. On the **Options** tab, you can open a window and find more advanced Word options. From here, you can even send feedback to Microsoft about things you like or dislike about the application. All these options look quite different on the Mac version.

Differences in features

On occasion, you may notice features available on the PC version of Word that are not available on every Mac version. A prime example of this is embedding fonts in documents, which has been available for many past versions of Word on PC but has only become recently available on Word for Mac for the Office 2019 and Microsoft 365 versions. So, if you are using an older version of Office, that particular feature may not be available.

On Word for Mac 2016 (version 16.16.27), inside the **Save Options** window (**Word menu > Preferences > Save**), you will see that there isn't an option to embed fonts anywhere in this window. If you are a Visual Basic developer, there are also differences in the object model between Mac and Windows versions of Office, so some macros may need to be rewritten or may not run at all on Mac:

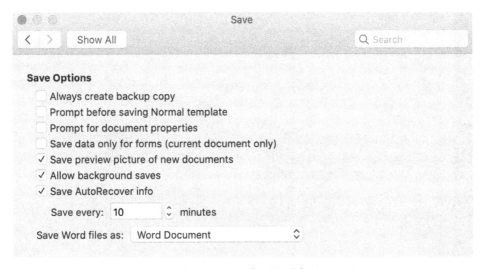

Figure 1.9 – Save Options for Word for Mac 2016

Now, compare this to the Microsoft 365 Word for Mac version:

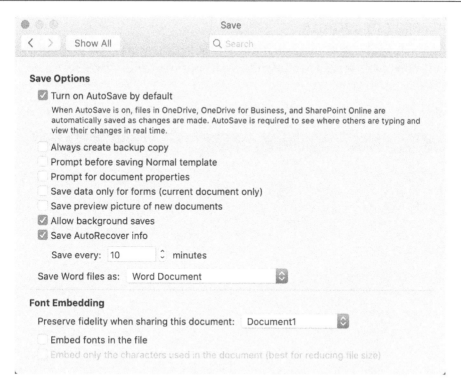

Figure 1.10 – Save Options for Microsoft 365 Word for Mac

At the bottom of the **Save Options** window in the Microsoft 365 version of Word for Mac, there is a new section for **Font Embedding**.

So, the version of Word will determine what features you have and when you will receive updates. The operating system will determine where features are located, how those features look, and, to a lesser extent, how those features behave.

So, as you can see, the differences within operating systems may be based on the version rather than the operating system. As such, you need to know what version of Word you and others (as well as books and help articles) are using. In the next section, we will explain a bit more about the version we will be using throughout this book.

Differences in Appearance

To make matters slightly more confusing, you may notice that your copy of Microsoft 365 Word on Windows 10 may look different from your friend's or coworker's copy of Microsoft 365 Word on Windows 10.

Have a look at the following screenshot:

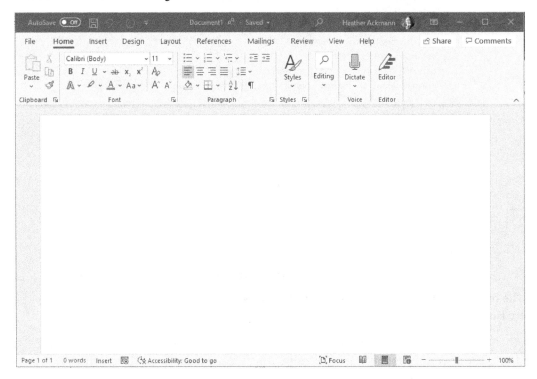

Figure 1.11 – Microsoft 365 Word on Windows 10

Notice the buttons and appearance of the Ribbon. Also, notice the Quick Access Toolbar in the upper left-hand corner. Now, compare the preceding image to the following image:

Figure 1.12 – Microsoft 365 Word on Windows 10 (Visual Refresh)

These differences are due to an update announced for select Windows 10 and Windows 11 Office apps (which includes Microsoft Word) referred to as Visual Refresh. Although things may look different, most of the functionality has remained the same with subtle differences here and there. With this refresh, Microsoft is trying to keep visual continuity and a consistent user interface between Word no matter which version you have.

The most striking difference you will encounter is that the color of the top bar of Word has changed from its traditional blue, to white, and the Quick Access Toolbar is hidden by default. If you use another theme, such as Dark Grey, then that theme will be consistent across all main Office apps and Windows.

Also, the **Undo** and **Redo** buttons have now moved to the **Home** tab, just before the Clipboard (cut and paste) commands:

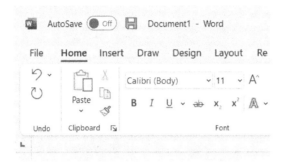

Figure 1.13 – Missing QAT and Undo/Redo Buttons

If you would like to add commands or show the Quick Access Toolbar once again, there is now a menu underneath the Ribbon where you can do just that:

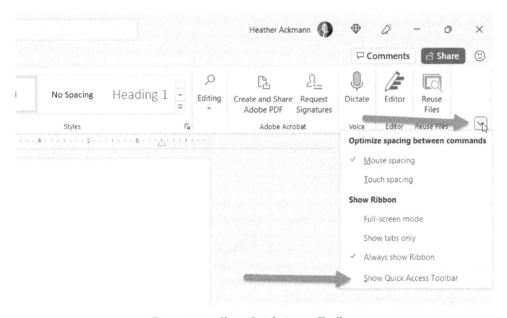

Figure 1.14 – Show Quick Access Toolbar

Just click the **Ribbon Display Options** drop arrow to the bottom right corner of the Ribbon to open a small menu. Towards the very bottom of the menu, you will see an option labeled **Show Quick Access Toolbar**. Select that option and your Quick Access Toolbar will appear as a small arrow either above or below your Ribbon. There, you can click and add commands just like you used to.

Now that we've learned a bit about what version we are using and how different versions of Word may look and act, let's learn how to use this book a bit more.

About this book

In this book, we will be using Microsoft 365 Word on PC for all the screenshots and demonstrations. The advice, tips, and tricks in this book are designed to be helpful regardless of the version of Word you are using. If, however, a piece of advice or a set of instructions do become version-specific, we will offer a version note and any suggestions, like this:

> **Note – Mac Users**
>
> If you are using Word for Mac, this feature is not available yet. If you want this feature, tell Microsoft by either sending a frown or by visiting `http://word.uservoice.com`.

Summary

Microsoft Word has been around since 1983 and has been growing, changing, and adapting ever since. Word is now available on multiple platforms and devices, allowing you to access your documents on the go from any device, regardless of connectivity.

If you are a Microsoft 365 subscriber, you can be assured that you will be one of the first to get the latest updates and features that Word has to offer. If this is not important to you, or your Word usage is minimal, perhaps the perpetual, classic, non-subscription-based option is better for you. Whichever version you choose and use, you will find that Microsoft Word will be a useful tool to learn and have.

In this chapter, we have given you a look at the many versions of Word to help you understand how the version you have will work for you. In future chapters, we will explore how to make the newest features of Word help solve some common everyday productivity problems.

2
Working with Others Remotely (Sharing and Collaboration)

These days, it seems that everything is all about "the cloud." That term can be confusing because it often refers to many different services and platforms. In this chapter, we will be looking exclusively at Microsoft's cloud storage options – specifically, OneDrive, SharePoint, and Teams, and how you can use them to store, access, and collaborate on all your Word documents.

This chapter will cover the following main topics:

- Introduction to cloud storage
- Saving Word documents to the cloud
- Accessing and sharing Word documents, OneDrive, SharePoint, and Teams
- AutoSave
- Retrieving unsaved documents

Introduction to cloud storage

Cloud storage refers to a secure, shared location where files are stored. Once stored, they can then be accessed from anywhere if you have a connection to the internet. Now, documents aren't really stored in a mythical place called "the cloud." They are stored on secure servers all over the world. The Microsoft cloud storage option is called **OneDrive** and it can be used alone or as part of SharePoint or Teams.

Once your files are stored in OneDrive, they are automatically backed up and are accessible from any mobile device that has a connection to the internet. Files stored in OneDrive can be shared with an individual, a group, or your entire organization. Once a document has been shared, you can work with multiple people using the latest collaboration features that Word has to offer, such as tracking changes, reviewing, and commenting. A document that's shared to OneDrive can also be edited by multiple people in real time.

Before cloud storage, files were saved locally, either on your desktop PC or to a local network server. Files saved in this manner could be lost in the event of equipment malfunctioning or other mishaps, such as forgetting to save frequently. Using Word in conjunction with OneDrive helps prevent these kinds of losses.

Once your documents have been saved to OneDrive, you could experience a catastrophic disaster with your computer, and your files would still be safely stored on Microsoft's secure servers.

Microsoft's OneDrive cloud storage protects your files from equipment failures, theft, and human error. It also allows you to collaborate no matter where you are, or what device you are using.

Cloud storage provides a convenient and secure way to save and access your documents. In the next section, we will look at how to use Word to save documents to OneDrive, SharePoint, and Teams.

Saving Word documents to the cloud

When saving a Word document for the first time, you have a variety of options regarding where you can save it. It could be saved locally on your PC or Mac, or in OneDrive, SharePoint, or Teams. Word makes it easy for you to save your document to OneDrive.

When a site is created in SharePoint, the document library is created in the site's OneDrive. Everyone who is a member of that SharePoint site has access to files stored in any libraries that have been created on that site.

When a new team is created in Teams, users can start saving files directly within the Teams chat and Teams channel. These files will then be available to other members of the team to view and edit.

Saving to OneDrive

To save a new Word document to the cloud for the first time, you will want to go to the **File** tab on the far left-hand side of the ribbon. This will open what's known as the **backstage view**. From here, you will see a column of options on the left-hand side of the page, including **Save** and **Save As**. Select **Save As**.

At the top of the page in large letters, you will see **Save As**. Below that, you will see a list of the various places where you can save this document. Typically, you will see a list of your OneDrive accounts. There can be multiple OneDrive for Business accounts and a single personal OneDrive account on the same computer. You will also see any SharePoint sites that you have permissions for listed.

The following screenshot shows the **Save As** page with **OneDrive for Business** selected, as well as the **Documents** folder:

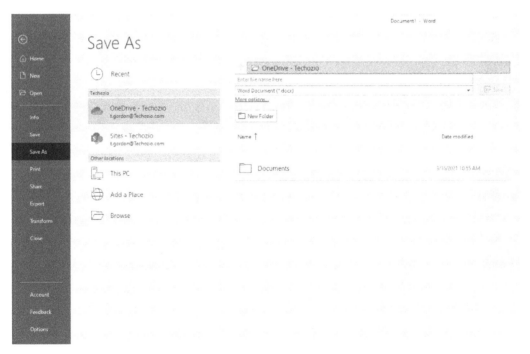

Figure 2.1 – Backstage view of the Save As page with OneDrive selected

Once you choose the specific OneDrive account you wish to save to, you will see a list of folders you have in that OneDrive. Then, you can select the folder you wish to save to or create a new folder using the **New Folder** button.

Once you have selected the specific folder, it will open and show a list of documents saved there. At this point, you will want to make sure that you enter the name of the document in the name field at the top of the screen, where it says **Enter file name here**.

Now, if you click on the **Save** button to the right, your document will be saved to your OneDrive cloud storage, assuming you are connected to the internet. If you aren't, the document will be stored on your computer in the proper OneDrive folder. Once you are connected to the internet again, OneDrive will automatically upload your document to OneDrive in the cloud.

The following screenshot shows the **Save As** page with OneDrive for Business selected, as well as the contents of the **Documents** folder. You can also see the new document's name and the **Save** button:

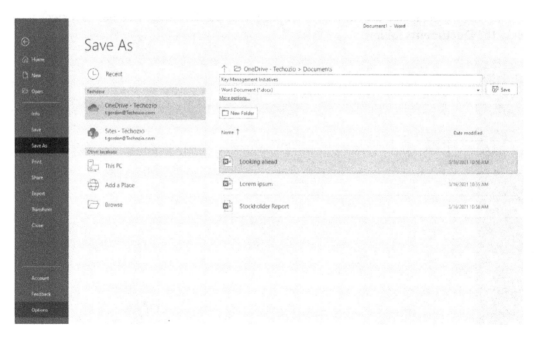

Figure 2.2 – Backstage view with the Documents folder selected and showing files

Next, let's see how to save documents to SharePoint and Teams.

Saving to SharePoint and Teams

Once a document has been saved to SharePoint or Teams, members of the site can access the site either from OneDrive, through the SharePoint site, or within Teams. No matter which app a document is accessed from, any edits will be saved automatically. Only one copy of the document exists, making it much easier for multiple people to collaborate on a file.

If a document has been saved to SharePoint, once edits have been made, SharePoint will save versions of the document. There are many options for versioning in SharePoint, and they can all be set by your SharePoint administrator.

To save a new document to a document library in SharePoint or Teams, you will need to go to the **File** tab on the far left-hand side of the ribbon to open the backstage view. From here, you will want to select **Save As**.

At the top of the page in large letters, you will now see **Save As**. Below that, you will see a list of OneDrive and SharePoint accounts. You can have multiple SharePoint accounts connected to Word. At this point, you will want to select the desired SharePoint account.

Once you've selected a SharePoint account, you will see a list of all the SharePoint sites you are a member of, as well as the Teams sites that have been created in SharePoint. You can now select the desired SharePoint site.

The following screenshot shows a list of SharePoint and Teams sites the user is a member of:

Figure 2.3 – A list of SharePoint and Teams sites

After you have selected a site, you will see the list of document libraries. Select the document library you want; you will see a list of documents already in that folder.

Name the document and select **Save**. The document will now be shared with everyone who is a member of the SharePoint or Teams site.

Sharing a Word document

Microsoft 365 and Word make it easy to share documents within your organization, but you can also share with people externally as well. You simply need to have their email address.

When you decide to share a document saved in OneDrive, there are many options you must consider, such as who has access to the document, and what permissions will they have. Do you want them to be able to edit the document or just read it? Will they be allowed to share the document's link? Sharing is a great feature, but you need to make sure that you understand all the available options.

You can share a document while it's open in Word. The **Share** button appears right above the ribbon, in the top-left corner of the page.

The following screenshot shows the **Share** button in the top-left corner in Word:

Figure 2.4 – The Share button in Word

You can also access the share options in the backstage view by clicking on **Share**. Once you click **Share** in either place, the share dialogue box will appear.

The following screenshot shows the share dialog box in Word:

Figure 2.5 – The share dialog box

The share dialog box allows you to select options for how you want to share the document.

At the top, you will notice that it says **Send link**. This is because that is how the document will be shared. An email will be sent to the recipient with a link to the document in OneDrive.

Next, you will see a box with **Anyone with the link can edit** written inside it. This is the default option and it means that anyone within your organization, as well as people outside of it, who have that link will have access and full editing permissions to the document.

Below this, you will see a space to add recipients. If you are sending to someone within your organization, once you begin to enter their name, the dialog box will search your organization for similar names, and you can simply choose the ones you want. If you plan to send the link to someone outside of your organization, you will need to add their email address manually.

Beneath the recipients list, there is a place to add a message that they will see. This will appear in the body of the email.

Now, you will see the **Send** button. When you click this button, the link will be sent to all the recipients on the list.

You will notice that there is also a button called **Copy link**. Clicking this will copy the link to the clipboard, allowing you to paste it wherever you need to.

At the very bottom of the dialog box is an option called **Send a copy**. If you select this, you will see a pop-up menu with two options: **Word document** and **PDF**.

Selecting the **Word document** option will send a copy of the document as a Word document. Therefore, the recipient will not have access to the original document, only a copy of it.

Selecting the **PDF** option will create a PDF version of the document and send that. This PDF is essentially a read-only version of the document.

Anyone with the link

The **Anyone with the link** option might be exactly what you need, but you also might not want the person you are sharing with to be able to edit the document.

If you want to change this option, you will need to click where it says **Anyone with the link can edit**. This will open the same dialog box but with several more options.

The following screenshot shows the share dialog box with **Anyone with the link** expanded to show all the available options:

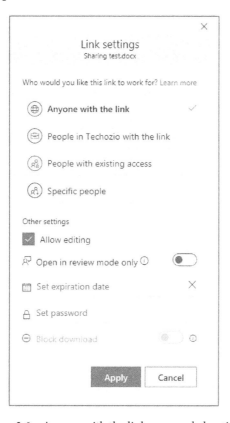

Figure 2.6 – Anyone with the link – expanded options

Further down the dialog box, you will see a checkbox for **Allow editing**. This box is checked by default. If you want to stop people from being able to edit this document, you can uncheck the box.

Below that, you also have the option to **Open in review mode only**. If you select this option, the recipient will only be able to make comments or suggest edits. If they already have edit permissions to the document, this will not prevent them from being able to make edits.

You can also set an expiration date for the link. This option is shown below the **Open in review mode only** button. After a specified date, the link will no longer work.

For even more security, you can set a password for the document. You will find this option near the bottom of the dialog box. When creating a password, it is important to share the password with the intended recipient so that they can open the document.

The last item in the dialog box is the **Block download** option. By default, this will be grayed out. To be able to enable this option, you must uncheck the **Allow editing** checkbox. Once you've done this, you can click the **Block download** button to enable it. This will prevent people from downloading a copy of the document.

Once you have selected the options you want, click the **Apply** button at the bottom; all your choices will be saved.

People in (your organization) with the link

The second option in the dialog box is **People in (your organization) with the link**. This means that only people in your organization who are signed in with their organization credentials will be allowed access to the document using the link. If somebody shares the link with someone outside of your organization, that person will not be able to access the document.

If this option is selected, you will also see the **Allow editing** checkbox, the **Open in review mode only** button, and the **Block download** button.

The following screenshot shows the share dialog box with the **People in (your organization) with the link** option selected:

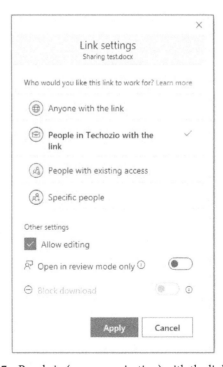

Figure 2.7 – People in (your organization) with the link selected

People with existing access

The third option in the share dialog box is **People with existing access**. This means only people who already have access to this document can use the link – for example, sharing a document that is in an already shared folder with someone who has access to that folder. They already have access to the document, but they might not realize that it exists. This option can only be used by people within your organization and has no additional options.

The following screenshot shows the **People with existing access** option selected:

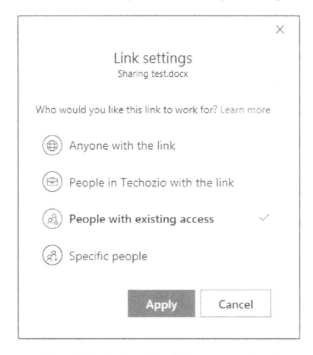

Figure 2.8 – People with existing access selected

Specific people

The final option is **Specific people**. This option is best used when you want to limit who has access to the document. Only the people who you have identified by adding their names and email addresses will be able to use this link. This is also a great option to use for sharing outside of your organization. It will ensure that the link will not work if those recipients send it to others.

The **Specific people** option also provides the **Allow editing** checkbox, the **Open in review mode only** button, and the **Block download** button.

The following screenshot shows the **Specific people** option:

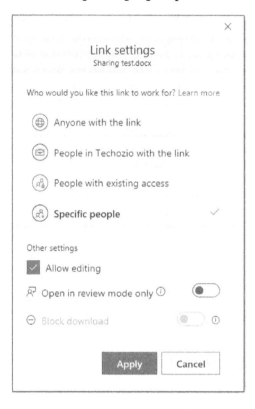

Figure 2.9 – Specific people selected

There are many options to consider when sharing a document, especially if the document contains sensitive or confidential material. These sharing options are the same throughout all of Microsoft 365.

> **Important note**
>
> It is important to note that you may not see all these options in your organization. These sharing options can be modified or even disabled by your organization if they feel the need to do so for security reasons.

The ability to share and collaborate, and the many ways we can access our files, is what makes Microsoft 365 so powerful. Next, we will talk about how to access documents in OneDrive, SharePoint, and Teams.

Accessing and sharing Word documents, OneDrive, SharePoint, and Teams

Once you have saved a document to OneDrive, it will be available anywhere, at any time, on any device, so long as you have a connection to the internet. You can log in to your Microsoft 365 account, or a personal Microsoft account, and access your OneDrive using any of the four most popular browsers; that is, Edge, Chrome, Firefox, and Safari.

On a desktop or laptop, you can use the OneDrive Sync app to sync some or all of your OneDrive folders to your computer. The Sync app is available for both PC and Mac. Microsoft also has OneDrive mobile apps for both Android and iOS.

Wherever you are, and no matter what device you use, any edits made to a Word document saved in OneDrive will be saved across all your devices. If you are not connected to the internet, the edits will be saved locally and once you are connected, your edits will be synced automatically. This is also true of any shared documents in OneDrive.

Word will also save a version history of your documents that have been saved in OneDrive. This version history can be accessed from the backstage view in the **Info** section.

SharePoint and Teams

Accessing Word documents from SharePoint and Teams can also be accomplished from a browser or mobile app. Both are part of Microsoft 365 and have mobile apps.

Once you are on the desired SharePoint site, you will need to find the document library where the document is stored. Then, you can select and open it using either Word Online, the Word desktop app (if you have it installed), or the Word mobile app.

The following screenshot shows the backstage view of Word and a selected SharePoint document library containing Word documents:

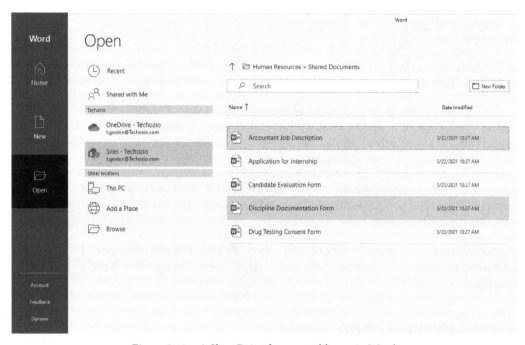

Figure 2.10 – A SharePoint document library in Word

Although Teams uses both SharePoint and OneDrive to store documents, accessing documents within Teams is a different experience than SharePoint. Unlike SharePoint, Teams has its own desktop app. You can go directly to the SharePoint site created by Teams to access your documents, but Teams has many good, collaborative features and is a great way to share files.

To access documents in Teams, you will need to select the correct team and channel. Each Teams channel will have a **Files** section. Once you select the **Files** section, you may see files, file folders, or both listed. You can then select the desired document to open it.

The following screenshot shows the **Files** section in the Teams desktop app:

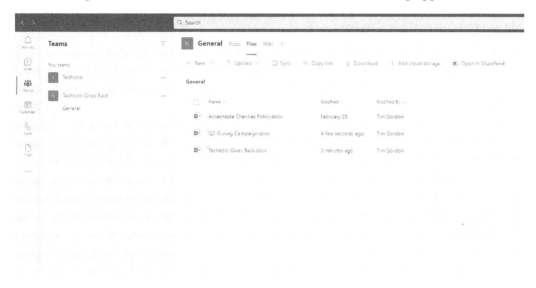

Figure 2.11 – The Files section in the Teams desktop app

When you open a Word document in either the Teams desktop app or Teams online, the document will open in Word online, within the Teams app.

The following screenshot shows a document open for editing in Word online, within the Teams desktop app:

Figure 2.12 – Word Online in the Teams app

Cloud storage, specifically OneDrive, has made it possible for us to collaborate seamlessly wherever we are. In this next section, we will see another great feature that has also been made possible by OneDrive: AutoSave.

AutoSave

AutoSave is a wonderful feature designed to help save you from that "oops" moment when you close a document and afterward, you realize that you've forgotten to save your work. You might be able to recover some of those lost changes, but you might not get them all, which can cause you to lose many hours of work. With **AutoSave**, you never have to fall victim to this again.

When working with a document in Word for the Web, any edits that are made are saved automatically by default, and you have no choice about it. Word 2019 does not have an autosave feature; you must save any changes manually using the **Save** button.

AutoSave is always on, unless it's not

AutoSave is part of Microsoft 365 Word. When you save a Word document to OneDrive, the **AutoSave** feature of Word is enabled by default. From that moment on, any changes you or your colleagues make to that document will be saved automatically, but this can be turned off.

When you first create a document in Word 365, it is necessary to give it a name and save it somewhere. If you save it to OneDrive, a SharePoint document library, or Teams site, the **AutoSave** feature will be enabled. If you save the document anywhere else, such as a local folder on your computer, you will not have the ability to use **AutoSave**.

AutoSave only works if a document has been saved to OneDrive or SharePoint. This allows **AutoSave** to continuously save as you edit. The same is true if the document has been shared and other users are editing it at the same time. If you decide to turn **AutoSave** off, your edits will not be saved until you turn it back on, or until you save the edits manually using the **Save** button.

The **AutoSave** button can be seen in the top-left corner, above the ribbon. If it is on, you will see that it is filled in white and specifies **On**. If it's off, it will not be filled in and will state **Off**.

The following screenshot shows the **AutoSave** button in the **On** position:

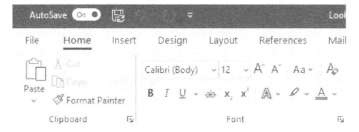

Figure 2.13 – AutoSave on

If **AutoSave** is on, you can rest assured that any edits will be saved without you having to take any action.

Turning AutoSave off

You might be wondering why anyone would want to turn **AutoSave** off. Consider this scenario: you are working on a document that is being shared with colleagues, either in SharePoint or Teams. You are just beginning to work on a new section, or perhaps you want to update an existing one, but the document has been saved at least once, and **AutoSave** is on.

Every change you make to the document is now overwriting the saved version and is being pushed out to anyone else who has access to it. The original is now gone. This could potentially be a bad thing, and this is only one scenario.

If you are not sure that you are ready to overwrite the current document, it is easy to turn off **AutoSave**. All you need to do is click on the **AutoSave** button and it will be turned off until you click it again to turn it on.

Another option would be to save a copy of the document and do your editing there. Once you have finished, you can copy and paste the changes into the original document.

The following screenshot shows the **AutoSave** button in the **Off** position:

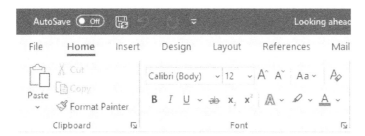

Figure 2.14 – AutoSave off

AutoSave is a truly great feature that can save countless problems, but it can potentially cause them as well. Knowing how **AutoSave** works, as well as how to turn it on and off when necessary, will help you protect your work. Accidents do happen, however, but fortunately, Word can help you retrieve and restore previous versions.

Retrieving unsaved documents

If you haven't saved a document to OneDrive or one of the other cloud options, you might experience a situation where you lose your unsaved documents. Word has an **AutoRecover** feature that can help you avoid such a disaster.

When disaster strikes

There are many reasons why a document's changes could be lost. Word could have experienced a crash, closing suddenly before you saved the document, or your computer could have crashed or lost power, causing you to lose your work. Whatever the reason, Word can help by recovering the changes you made the last time AutoRecover saved the document.

Once you've experienced a crash or lost a document due to Word closing abruptly, you will need to open that document again. At this point, the **Document Recovery** panel should be open on the left, and you should see a list of recovered versions of the document, along with the original, which is the last saved version.

The following screenshot shows the **Document Recovery** panel on the left, showing saved versions of the document:

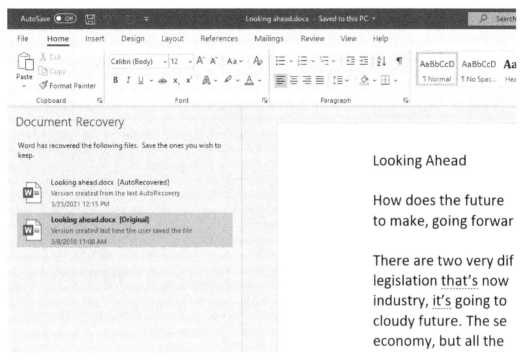

Figure 2.15 – The Document Recovery panel

To recover the document, select the most recent version. You should see the date and time beneath the document's title.

Once you click the version you want, it will open. Above the document, you will see a yellow bar across the top of it. You will see the words **RECOVERED UNSAVED FILE** and a blue **Save** button.

The following screenshot shows the yellow **RECOVERED UNSAVED FILE** bar and the **Save** button:

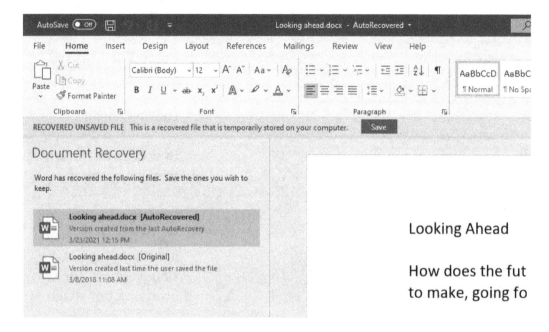

Figure 2.16 – The RECOVERED UNSAVED FILE bar

If this is the version you want to keep, click the blue **Save** button on the yellow bar; Word will save this as the currently saved version.

You might like to save this as a different version of the document, and not make it the current saved version. To save the document, click on the **File** tab; then, from the backstage view, select **Save As**. You will be prompted to save the document in the location of your choice.

If you decide not to save the recovered document, you can simply close the document and choose to delete the recovered file.

Changing AutoRecover settings

By default, Word's AutoRecover feature saves your open documents every 10 minutes to the AutoRecover file location. This is typically located at `C:\Users\[UserName]\AppData\Roaming\Microsoft\Word\`.

It is possible to change both settings.

Changing the AutoRecover interval

To change the AutoRecover interval, follow these steps:

1. Click the **File** tab to go to the backstage view.

2. Near the bottom of the column, on the left, click **Options**.

3. This will open the **Word Options** window. From the column on the left, click **Save**.

4. In the **Save Documents** section, you will see **SaveAutoRecover information every 10 minutes**. Add a new value or use the arrows to increase or decrease the value.

5. Click **OK** at the bottom right to save the changes.

The following screenshot shows the Word Options window open on the **Save** section:

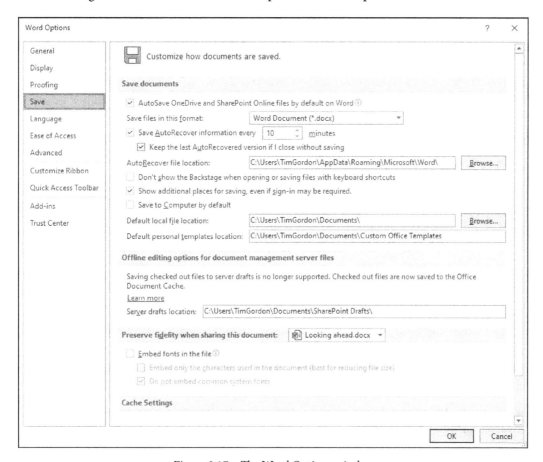

Figure 2.17 – The Word Options window

Changing the AutoRecover location

To change the AutoRecover location, follow these steps:

1. Click the **File** tab to go to the backstage view.

2. Near the bottom of the column on the left, click **Options**.

3. This will open the **Word Options** window. From the column on the left, click **Save**.

4. In the **Save Documents** section, you will see **AutoRecover file location**, as well as a box with the path to where your files are saved. To save to a different location, either type in the desired path or use the **Browse** button on the right to navigate to the desired location.

5. Click **OK** at the bottom right to save the changes.

It's always best to save your documents to OneDrive, but it may not be the right choice for you. If you are not saving your documents to OneDrive, the AutoRecover feature in Word can really help. Remember, though: by default, it only saves every 10 minutes. This may cause you to lose some of your most recent work in the event of an unforeseen incident that causes a loss. Consider shortening the time between save intervals, especially if your system is unstable.

Summary

At the beginning of this chapter, we provided an overview of cloud storage – specifically OneDrive and its impact on sharing and collaboration in Microsoft 365 and Word. We reviewed the benefits of saving to OneDrive and then showed you how to use Word to save documents to OneDrive, SharePoint, and Teams.

Next, we saw how documents can easily be shared with people inside your organization, as well as outside of it. We examined the sharing options and saw that there are ways to limit access to documents, as well as whether they can be downloaded or shared further.

We talked about how to access Word documents saved in OneDrive, SharePoint, and Teams from within Word itself, making it easy to retrieve them from one location. We also saw how when accessing a Word document from the Teams app, Word Online will open within Teams. This makes it easy to review and edit documents within Teams.

AutoSave is another great Word feature made possible by OneDrive. We learned that AutoSave is enabled by default once a document has been saved to OneDrive. AutoSave can be very helpful but may not always be what you need when creating or editing your Word documents, which is why we also showed how it can be turned off if necessary.

Lastly, we explored how Word can help you retrieve unsaved documents with the AutoRecover feature. AutoRecover is set to automatically save open documents every 10 minutes, but we showed you how you can change that interval, as well as how to change where recovered documents are saved. We also looked at how to recover an unsaved document when the worst happens.

In the next chapter, we will explore how to review documents when working collaboratively with others. We will explore how to track changes, view markup, and explain how to use the reviewing pane. You will learn how to compare and combine multiple versions of the same document, and then learn about notes, comments, and how to mention someone to get their attention.

3
Reviewing Documents Remotely

The collaborative features of Microsoft 365 have transformed the way we work today, and being able to work remotely on any device, anywhere, is one of its key features. In the previous chapter, we learned about using Microsoft's cloud storage solution known as OneDrive, and how, by using it to store our documents, we can take advantage of the many collaborative features of Word Online. In this chapter, we will explore how Word makes the task of working with others easier by giving you the tools to give feedback, track changes, and view, compare, and combine documents with colleagues around the globe in real time or whenever. Word truly is a magnificent collaborative tool.

This chapter will cover the following main topics:

- Using Track Changes
- Commenting
- Mentioning others in comments
- Viewing, comparing, and combining changes

Using Track Changes

Track Changes does exactly what its name suggests: it allows you to track the changes that have been made to a document, either by you or by others that the document has been shared with. It can show you the changes that have been made to the document in different colors, some of which are based on each specific author. **Reviewing Pane** shows a list of all the changes and the name of the person who made the change. You can also accept or reject specific changes. However, to make all this happen, you must turn **Track Changes** on.

Turning on Track Changes

To turn on **Track Changes**, you must go to the **Review** tab on the ribbon. Near the center, you will see the **Tracking** section; to the left is the large **Track Changes** button.

The following screenshot shows the **Track Changes** button unselected:

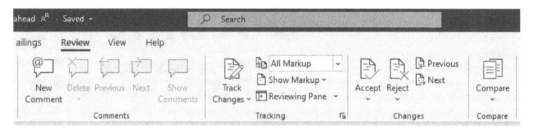

Figure 3.1 – The unselected Track Changes button

The button is divided into two parts, an upper and a lower part. If you click the upper portion, that will turn on **Track Changes**, and from that point on, all changes that are made to the document will be recorded, unless someone turns it off.

The following screenshot shows the **Track Changes** button with the upper portion highlighted:

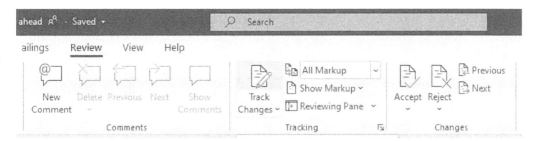

Figure 3.2 – The Track Changes button, with its upper portion highlighted

This brings us to the lower portion of the button. If you click on the lower part of the **Track Changes** button, it will show you two options. One is to simply turn on **Track Changes**, while the second is the option to **Lock Tracking**.

The following screenshot shows the lower **Track Changes** button selected, as well as the **Lock Tracking** option:

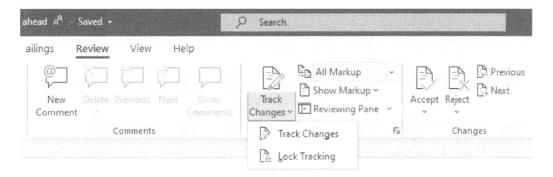

Figure 3.3 – The Lock Tracking option

If you select this option, you will be prompted to create a password, which can prevent others from turning off **Track Changes**.

Once **Track Changes** is on, by default, **All Markup** is selected and you will begin to see any changes that are made to the document highlighted in different colors. Different types of changes will be shown in different colors, and some changes will be a specific color for a particular editor. You will also see a panel on the right that shows formatting changes and the editor's name. In the left margin, you will see marks indicating where there have been insertions and deletions.

The following screenshot shows a document with **Track Changes** on and **All Markup** selected. Two editors have made changes, so we can see the markup in two colors, one for each editor:

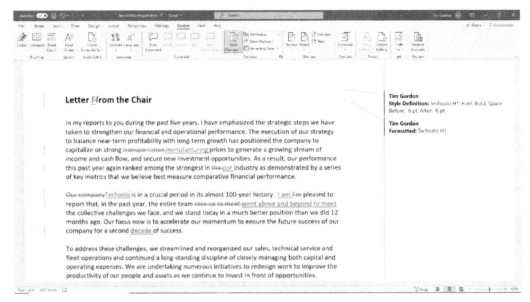

Figure 3.4 – All Markup

To change which markup you see, you will need to select the drop-down arrow to the right of the **All Markup** option. You will then have three additional choices: **Simple Markup**, **No Markup**, and **Original**.

The following screenshot shows these markup menu options:

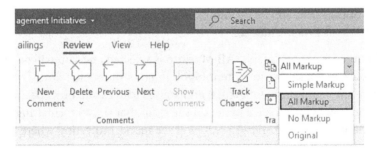

Figure 3.5 – The markup menu

Let's take a look at these in more detail:

- **Simple Markup** will close the panel on the right and show only the changes in the document, as well as the insertion and deletion marks in the left margin.

- **No Markup** will show the document in its current state, with all changes and no markup visible.

- **Original** will show the document in its original state before any changes were made.

Beneath the markup selection box is the **Show Markup** menu. If you click it, you will see a list of options that you can use to customize which types of markup you see.

The following screenshot shows the **Show Markup** menu:

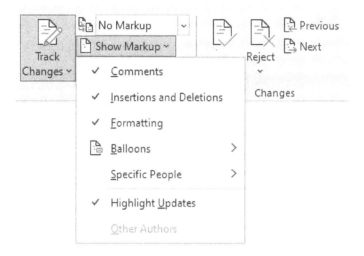

Figure 3.6 – The Show Markup menu

Below the **Show Markup** menu, you will see various options for **Reviewing Pane**. When you click the arrow to the right of this option, you will be presented with the choice of displaying **Reviewing Pane** vertically or horizontally.

The following screenshot shows the **Reviewing Pane** options:

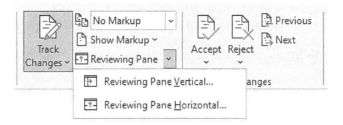

Figure 3.7 – Reviewing Pane options

For this chapter, we will choose to display **Reviewing Pane** vertically, and it will open on the left-hand side of the document. If you choose the horizontal option, it will open at the bottom of the document.

The following screenshot shows **Reviewing Pane** open vertically on the left:

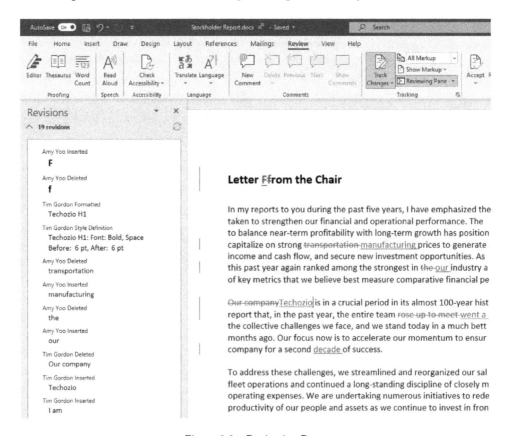

Figure 3.8 – Reviewing Pane

Reviewing Pane displays a list of all the changes that have been made, and which editor made them.

Once a document has been submitted for review, you can go through the changes one by one, and then accept or reject them individually. You can find those options in the **Changes** section of the ribbon. The **Changes** section appears to the right of the **Tracking** section.

The following screenshot shows the **Changes** section of the ribbon:

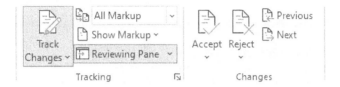

Figure 3.9 – The Changes section

You can advance through these changes by using the **Previous** or **Next** buttons in the **Changes** section. Once you have made your choice, you can click either the **Accept** or the **Reject** button, depending on which action you desire. You will then automatically advance to the next change in the document. Once a change has been accepted or rejected, the markup for that change will no longer be displayed, and it will be removed from **Reviewing Pane**.

Beneath each **Accept** and **Reject** button, there is a small downward pointing arrow. If you select this arrow, it will reveal a menu of additional options for each button. The **Accept** button provides the following options:

- **Accept and Move to Next**: This option accepts the changes and advances you to the next change.

- **Accept This Change**: This option accepts the change and does not advance you to the next change.

- **Accept All Changes Shown**: This option accepts all the changes that are displayed. If you have changed which changes are displayed in the **Show Markup** menu, all changes may not be accepted.

- **Accept All Changes**: This option will accept all the changes in the document.

- **Accept All Changes and Stop Tracking**: This option will accept all the changes in the document and stop tracking changes.

The following screenshot shows the **Accept** options menu:

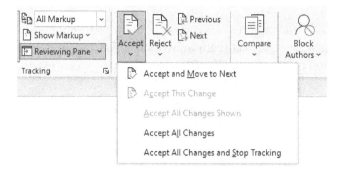

Figure 3.10 – The Accept options menu

Similarly, the **Reject** button provides the following options:

- **Reject and Move to Next**: This option rejects the changes and advances you to the next change.

- **Reject Change**: This option rejects the change and does not advance you to the next change.

- **Reject All Changes Shown**: This option rejects all changes that are displayed. If you have changed which changes are displayed in the **Show Markup** menu, all changes may not be rejected.

- **Reject All Changes**: This option will reject all the changes in the document.

- **Reject All Changes and Stop Tracking**: This option will reject all the changes in the document and stop tracking changes.

The following screenshot shows the **Reject** options menu:

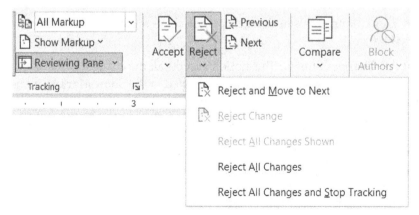

Figure 3.11 – The Reject options menu

Being able to track changes that have been made to a document by multiple editors is a wonderful way to collaborate on a document. **Track Changes** allows us to make decisions about which changes are accepted and rejected, and it can also help us prevent others from turning off **Track Changes**.

Along with tracking changes in a document and showing markup, we can leave comments for other authors. Comments will appear in an expanded right-hand margin, along with information about formatting changes that have been tracked. In the next section, we will look at how to work with comments in a document.

Commenting

Commenting in Word is a great way for collaborators to communicate questions, feedback, and other comments to each other directly in the document. A comment can be added to a particular passage or section, and others can respond to it by replying directly to the comment. Comments appear in an expanded right-hand margin and can be deleted or hidden at any time.

To add a comment, select the **Review** tab from the ribbon and go to the **Comments** section. Place your insertion point (the blinking line) in the document where you want your comment to be or select the specific text. Then, from the **Comments** section, click **New Comment**.

The following screenshot shows the **Comments** section of the **Review** tab:

Figure 3.12 – The Comments section

You will see a colored line drawn from the spot of your insertion point to the now expanded right margin, where there will be a balloon with space to add your comment. The insertion point should appear in the balloon. At this point, you can type your comment.

In the balloon, either your name will appear, the name you signed into Word with, or simply the word **Author**. Beneath this, you will also see the **Reply** and **Resolve** buttons.

The following screenshot shows a comment with the author's name:

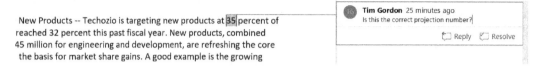

Figure 3.13 – Comment with the author's name showing

The following screenshot shows a comment with the word **Author** instead of a name:

Figure 3.14 – Comment with the word Author showing instead of a name

You can also add a comment by right-clicking the document and selecting **New Comment** from the pop-up menu.

If you are signed into Word with your Microsoft 365 credentials, and you are still only seeing **Author** instead of your name, this could be due to your privacy settings in Word.

Changing the privacy settings in Word

To change your **Privacy Settings** in Word, you need to go to the **File** tab on the ribbon and click on **Options**, which is at the bottom of the page in the left-hand corner. The **Word Options** window will now appear.

The following screenshot shows the **Word Options** window:

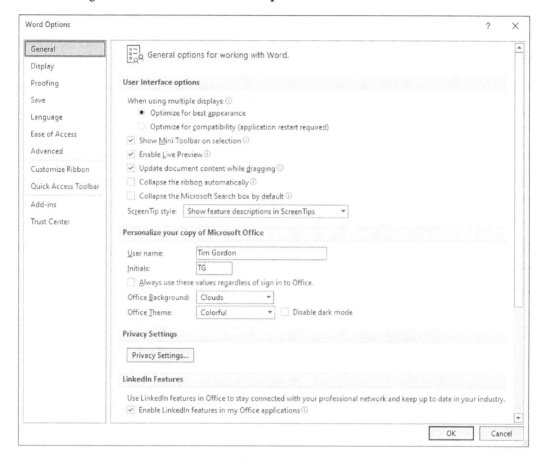

Figure 3.15 – The Word Options window

In the **Word Options** window, you need to select **Trust Center** from the list of options on the left and click the **Trust Center Settings** button on the right-hand side. The **Trust Center** window will now open.

From here, you will need to go to **Privacy Options** from the menu on the left.

From the **Privacy Options** settings, go to the **Document-specific settings** section and make sure that **Remove personal information from file properties on save** is unchecked. Then, click **OK** twice to return to the document.

The following screenshot shows **Trust Center** and the **Privacy Options** settings window:

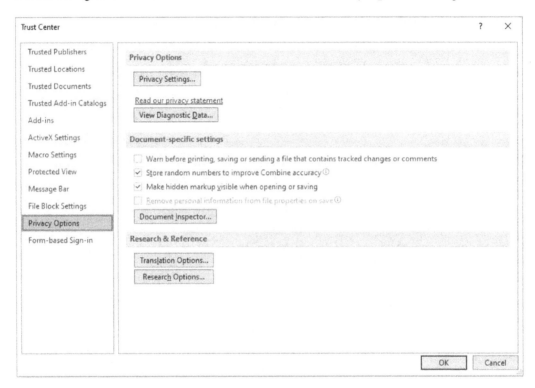

Figure 3.16 – The Privacy Options window

The document should now show the names of all collaborators. This option is document-specific, and you might want to make sure that sharing this personal information is allowed within your organization. If the author's name is still not showing, there may be other account issues.

Replying to comments

For this example, let's assume that we are collaborating with colleagues, and someone has posted a question using a comment. We have the answer to that question and wish to reply.

To reply to a comment, you will need to move your mouse near the comment in the right-hand margin. The comment balloon will appear, and you will see the **Reply** button beneath the text of the comment. If you click the **Reply** button, you can type your response. The **Reply** and **Resolve** buttons will appear beneath the reply.

The following screenshot shows a comment reply:

Figure 3.17 – A comment reply

Other collaborators can continue to comment and reply as desired. If a thread of comments eventually ends, an author can mark the comment or comments as resolved.

Resolving and reopening a comment

To mark a comment or comment thread as resolved, you simply need to click the **Resolve** button beneath the last comment. The comments will now appear grayed out, and each editor's comments will be collapsed. A small gray downward pointing arrow will appear next to each comment. Clicking on such an arrow will expand that comment.

Resolving a comment thread does not prevent editors from continuing to reply to comments. Resolving a thread is done to tell everyone that the topic needs no further discussion.

The following screenshot shows comments that have been marked as resolved:

Figure 3.18 – Resolved comments

If there comes a time when an editor wishes to continue a comment thread once it has been resolved, they can reopen the thread using the **Reopen** button.

To reopen a comment thread, click somewhere in the comments; the **Reply** and **Reopen** buttons will appear at the bottom. If you click the **Reopen** button, the comment thread will be active again.

The following screenshot shows the **Reopen** button within a resolved comment thread:

Figure 3.19 – The Reopen button

Showing or hiding comments

In the **Comments** section, there is a **Show Comments** button. By default, it will be grayed out. The **Show Comments** button's status has a direct relationship to which markup option has been selected in the **Tracking** section.

If we go to the **Review** tab and look at the **Tracking** section, by default, **All Markup** will be selected in the markup menu. If you select the **Simple Markup** option, the **Show Comments** button will no longer be grayed out. The expanded right-hand margin will collapse, and any comments will now appear only as callouts in the normal right-hand margin.

The following screenshot shows a comment as a callout with **Simple Markup** selected and the **Show Comments** button available:

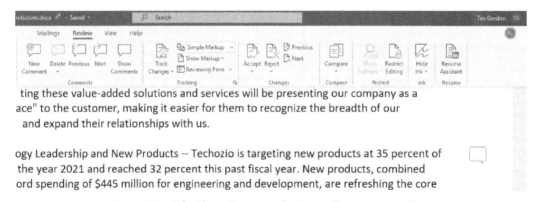

Figure 3.20 – The Show Comments button and a comment callout

If you select the **Show Comments** button now, the right-hand margin will expand, and the comments will be fully displayed. If **Track Changes** is on, any markup will still be hidden.

Reviewing and deleting comments

If your document contains several comments, you can review them quickly by using the **Previous** and **Next** buttons, which can be found in the **Comments** section of the **Review** tab.

If you need to delete a comment, once it has been selected, you can use the **Delete** button in the **Comments** section to delete it. You can also use the **Delete** button to delete comments that have been resolved.

Comments are a great way to communicate ideas and questions with colleagues directly in a Word document, but if you really want to grab someone's attention, you might want to use @mention in your comments. In the next section, we will explore how to mention someone in a document.

Mentioning others in comments

So far, we have seen how helpful it can be to use comments when collaborating on a document. However, a comment is only effective if the person it is intended for sees it. If you really need to get somebody's attention in your organization with a comment, you can @mention them.

When you use the @ symbol before someone's name in a comment, they will receive an email, alerting them that someone has mentioned them in a document. The email will also contain a link to the comment in the document. @ mentioning only works with Word 365 and other Microsoft 365 apps, and you must be signed in to your Microsoft 365 account. @mention does not work in Office 2019 or older versions. @mention also works across different platforms, such as Android, iOS, and Mac.

If you want to @mention someone in a comment, then you should create a new comment, enter the @ symbol, and begin to type the first few letters of the person's name. Their name should appear. At this point, you can simply select their name to @mention them in the comment.

Another great option of the @mention feature is that you can assign a task to someone. We will explore this a little later in this section.

The following screenshot shows the @mention feature and the name to select:

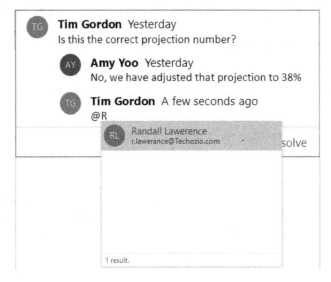

Figure 3.21 – The @mention feature

Once you have selected the name, you can complete your comment. This comment will highlight the @mention name as a hyperlink that, if clicked, will bring up that person's contact information.

The following screenshot shows the completed comment with an @mention:

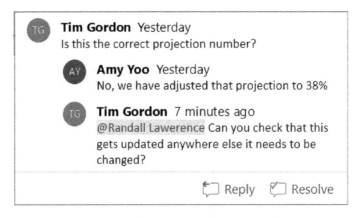

Figure 3.22 – The @mention feature completed

The person mentioned in the comment will now receive an email, alerting them that they have been mentioned. The email will also have a link to the comment in the document.

The following screenshot shows an @mention email:

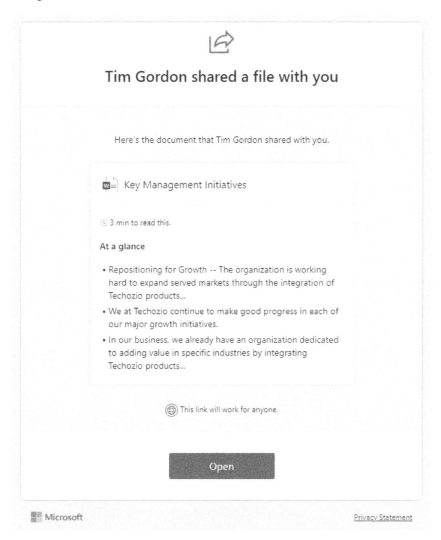

Figure 3.23 – The @mention email

By clicking **Open**, the email recipient will be taken to the document and the comment.

@ mentioning someone in a comment is a great way to ensure that person is alerted to the comment. @mention automatically sends an email to the user, which provides them with an easy way to access the document with a link.

@mention also makes it easy to assign a task to a collaborator. In either a comment or a reply, the **Assign to** box and button will appear.

The following screenshot shows the **Assign to** button. It has been checked and we are ready to click the **Assign** button:

Figure 3.24 – The Assign task to (name) checkbox and button

Once the task has been assigned, you will see the assignment in the comment box:

Figure 3.25 – Task assigned

The person to whom the task was assigned will also receive an email, informing them that the task has been assigned to them.

You will now see a radio button at the top of the comment window. Once the task has been completed, click this button; the task will be marked as completed:

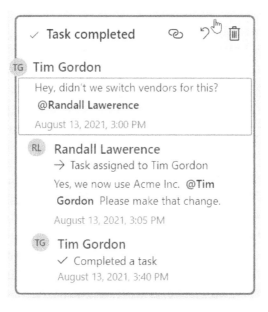

Figure 3.26 – Task completed

Once the task has been completed, the assigner of the task will also receive an email, telling them that the task has been completed. In the next section, we will explore how to view, compare, and combine changes from multiple versions of the same document.

Viewing, comparing, and combining changes

We have seen how to use **Track Changes**, and how it can be very helpful when collaborating on a shared document with multiple authors. But think about this scenario – you have sent a document out for revision to multiple authors, and they have sent you revised versions of the document. Word gives us the tools we need to work with multiple versions of the same document, and we can also use **Compare** and **Combine** to compare two versions of a single document saved in OneDrive.

> **Documents saved to OneDrive versus documents saved locally**
>
> If the document you are working with has not been saved to OneDrive, only the **Compare** and **Combine** options will be present. Saving previous versions of documents is done automatically in OneDrive. Documents saved to your local computer will not save previous versions of the document.

To compare or combine two versions of a document, you must select the **Review** tab on the ribbon and go to the **Compare** section. Upon clicking the **Compare** button, you will have several options to choose from. If the document has been saved to OneDrive, you will have five options:

- **Major Version**: This will compare the current version with the last published version. Publishing a document version is a common feature in SharePoint.

- **Last Version**: This will compare the current document with the last version that has been saved to OneDrive.

- **Specific Version**: This will allow you to choose which of the previous versions of the document you wish to compare to.

- **Compare**: With this option, you will need to select the original document, as well as a revised version of the document to compare it to. Word will then create a new version of the document, showing what has been changed between the original and the revised version. Neither document will be changed, but you can save the comparison version as a new document. This is also referred to as the **legal blackline**.

- **Combine**: This option is similar to **Compare** but allows us to combine documents that have **Track Changes** turned on.

The following screenshot shows the **Compare** options in a document saved to OneDrive:

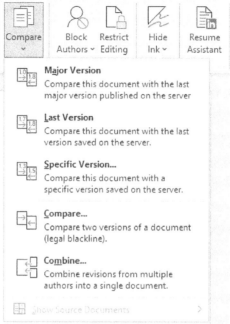

Figure 3.27 – The Compare options menu

Comparing documents

To begin with, we will look at two variations of the same document that's been revised by two different authors. We will begin by selecting the **Compare** button and choosing the **Compare** option. The **Compare Documents** window will open, and you will need to select **Original document** and **Revised document**.

The following screenshot shows the **Compare Documents** window:

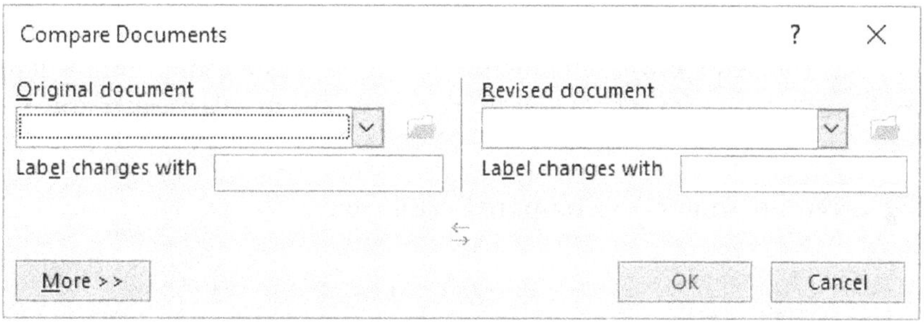

Figure 3.28 – The Compare Documents window

You can now navigate to **Original document** by selecting the folder icon on the left, and then select **Revised document** by selecting the folder icon on the right. Once both files are selected, you can change the comparison settings by clicking the **More** button in the lower-left corner of the window.

The following screenshot shows **Comparison settings**, with the default options selected:

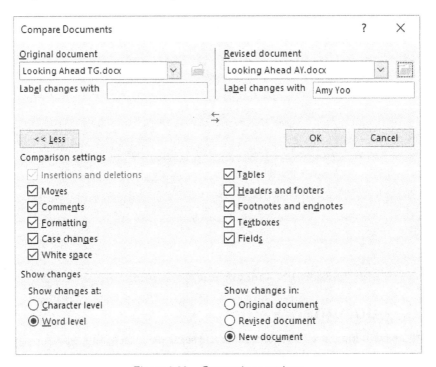

Figure 3.29 – Comparison settings

In the preceding screenshot, you can see that under **Revised document**, we have the name of the editor in a textbox, preceded by **Label changes with**. This indicates that Word recognizes the editor and will label their changes with the name shown in the box.

Now, we can click the **OK** button. Word will open both the original document and the revised document. The new **Compared Document** will be created, and Word will open the **Compare Result** view. A lot is going on in this new view, so let's break it down into its various parts.

The following screenshot shows the **Compare Result** view:

Figure 3.30 – The Compare Result screen

On the left, we can see the **Revisions** pane. This is where we will see a list of all the revisions that have been made by the reviewer in the revised document. We will also see that they are labeled with the reviewer's name.

The following screenshot shows the **Revisions** pane:

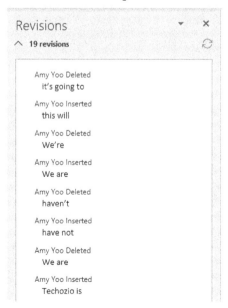

Figure 3.31 – The Revisions panel

On the right, we can see two panels: **Original Document** and **Revised Document**. No changes are shown in these panels, as shown here:

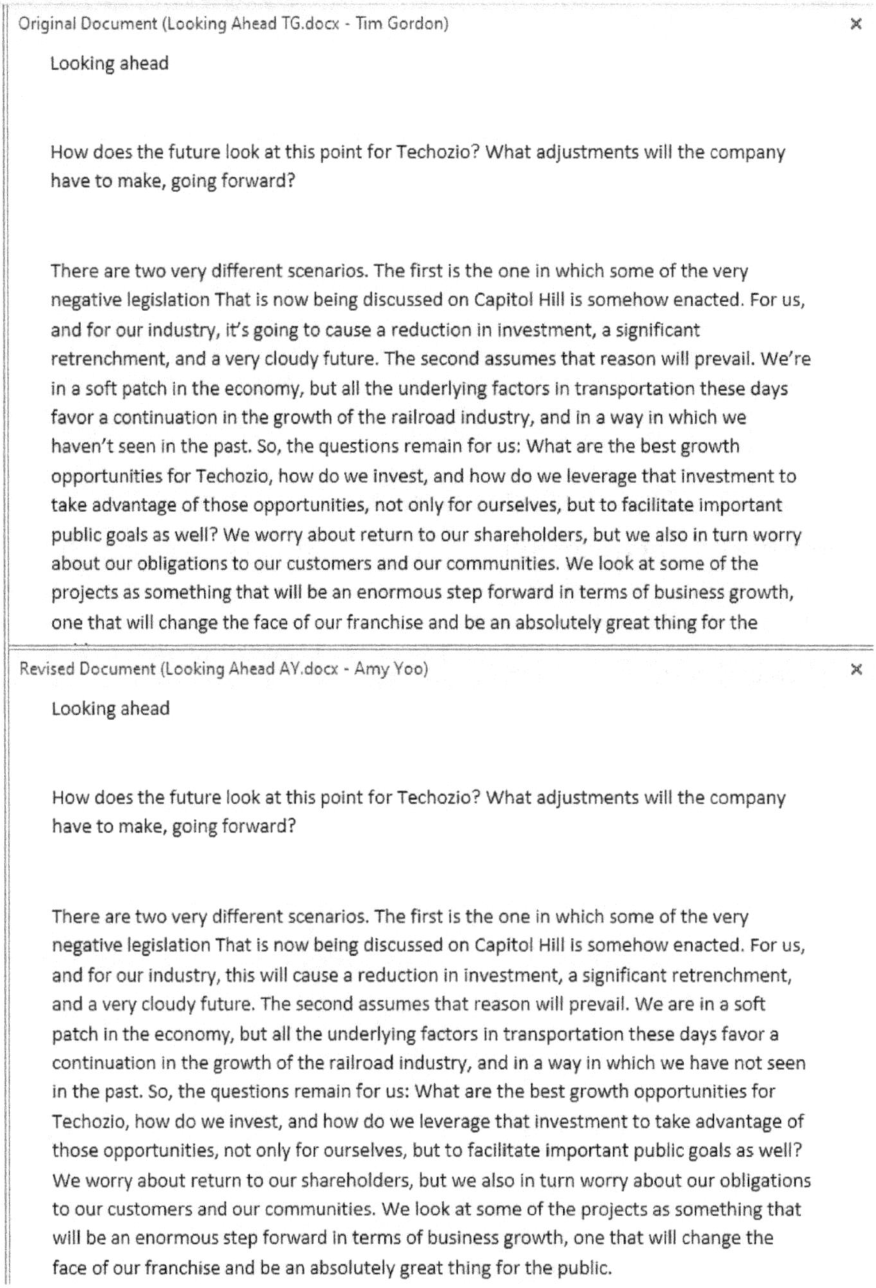

Original Document (Looking Ahead TG.docx - Tim Gordon)   ×

Looking ahead

How does the future look at this point for Techozio? What adjustments will the company have to make, going forward?

There are two very different scenarios. The first is the one in which some of the very negative legislation That is now being discussed on Capitol Hill is somehow enacted. For us, and for our industry, it's going to cause a reduction in investment, a significant retrenchment, and a very cloudy future. The second assumes that reason will prevail. We're in a soft patch in the economy, but all the underlying factors in transportation these days favor a continuation in the growth of the railroad industry, and in a way in which we haven't seen in the past. So, the questions remain for us: What are the best growth opportunities for Techozio, how do we invest, and how do we leverage that investment to take advantage of those opportunities, not only for ourselves, but to facilitate important public goals as well? We worry about return to our shareholders, but we also in turn worry about our obligations to our customers and our communities. We look at some of the projects as something that will be an enormous step forward in terms of business growth, one that will change the face of our franchise and be an absolutely great thing for the

Revised Document (Looking Ahead AY.docx - Amy Yoo)   ×

Looking ahead

How does the future look at this point for Techozio? What adjustments will the company have to make, going forward?

There are two very different scenarios. The first is the one in which some of the very negative legislation That is now being discussed on Capitol Hill is somehow enacted. For us, and for our industry, this will cause a reduction in investment, a significant retrenchment, and a very cloudy future. The second assumes that reason will prevail. We are in a soft patch in the economy, but all the underlying factors in transportation these days favor a continuation in the growth of the railroad industry, and in a way in which we have not seen in the past. So, the questions remain for us: What are the best growth opportunities for Techozio, how do we invest, and how do we leverage that investment to take advantage of those opportunities, not only for ourselves, but to facilitate important public goals as well? We worry about return to our shareholders, but we also in turn worry about our obligations to our customers and our communities. We look at some of the projects as something that will be an enormous step forward in terms of business growth, one that will change the face of our franchise and be an absolutely great thing for the public.

Figure 3.32 – The Original and Revised documents

In the center is the newly created **Compared Document**. This is where we can see all the changes from **Revised Document** applied to **Original Document**.

The following screenshot shows **Compared Document**:

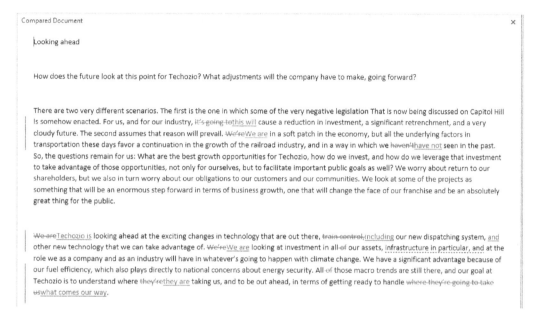

Figure 3.33 – Compared Document

As you scroll through any of these documents, you will notice that all three will scroll in sync, so you will be looking at the same place in all three documents simultaneously.

If you feel like there is too much going on here, you have options to hide some of these panels. If you click the **Compare** button, at the bottom of the list, you will see the option to **Show Source Documents**. Click this to see a menu of those options.

The following screenshot shows the **Show Source Documents** menu:

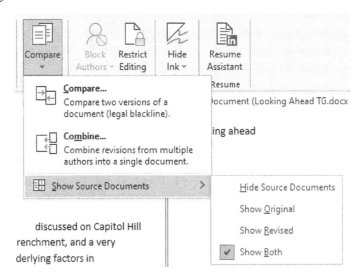

Figure 3.34 – The Show Source Documents menu

The options are as follows:

- **Hide Source Documents**: This will hide both the original and the revised documents, leaving only **Compared document**.

- **Show Original**: This will hide **Revised Document** and only show **Original Document** in a panel on the right.

- **Show Revised**: This will hide **Original Document** and only show **Revised Document** in a panel on the right.

- **Show Both**: This is the default view, and it shows both **Original Document** and **Revised Document** in the panel on the right.

Once you've selected your desired option, the screen view will change.

The following screenshot shows the screen view with the **Hide Source Documents** option selected:

Figure 3.35 – The Hide Source Documents option

You can now go through the revisions on the **Revisions** pane one by one, and either accept or reject them using the **Accept** and **Reject** buttons in the **Changes** section. Changes that are accepted are then merged into the new **Compared Document**, which you can now save as you wish.

If you have more revised versions of the original document, you can compare the version you just saved with an additional revised version to continue comparing and merging documents from multiple authors.

Comparing versions of the same document

Once a document has been saved to OneDrive and **Autosave** has been enabled, any edits are saved automatically, and a new minor version of the document is created when it is closed. You can compare previous versions of a document saved in OneDrive by going to the **Review** tab on the ribbon and selecting **Compare**.

Once the **Compare** button is selected, you have the option to compare the current version to the last **Major Version**, if you have published major versions available.

You can also choose to compare the current document to the **Last Version** document that was created and saved to OneDrive. From this point on, the process will be the same for comparing documents, as we discussed earlier in this chapter.

Lastly, you have the option to compare the current document to a **Specific Version**. If you select this option, you will be presented with a list of previous versions to choose from.

The following screenshot shows the **Versions saved** window:

No.	Modified ▼	Modified By	Size	Comments
6.0	4/7/2021 2:23 PM	Tim Gordon	29.1 KB	
5.0	4/7/2021 2:17 PM	Tim Gordon	28.7 KB	
4.0	4/7/2021 2:13 PM	Tim Gordon	29.3 KB	
3.0	4/7/2021 11:42 AM	Tim Gordon	27.7 KB	
2.0	4/7/2021 11:36 AM	Tim Gordon	27.3 KB	
1.0	3/16/2021 10:56 AM	Tim Gordon	28.8 KB	

Versions saved for Stockholder Report.docx

Versions saved to: https://techozio-my.sharepoint.com/personal/t_gordon_techozio_com/Documents/Stockholder Report/

More >>>   Compare   Close

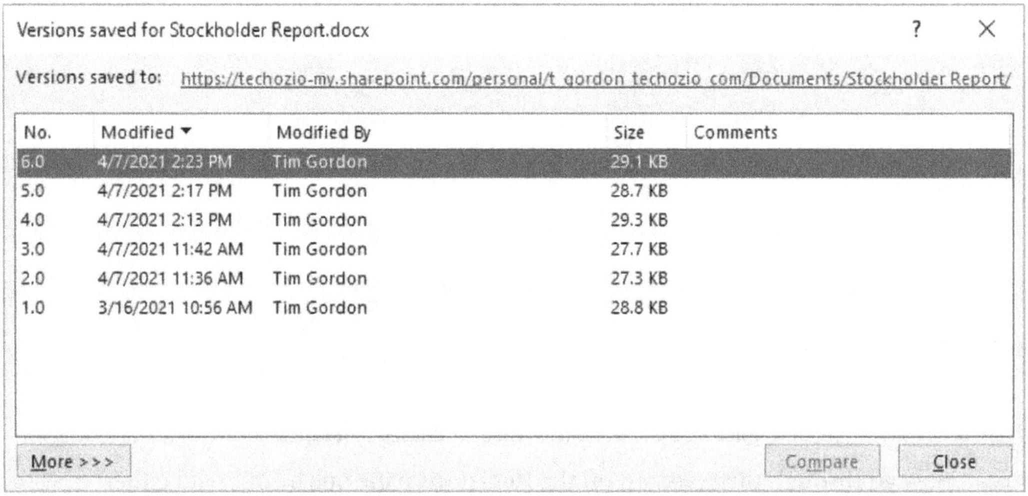

Figure 3.36 – The Versions saved window

You can now select a version to compare to and compare the two documents, as we described earlier in this chapter.

Comparing documents with tracked changes

So far in this chapter, the examples I have used to compare documents have been with documents that do not have **Track Changes** turned on. If you attempt to compare documents with tracked changes, the following dialog will pop up, and you will need to choose whether to proceed or not:

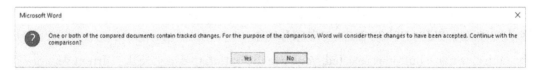

Figure 3.37 – The tracked changes popup

What this is telling you is that if there are tracked changes in either document, Word will assume that those changes have been accepted when creating the new compared document and they will be applied. You can then continue to compare the documents as you normally would.

This may present a problem for you, which is why you might want to consider using the **Combine** option for documents with tracked changes.

Combining documents

The **Combine** option, while similar to **Compare**, is best used when at least one of the documents has **Track Changes** turned on. As the name implies, the **Combine** option will combine different versions of the same document from multiple editors and create a new, combined version while leaving the other versions intact.

To combine documents, you must go to the **Review** tab on the ribbon and select the **Compare** button. You will see a menu of choices, and near the bottom will be the **Combine** option. If you click on it, the **Combine Documents** window will appear, as follows:

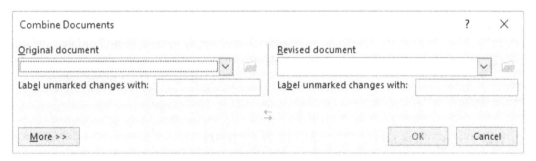

Figure 3.38 – The Combine Documents window

You will now need to select **Original document** by clicking the folder icon on the left and navigating to the correct document. Next, select a **Revised document** that you wish to combine it with by clicking the folder icon on the right and navigating to the correct document. Once both documents have been selected, click the **OK** button in the lower right. At this point, the new combined document will be created.

The **Combine Result** view will now be displayed on your screen. This will include the **Revisions** pane on the left, the **Original Document** and **Revised Document** panels on the right, and **Combined Document** in the center. Unlike the **Compare** option, tracked changes are not assumed to be accepted when combining documents.

The following screenshot shows the **Combine Result** view:

Figure 3.39 – The Combine Result view

You can now go through the revisions on the **Revisions** pane one by one, and either accept or reject them using the **Accept** and **Reject** buttons in the **Changes** section. Changes that are accepted are then merged into the new **Combined Document**, which you can now save as you wish.

Combining documents with tracked formatting changes

Something that you need to be aware of when combining documents that have tracked formatting changes is that Word can only retain one set of formatting in the combined document. If you choose to combine documents with tracked formatting changes, you will encounter a pop-up window that will force you to select the formatting changes from one of the selected documents.

The following screenshot shows the formatting choice popup:

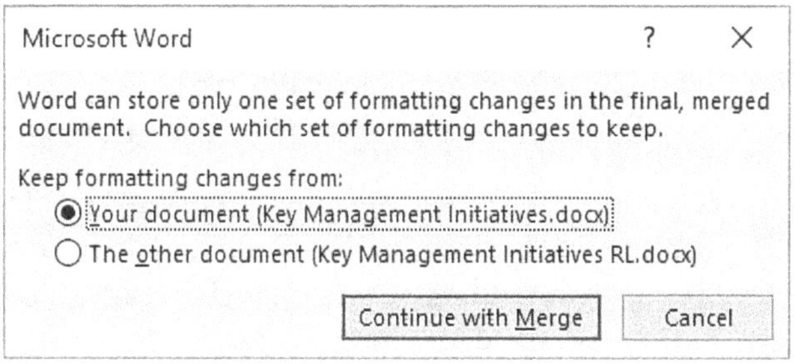

Figure 3.40 – The formatting choice popup

You will now need to select which document's formatting changes you want Word to apply. It is important to understand that this only applies to formatting conflicts. For example, if you choose to retain the formatting from the original document, formatting from the revised document will still be applied to the new document, unless it conflicts with formatting that's already been applied to the original document. In that case, Word will retain the formatting of the original document.

Now, you can go through the revisions and accept or reject them as you desire, and then save the new combined document.

Summary

In this chapter, we focused on collaborating with others on Word documents. We began by learning how to enable **Track Changes**, which uses markup to show changes made by other editors, and how to use **Reviewing Pane** to accept or reject those changes.

Next, we looked at how to use comments to get feedback, ask questions, and have a discussion with editors directly in the document. We also learned about using @mention in a comment to alert someone by email that they have been mentioned.

Lastly, we explored how to view, compare, and combine multiple versions of the same document, and then learned about the differences between comparing and combining, as well as the best case for each.

Being able to track changes and see markup is invaluable when working with multiple authors and editors. When I think about my own experience of writing this book with my co-author, as well as editors in various countries, without the tools we just learned about in this chapter, this book would have been extremely difficult to put together. As I said at the beginning of this chapter, the collaborative tools in Word are transformative.

In the next chapter, we will focus on skills that will let you work more effectively alone. You will learn how to use features such as **Navigation Pane** to help locate items, and will also learn how to use features such as reading view, immersive reader, and focus to work more effectively alone in an increasingly distracting world.

4
Concentrating Better with Microsoft Word

Ironically, while trying to make employees more connected, today's work environments can be quite distracting. Between open office spaces and constant messages, notifications, and interruptions, it can be difficult to focus on the work we are assigned and get things done. Sometimes, working from home isn't any better. It is difficult to separate our work lives from our personal lives, especially with tight living quarters where we can't easily draw clear physical boundaries between spaces. Not everyone has a home office where they can shield themselves from the piles of dirty dishes, laundry, or a pet begging for food. Everywhere we go, it seems, there are so many things to do and so many distractions. It is just so difficult to focus sometimes.

Luckily, Microsoft Word has built a variety of tools that can help you to focus and work more effectively and efficiently when you are reading, editing, or writing in a distracting environment.

In this chapter, we will cover the following tools:

- The Navigation pane

- Dictate

- Immersive Reader

- The reading view

- Focus

When used effectively, each of the preceding tools can help you become more productive by saving time. Additionally, they can help improve your focus by guiding your eyes and eliminating any distractions within the computer interface while you are working in Microsoft Word.

We will explore the first two tools from the perspective of how they can help us save time when working with long documents.

The Navigation pane

The **Navigation Pane** is not a new feature in Word. It has been around in one form or another since the Office 2007 version, where it was formerly called the **Document Map**. Even though its name and appearance have been updated from version to version, its primary purpose hasn't changed: it's there to help you locate things more quickly within your Word document.

By default, your Navigation pane will be hidden, so you will need to turn it on to use it no matter what version of Word you are using.

Turning on the Navigation pane

To turn on the Navigation pane, perform these steps:

1. For newer (or currently supported) versions of Word, open the document you are planning to review, edit, or continue writing in.

2. Click on the **View** tab.

3. In the **Show** group, click on the **Navigation Pane** checkbox to open the **Navigation pane**.

The Navigation pane should open and automatically dock to the left-hand side of your screen.

If the pane isn't docked, you can hover your mouse cursor over the topmost portion of the pane until your cursor changes into a cross with four arrows:

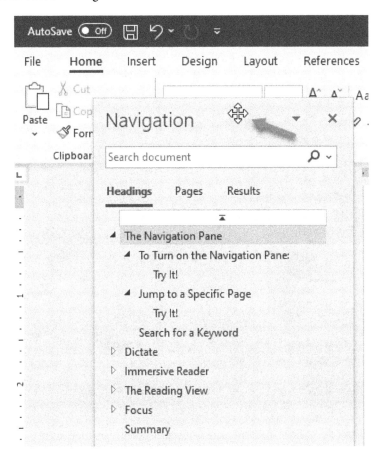

Figure 4.1 – Docking the Navigation pane

Then, click and drag the pane to the left-hand side of your screen until the panel snaps into place.

> **Important note**
>
> If you are using Office 365 Word for Mac, the steps for opening the Navigation pane will be nearly identical (click on **View** and check the box next to **Navigation Pane**). The only difference is that the area containing the checkbox for the Navigation pane is not labeled as the **Show** group.

If you are starting from a new blank document, the Navigation pane will contain simple explanatory text along with quick-start instructions about how to use the Navigation pane:

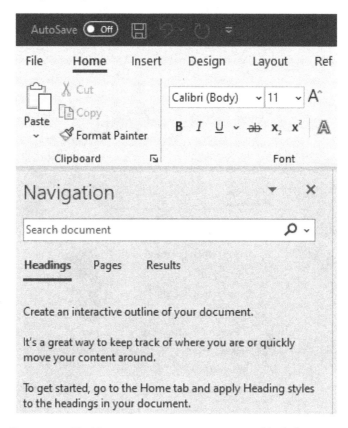

Figure 4.2 – The Navigation pane as it appears on a blank document

In order to get the most value out of the Navigation pane, your document will need to be formatted with **heading styles**. If you are unfamiliar with how to apply headings or the concept of styles, we will cover these topics, in depth, in *Chapter 8, Saving Time and Ensuring Consistency with Styles*.

When styles are applied to a document, you can use those headings to navigate or "jump" to that section of the document more quickly.

Try it!

If you would like to try out the Navigation pane and follow along with the steps and screenshots in this book, simply open Microsoft Word and create a new document using the **Welcome to Word** template from Microsoft:

Figure 4.3 – Creating a new document based on the Welcome to Word template from Microsoft

Once you have downloaded and opened the **Welcome to Word** template, go to the **View** tab and check **Navigation Pane**:

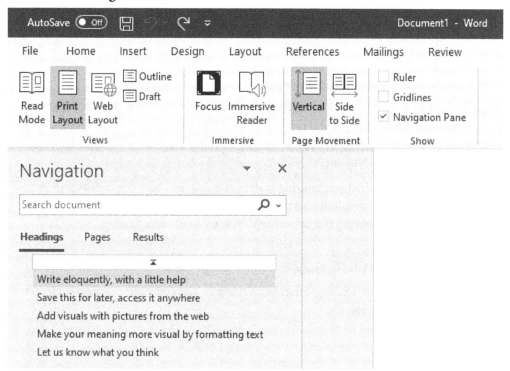

Figure 4.4 – The Headings tab in the Welcome to Word Navigation pane

Inside the Navigation pane, you will find five headings. You can click on or select the fourth heading, **Make your meaning more visual by formatting text**, to quickly jump to that section of the document:

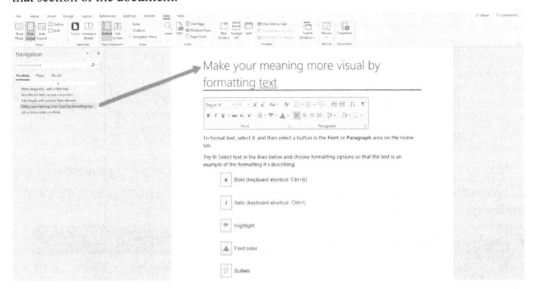

Figure 4.5 – The fourth heading, Make your meaning more visual by formatting text

Clicking on the fourth heading in the Navigation pane will move your cursor to that position within the document. As you can see, formatting a document with heading styles not only makes documents visually appealing, but it makes it easier to navigate through documents via the Navigation pane.

For documents that do not include heading styles (as beginners to Microsoft Word often forget or do not know they should format documents with styles), Microsoft has included other ways in which to navigate a document within the Navigation pane.

Jumping to a specific page

In addition to navigating via headings, users can jump to a specific page within their document from the Navigation pane.

Try it!

To follow along with this section, open Word and create a new Word document from the **Modern newspaper** online template:

Figure 4.6 – Searching for the Modern newspaper online template

This specific template does not come pre-styled with any headings:

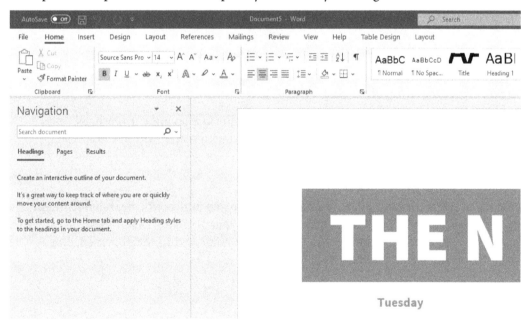

Figure 4.7 – The Modern newspaper template

When you open the Navigation pane for the first time, the pane won't appear to be very useful for navigating through the document. However, if you click on the **Pages** tab, you can quickly scroll through a thumbnail view of the document. Using this, you can click on any thumbnail to jump to a specific page:

Figure 4.8 – Clicking on page 4 to jump to page 4 in the document

So, scroll down the Navigation pane and click or tap on page 4. This will move your selection cursor to the top of the page on page 4.

But what if you are looking for something really specific in a document? Perhaps someone's name? Well, you can use the Navigation pane to search within a document, too.

Searching for a keyword

At the top of the Navigation pane, you might have already noticed the **Search document** box. Click inside that box and type in the name Mirjam Nilsson and press *Enter*. Word will search and highlight every instance of that name within the document and display the results within the **Results** tab:

Figure 4.9 – Displaying the Result 1 of 8 results for the Mirjam Nilsson search

To jump to any specific instance of `Mirjam Nilsson` within the document, all you have to do is click or tap on that instance in the **Results** pane and your insertion point or cursor will move to that section of your Word document. This will save you time by limiting the scrolling and keystrokes you have to make on your computer. That might not sound like much, but all those precious seconds add up over the course of a workweek. Sometimes, it can make the difference between meeting or missing a deadline.

There are other ways in which you might be able to save time as well. If you are not the fastest or most proficient typist, you could benefit from Word's Dictate feature.

Dictate

For Microsoft 365 subscribers who speak faster than they type, you might find Word's Dictate feature helpful when drafting documents in the early stages of writing. It is a useful way to get your thoughts and ideas onto paper quickly, without having to scrutinize or worry about sentence-level correctness, structure, or formatting.

What you will need before getting started

To compose documents using the Dictate feature, for best results, you will need *a quiet environment*. Other voices in the room have the potential to get picked up on the microphone. That said, for even better results, you will need a good microphone. While we have had success using the built-in microphones on our laptops, we have found that a headset microphone works best.

Starting dictation

To set up the dictation feature, perform these steps:

1. From the **Home** tab, in the **Voice** group, click on the **Dictate** button, which appears on the right-hand side of the ribbon:

Figure 4.10 – The Dictate icon looks like an old-fashioned microphone

You should hear a sound indicating that the dictation feature has been turned on. Additionally, the **Dictate** icon will turn white and display a red circle to indicate that it is listening:

Figure 4.11 – The white Dictate icon with a red circle

2. Begin speaking.

Dictation will capture everything you say. If you'd like to include special characters such as punctuation, simply say the name of or phrase for the punctuation mark.

> **Tip**
> For a complete list of punctuation phrases, please refer to the following Microsoft Support article: `https://support.microsoft.com/en-us/office/dictate-your-documents-in-word-3876e05f-3fcc-418f-b8ab-db7ce0d11d3c#Tab=Windows`.

Personally, I find thinking about things such as punctuation to be difficult. This is because it just slows me down and defeats the purpose of why I use this feature. So, I recommend ignoring punctuation completely and saving that step for later on when you are ready to edit.

When you are ready to stop dictation, simply click on the **Dictate** button again.

> **Important note**
>
> *No Microsoft 365 subscription, no problem!* If you open Microsoft Word and don't see the **Dictate** button on your ribbon, then chances are that you either don't have a Microsoft 365 subscription or you don't have an operating system that supports dictation in Office. If that's the case, don't worry. You can still use the dictation feature via Word for the Web. Just go to Office.com and sign in to your free Microsoft account. Word for the Web will have all of the latest dictation features and a few more options that are not available on Windows or macOS, such as the ability to format text, undo, and delete words and phrases using voice commands.

Saving time with any of the features we've described so far, be it through Dictate or the Navigation pane, will take a little practice and getting used to before you start seeing it really pay off in the long run.

The next three tools are beneficial not because they will necessarily save you a lot of time, but they will enable you to make the most of your time by helping you stay focused on your task within distracting environments.

Immersive Reader

The Immersive Reader tool is primarily designed to help improve reading comprehension for people with learning differences and people who are reading a non-native language. I've found, though, that this tool is quite useful for anyone, especially adults who struggle to stay focused in busy or distracting environments, such as in open office spaces or while working at home with kids in the house. If I must read a document and I am having difficulty concentrating, I can just pop in some headphones, turn on Immersive Reader, and Word will read aloud my document to me while highlighting the words.

Using the Immersive Reader tool

You can use the Immersive Reader tool to read an entire document or just a small section of text. Simply tell Word where to begin:

1. Move your insertion point to where you'd like Word to begin reading, or simply select the text you'd like to read.

2. Click on the **Review** tab.

3. In the **Speech** group, click on the **Read Aloud** button.

    This will open a small toolbar underneath the ribbon with five buttons:

    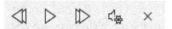

    Figure 4.12 – The Immersive Reader toolbar

4. Click on the settings icon (the speaker with the gear) to choose the reading speed and select a **voice style**:

    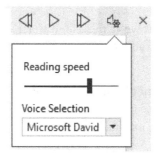

    Figure 4.13 – Moving the Reading speed bar and selecting a voice

5. Click on the **Play** button or use the keyboard shortcut of *Ctrl* + *Space* to begin the Immersive Reader.

Word should now begin reading aloud the text and simultaneously highlighting the words on the page as they are read. You can use the **Previous** button (*Ctrl* + *Right*) and the **Next** button (*Ctrl* + *Left*) to back up or jump to the next paragraphs in your Word document. The **Pause** button (*Ctrl* + *Space*) will stop the narration.

For kids and adults who want to read faster or prefer speed-reading, I've also found this tool to be quite useful. Like any muscle in your body, the muscles in your eyes must be trained to move faster. With regular practice, and by gradually increasing the reading speed, you can train your eyes to move along the page faster. Eventually, your eyes will move faster than this tool can move, and you can continue practicing without it.

If your goal is reading in Microsoft Word, and you want to improve either your focus or your reading speed, you could try switching to a view that ensures the best view for that specific task.

The reading view

Ordinarily, when you open Microsoft Word, the view you see your document displayed in is called **Print Layout**. This is simply what the document will look like when printed, where you can easily see the margins and the edges of the paper. However, that leaves a lot of wasted space within the screen and makes your eyes work much harder. You can change how your screen appears without changing how your document is formatted or how it will print.

Switching to the reading view

Switching to a view that is optimized for the task of reading allows you to customize the view that is suited for both the task and your specific needs. To switch views, perform the following steps:

1. Go to the **View** tab on the ribbon.

2. In the **Views** group, click on the **Read Mode** button:

Figure 4.14 – Clicking on the Read Mode button

This will immediately reflow your document, including any pictures, tables, and other elements the document might contain. Reading view does work best with text as the text will be resized to fit the view. Pictures, tables, and textboxes will retain their original sizes:

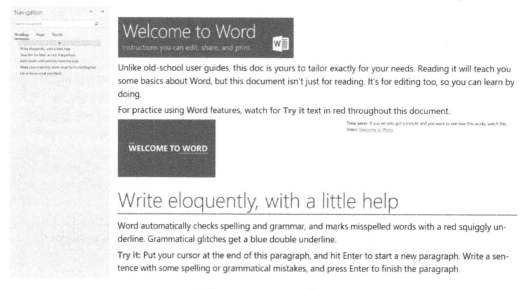

Figure 4.15 – The Welcome to Word template in the reading view

The reading view has a very minimal interface. In fact, the ribbon is completely gone, leaving only three menus: **File**, **Tools**, and **View**. I like to keep my **Navigation pane** open as a kind of table of contents. If you would like to do the same, or if you would like to turn it on or off from this view, you can find it in the **View** menu:

Figure 4.16 – The View menu

In addition to the Navigation pane, the **View** menu has a lot of other useful tools, including Immersive Reader (**Read Aloud**), a **Show Comments** button where you can turn on or off contributor comments for review, adjust things such as the column width, change the text spacing, or display the syllables between words.

But perhaps best of all, you can adjust the page color to help ease any eye strain for long or late-night reading and reviewing sessions:

Figure 4.17 – Changing the page color to Sepia

You have three options for your page color: **None**, **Sepia**, and **Inverse**. Personally, I am a fan of **Sepia**. Depending on your individual needs and the time of day or night, you might find other page colors more helpful in different environments.

Getting out of the reading view

To get back to the previous **Print Layout** view, there are several ways to get there:

- Go to your **View** menu and click on **Edit Document**.
- Go to your **status bar** and click on **Print Layout**.
- Hit the *Esc* key on your keyboard.

The reading view is definitely a great way in which to focus on reading in Microsoft Word. However, if you simply want to eliminate some of the distractions on the screen and focus on the page while you are writing or editing rather than reading, you might want to try Word's new Focus feature.

Focus

Sometimes, when working within an application, it is easy to be distracted by buttons or things that change within the application. And since Microsoft 365 has the potential to change from month to month, we are always potentially at risk of being distracted by something new in the application. Luckily, one of those new changes is the addition of the **Focus** button.

The **Focus** button offers a distraction-free view in Word, which takes whatever view you were working in and turns off all toolbars and buttons, allowing you to continue writing, editing, or reading:

Figure 4.18 – The Focus view

It even hides the Windows taskbar, so all you see is your document framed in black and nothing else.

Turning on the Focus view

If you are someone who is often distracted by buttons or applications, or even just the clock on the taskbar, when reading or reviewing a document, the Focus view is something you should try out. From the **Print Layout** view, go to the **View** tab and click on the **Focus** button. Your view will instantly change, allowing you to continue working with minimal distractions.

If you do find that you need some tools or commands from your ribbon, the ribbon is still there—it has just been minimized and darkened. Simply hover your mouse toward the very top center of your screen, and your Word toolbars and menus will return temporarily, though they will still appear darkened:

Figure 4.19 – The Focus view with the ribbon displayed

When you are finished and once again ready to return to the distraction of the world, returning to Print Layout is very similar to the steps for getting out of the reading view.

Getting out of the Focus view

To get back to the previous Print Layout view, there are a few methods that you can use to get there:

- Hover over the top of your screen so that your ribbon returns. Go to the **View** menu and click on the **Focus** button again.

- Hover over the top of your screen so that your ribbon returns. Go to the **status bar** and click on **Focus**.

- Hit the *Esc* key on your keyboard.

Summary

In this chapter, we have given you a few different ideas to improve your productivity and your focus using some of the new and improved tools in Microsoft Word.

The Navigation pane is a great way to quickly scan your document's headings, jump to a section or a page, or even search for a keyword or phrase. I've even used it to highlight words in a document for faster visual scanning rather than using the **Find** box. There are so many uses for this pane beyond what it has been designed for—it's just waiting for your creativity and imagination to put it to good use.

Don't let the name fool you. Microsoft's learning tools, including Immersive Reader and features such as Dictate, Read Mode, and Focus, aren't just for students. Business professionals can also use these tools in busy or distracting environments. These tools are for everyone, to improve the reading, writing, and editing experience no matter the environment, device, or individual challenges we face.

In the next few chapters, we will be shifting gears a bit to discuss how to format different types of documents for different types of people and situations.

Section 2: Making Sense of Formatting Short and Long Documents

In this section, you will learn how to use common features for better organization, to work faster with automation tools, use graphics, and make a document accessible to all audiences.

This section comprises the following chapters:

5
Working with Short Documents

Technology has advanced dramatically, and with those advancements, how we write and communicate in the workplace has adapted and changed. The letter or memo, once a common form of business and interoffice communication, now seems in some business circles like an ancient relic, having been replaced with email and other communication and electronic tools. Unless you work in a field that still relies heavily on written documentation, you might find that your skills of writing short documents in programs such as Microsoft Word have atrophied a bit. So, when occasions arise where you need to write a short document, such as a cover letter or a résumé, "the old-fashioned way," you might have a difficult time getting started, struggle to get your document to look "just right," or have trouble finding the most efficient workflows. Or, worse, you might feel unjustly unqualified for the task.

The purpose of this chapter is to restore your confidence in writing short documents using Microsoft Word. We will revisit some forgotten forms of written communication to apply for jobs. These will help us to focus on a task and give us something easy to format. We will discuss ways in which to leverage Microsoft Word wisely to visually make the best first impression before someone has had a chance to read your document, talk, or meet with you.

In this chapter, we will cover the following key topics to help you write and work more efficiently with Microsoft Word:

- Starting from a template

- Formatting essentials for templates

- Saving time with Quick Parts

These key Microsoft Word topics, in combination with understanding some basic design and writing principles, will help you to hone and advance your skills as a business professional and become more efficient with your writing workflows.

Starting from a template

If you are pressed for time and the style and branding of your document don't matter, starting from a Microsoft template is a great way to begin. A template comes pre-formatted with a variety of elements: text, styles, page formatting, and even graphical elements, such as textboxes, sidebars, and pictures. You might even find placeholders. A lot of these time-consuming style and formatting choices have already been created for you. All you have to do is download the template and create a new document based on that template. In fact, you can make as many documents from that template as you like. The hardest part is finding the best template that suits your needs.

Browsing Microsoft Word templates

There are two locations where you can go to browse Microsoft Word templates. The first place is right from within Microsoft Word's **Home** screen. The second place is online from the Microsoft Office templates page, which can be found at `https://templates.office.com/en-us/templates-for-word`:

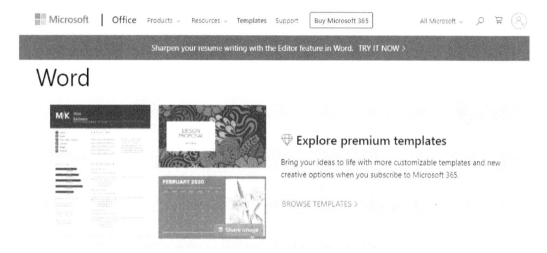

Figure 5.1 – Online Microsoft Office templates

Either location will work. You'll see the same templates in both locations. Subscribers to Microsoft 365 will have access to premium templates in both locations. Personally, I prefer to browse and download templates through Microsoft Word.

Downloading a template in Microsoft Word

To save time, staying within Microsoft Word to browse and download templates is simply easier. To browse and download a template right from within Microsoft Word, perform the following steps:

1. From any new or open Word document, click on the **File** menu on the ribbon.

    This will take you to Word's **Home** page.

2. At the top of the screen, underneath the greeting and **New**, you'll find some thumbnails of recently used templates, including the **Blank document** template. Underneath those thumbnails, there is a link that says **More templates →**. Click on the **More templates →** link:

Figure 5.2 – The More templates → link

This will take you to the **New** screen, where you can search for online templates or browse from a list of popular or suggested templates. To search for a specific type or kind of document, simply enter your keyword search into the **Search for online templates** box.

3. Type cover letter into the **Search for online templates** search box and press *Enter* on your keyboard to search:

Figure 5.3 – Searching for cover letter templates in Word

4. Scroll down to view more templates.

5. Click on a template thumbnail to view more details about a particular template.

6. Click on **Create** to download your chosen template:

Figure 5.4 – Headshot cover letter

Once you have clicked on **Create**, Word will download that template and open a new document based on that template for you to use and modify. Feel free to make any changes you wish. Any changes you make to the document that was created off the template will not impact the template itself, just the one document that was created from that template.

The template search results

Now that we know how to download a template, let's go back and discuss the search results from our cover letter search in a bit more depth. The results that are displayed will be a mix of everything that is tagged as being related to "cover letter" but not necessarily a "cover letter" in the strictest or most traditional sense. In other words, these templates don't always follow the style and conventions you might have been taught in school (depending on when and where you went to school). Not to mention, some of the results that are shown might not even be cover letters:

Figure 5.5 – The cover letter Word template search results

You might find some résumés or CVs mixed in, along with some non-traditional cover letters styled to match those résumés. In fact, you will need to scroll down to find what we would call a "simple and traditional" looking cover letter:

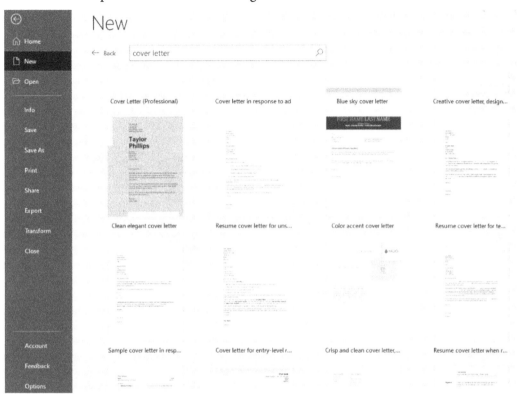

Figure 5.6 – Traditional cover letters

These cover letters, though they might not look like much at first glance, are better for a wider, more professional audience. Each one of these simple and plain-looking cover letters is designed with a specific situation, purpose, and audience in mind. For example, the **Resume cover letter when referred** template has starter text in the template to help guide you in writing the letter:

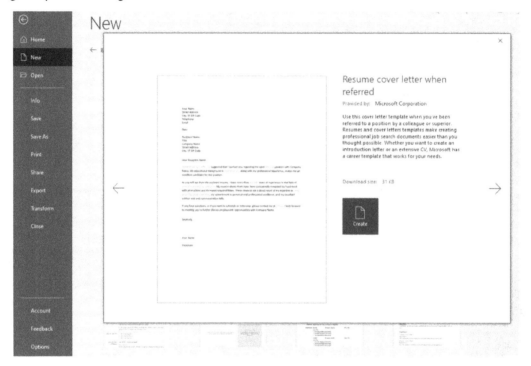

Figure 5.7 – Resume cover letter when referred

In other words, it will help not only with the formatting and structure of the letter, but it will also help you craft the content as well. Just make sure that you change the content to make it your own. Imagine someone from HR reading the exact same Microsoft-supplied template text, verbatim, from 50 applicants. How will that help you stand out? These templates are here to help give you an idea of what to write, not to write the letter for you. So, use these templates as a starting point to save time and to give you ideas about what you could write instead.

> **Important note**
>
> Business writing conventions vary greatly from culture to culture and from business to business. Before downloading and using any Word template (or taking advice from anyone online), be sure to check with trusted industry professionals in your region—that is, people who do what you do—regarding current writing conventions and requirements when applying for jobs and communicating with colleagues.

Going along with the same idea of standing out from the crowd, you might want to edit the visual appearance of your template, too. Many recruiters and HR representatives spend just a handful of seconds skimming through résumés and cover letters, so seeing a visually similar résumé or cover letter over and over won't help you. That doesn't mean you still can't save time and start from a template—you just need to know how these templates are built, so you can quickly and easily change their appearance.

Formatting essentials for templates

If the template doesn't quite match your needs, or if you are worried that your template will look like everyone else's document, you can still modify a template's appearance and placeholder text. In fact, even if the template does match your needs, I strongly encourage you to still modify the template to make it your own. Even with making modifications, templates still save time now (depending on how many changes you make) and in the future if you plan on reusing that template over and over.

> **Important note**
>
> There will be times when you will want to avoid starting from or even modifying a Microsoft-designed template. If your profession is design-centered or your personal brand is about originality and creativity, using someone else's template will not communicate those ideas. In these situations, start from scratch and design your own template.

As mentioned earlier, a template is comprised of a variety of elements, pictures, and, sometimes, placeholders. You can change any of these elements within the document without affecting the underlying template upon which the document is based. However, if you want the changes that you are making to be permanent, that is, you know you will want to make more documents that reflect those changes in the future, then you will need to modify or make those changes to the template rather than to the document you've created based on that template.

To know which type of document you are working with, that is, a document or a template, you can check the file extension of the file from the top title bar of Word:

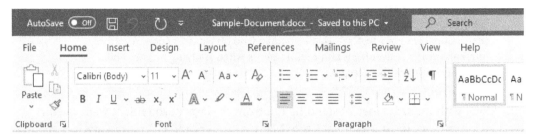

Figure 5.8 – The document file extension in the Word title bar (Windows only)

A file that ends in .docx is the default XML-based file format used for newer Word files (from Word 2007 and beyond). If you see the .dotx extension, then you are working with a template created for newer Word files—ones that do not contain macros. If, however, you see an extension of .dotm, you'll know that that template has been enabled for macros.

Alternatively, outside of Word, you can also view these file extensions from Windows File Explorer:

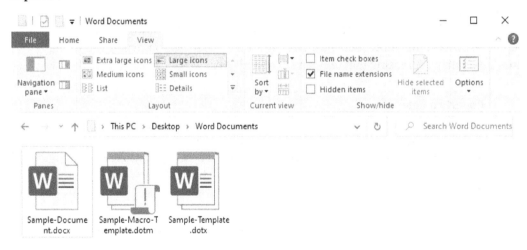

Figure 5.9 – Windows File Explorer

From outside of Word, you can also observe that different types of files will have different icons representing the kind of Word file each one is.

Important note

You will need to turn on file extensions if they are not already on. In Windows 10, click on the File Explorer (the little yellow folder icon), then click on the **View** tab. In the **Show/hide** group, check **File name extensions** to display file extensions. On a Mac, navigate to your **Finder** menu and click on **Preferences** to open the **Finder Preferences** window. From there, click on the **Advanced** tab and check the **Show all filename extensions** option box.

There are other extensions and file formats as well. If you would like to read more about other Office file extensions, please refer to the Microsoft documentation here: `https://docs.microsoft.com/en-us/deployoffice/compat/office-file-format-reference`.

Exploring a template

Now that we understand a little bit more about the differences between Word documents and templates, and how to identify which we are working on, we can move on to discuss how to save and edit the template files that you've downloaded from Microsoft.

To follow along, download the **Resume cover letter for temporary position** template by searching for the title of this letter in Word and then clicking on the **Create** button:

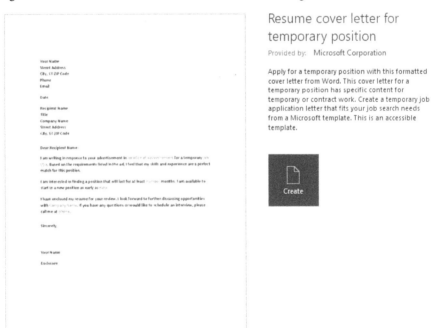

Figure 5.10 – Resume cover letter for temporary position

Once you've downloaded and created a new file based on this template, you will notice that this file does a few strange things right away. First, it might automatically populate your name at the top of the letter and in the closing part of the letter. Second, you might also notice that when trying to move your insertion point or cursor to the body of the letter, a huge portion of the first sentence is automatically selected at once:

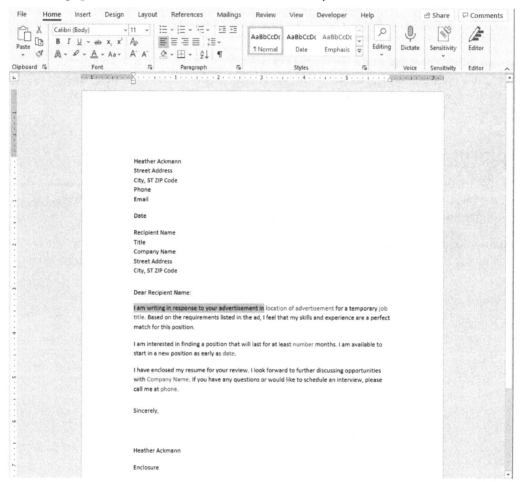

Figure 5.11 – The temporary position cover letter

If I begin typing with that portion selected, then what I type will replace that entire selection, making it difficult to edit only part of the sentence. This is because this template was created using **content controls**.

We could edit these controls within this one document, or if we think we would like to reuse this template again later, we could save this file as a template and then edit that template file.

Editing a template

To edit this file and make it our own so that we can reuse it again later, first, we are going to need to save this file as a template. That might seem counterintuitive since we thought we were downloading a template. But what was really happening was that Word had merely created a new document off of an online template.

Saving as a Word template

To save the template, perform the following steps:

1. Go to the **File** menu, and select **Save As**.

2. Give the template a name.

3. From the file type menu, select **Word Template (*.dotx)**.

   Upon selecting **Word Template (*.dotx)** from the list of choices, Word will automatically change your save location to the **Custom Office Templates** folder or another default save location set in your Word options:

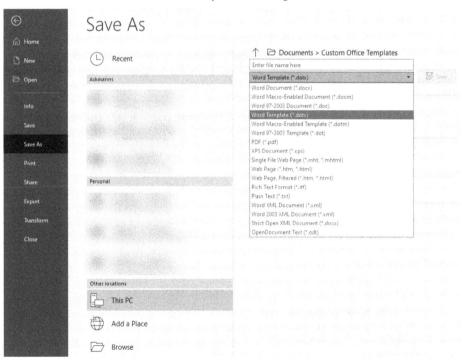

Figure 5.12 – Custom Office Templates

If you would like this template to appear in your personal templates area, keep this location.

4. Click on **Save** to save the file as a template. Then, open that template.

    If you look at the top title bar for that file, you should see the name of the template (rather than Document1.docx) and the file extension of .dotx at the end. If so, that means you are now editing the template:

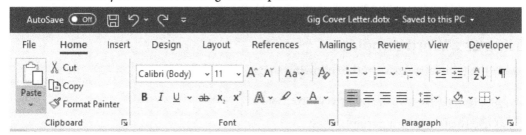

Figure 5.13 – Creating and opening the Gig Cover Letter template

Now that the template has been opened, we can begin making changes to our template for future use.

Editing the template's content controls

Most changes to a template will be exactly the same as formatting a regular document —unless the template was created using content controls. **Content controls** are like little buckets or containers that you can add to a template or form. They include descriptions, instructions, and restrictions for what kind of content users can enter into the control.

The cover letter we downloaded from Microsoft, **Resume cover letter for temporary position**, is crammed with content controls. To view, examine, and change these content controls, you will need access to the **Developer** tab on your ribbon, which is turned off by default.

Turning on the Developer tab

To turn on the **Developer** tab, perform the following steps:

1. Go to **File** and click on **Options**.

    This will open the options window to the **General** tab.

2. Click on the **Customize Ribbon** tab.

3. Underneath the **Customize the Ribbon** section, scroll down until you see **Developer**. Check the box next to **Developer** to add the **Developer** tab to your ribbon:

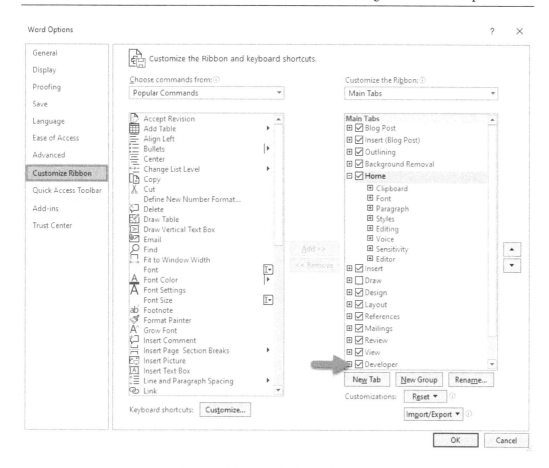

Figure 5.14 – The Developer checkbox

4.   Click on **OK**.

The **Developer** tab will now appear on your ribbon between the **View** and **Help** tabs.

> **Mac users**
>
> If you are a Mac user and would like to display the **Developer** tab, the steps
> you need to take are a little different from a PC. From the Word menu, select
> **Preferences**. This will open the **Word Preferences** window above your
> document. In the **Authoring and Proofing Tools** section, select **Ribbon &
> Toolbar**. On the right-hand side of the ribbon screen, underneath the **Main
> Tabs** section, scroll down and find the checkbox for **Developer**. Check the
> box next to **Developer** and click on **Save**. The **Developer** tab will then appear
> between **View** and the **Tell me** box on your ribbon.

Exploring the content control properties

Once the **Developer** tab has been turned on, navigate to the **Developer** tab and click on the **Design Mode** button. With design mode enabled, you will be able to view all of the content controls within your current document:

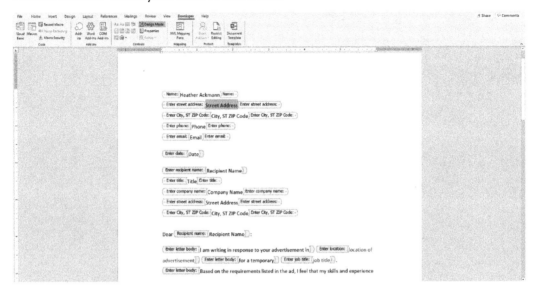

Figure 5.15 – The Developer design mode

As I mentioned earlier, this document is filled with content controls. If you would like to view the properties of the content controls or edit any of the properties of a specific content control, simply select a control from this design mode, and click on the **Properties** button:

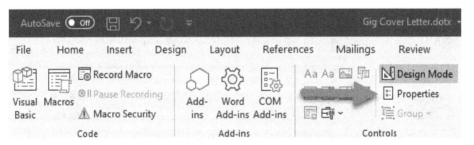

Figure 5.16 – The content control Properties button

This will open a separate floating window that contains all of the properties for your selected content control. These properties will vary depending on the property type that was created. Most of the content controls used in this template were **rich text content controls**, so their property options should look something like this:

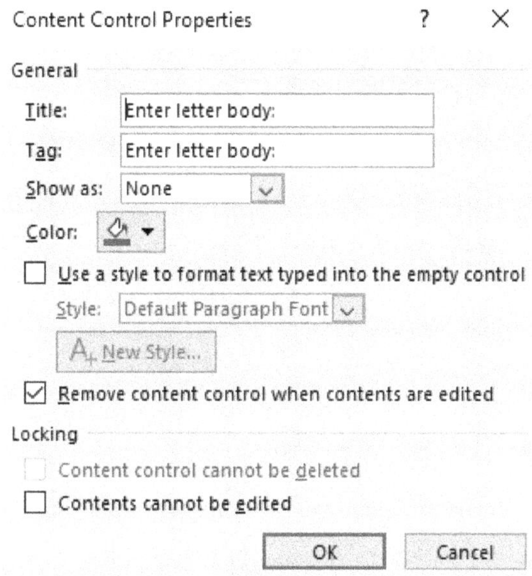

Content Control Properties   ?   ✕

General

   Title: Enter letter body:

   Tag: Enter letter body:

   Show as: None

   Color:

   ☐ Use a style to format text typed into the empty control

      Style: Default Paragraph Font

      A₊ New Style...

   ☑ Remove content control when contents are edited

Locking

   ☐ Content control cannot be deleted

   ☐ Contents cannot be edited

OK   Cancel

Figure 5.17 – Content Control Properties

In this specific template, all of the controls are set to **Show as: None**. This means that when the user selects the control, there is nothing that alerts them saying they are selecting a control. And when text is edited, the control is removed, which is why all of the text disappears.

If we want to change how this control behaves, the easier method is to change how the control is displayed or shown. So, instead of **None**, let's change it to **Bounding Box**:

Figure 5.18 – Show as: Bounding Box

To view what a bounding box looks like in our template compared to the other style, **None**, let's exit the design mode by clicking on the **Design Mode** button in the **Developer** tab once more:

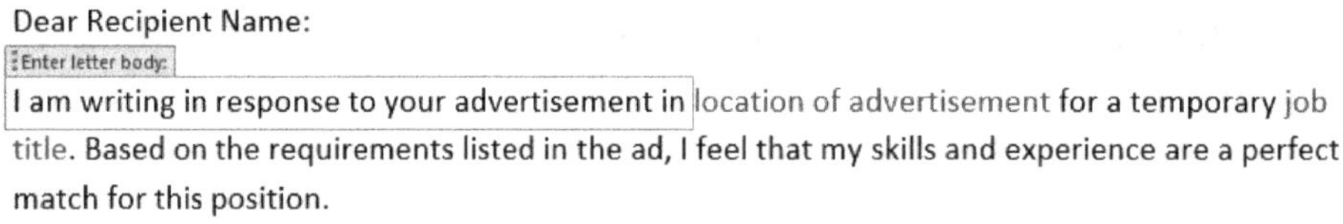

Dear Recipient Name:

Enter letter body:

I am writing in response to your advertisement in location of advertisement for a temporary job title. Based on the requirements listed in the ad, I feel that my skills and experience are a perfect match for this position.

Figure 5.19 – Bounding box around the first part of the letter

With a bounding box around the suggested text, it is easier to view where those controls are within the document. We can also view the tagged text above the control. This text can then be used to give users suggestions or help with what to write in these boxes.

If you would like to change what appears within the content controls of the letter (that is, the suggested text), you can turn **Design Mode** back on and edit the text that appears within the middle of the content control tags:

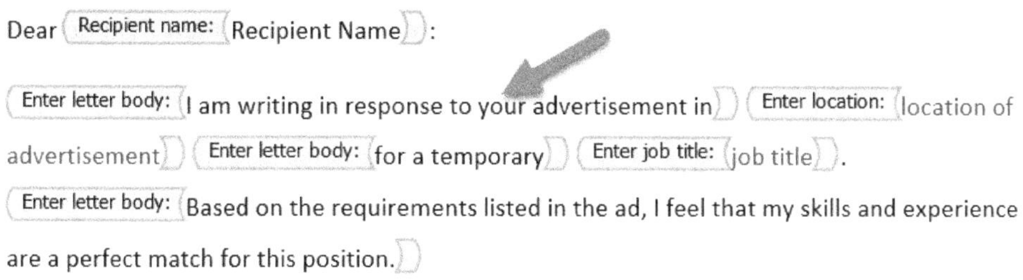

Dear (Recipient name: (Recipient Name)) :

(Enter letter body: (I am writing in response to your advertisement in)) (Enter location: (location of

advertisement)) (Enter letter body: (for a temporary)) (Enter job title: (job title)) .

(Enter letter body: (Based on the requirements listed in the ad, I feel that my skills and experience

are a perfect match for this position.))

Figure 5.20 – Editing the suggested text control

Just remember that as soon as the user selects this text in their document and begins typing, that text will disappear and be replaced with their own text. Alternatively, if the user chooses to not edit the text, whatever has been suggested, or the placeholder text that has been left, will remain.

Editing the suggested text content controls for your own use can help you to craft a more original letter tailored to your own needs, experience, and situation, while still enabling you to reuse the template for future letters.

While templates are a great timesaver, they aren't always the best solution for every situation. If you are looking to save time but have a little more control or say in the type of content you insert or create, you might want to consider exploring some of the content creation options available to you with Quick Parts.

Saving time with Quick Parts

If there is a portion of a document that you find you are reusing or copying and pasting frequently, such as your address, a disclosure, copyright information, a form, or even a decorative element, you can save that chunk of your document as a **Quick Part** and reuse that content over and over again with just a few clicks of your mouse. A Quick Part is simply a chunk of reusable content. In fact, Microsoft Word already comes preloaded with some Quick Parts that you can explore and use. Just open the **Quick Parts** gallery to view what Word already has available.

Exploring the Quick Parts gallery

To view what Quick Parts you already have available to you to add to your documents and templates, perform the following steps:

1. From the ribbon, click on the **Insert** tab.
2. In the **Text** group, click on the **Quick Parts** button.

This will open a small menu with four main options: **AutoText**, **Document Property**, **Field…**, and **Building Blocks Organizer…**:

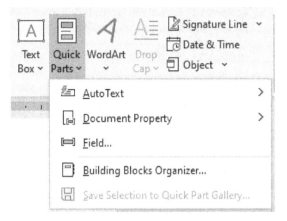

Figure 5.21 – The Quick Parts menu

If you've never used **Quick Parts** before, you might not have much to look at in your **AutoText** gallery besides your name and your initials. Any text that you would like to reuse, you can save to this gallery (which is much better than copy and paste). In the **Document Property** menu, you will find a list of properties or information that pertains to your Word document:

Figure 5.22 – The Document Property menu

If you ever need to reference the author of the document or when the document was published, you can insert this information here.

Fields are useful when you need Word to automatically update the information within your document. If you have ever inserted page numbers using Word's page number gallery, that is exactly what Word is inserting—a field code. With Quick Part field codes, you have a lot more fields in which to create your own combinations and customizations of fields:

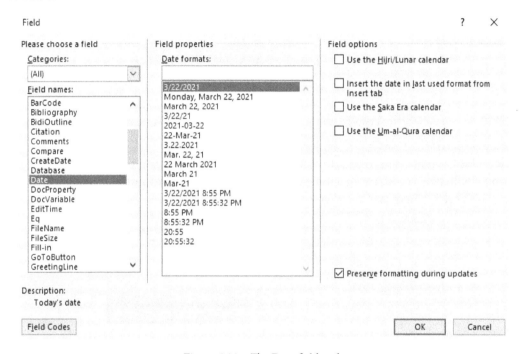

Figure 5.23 – The Date field code

The **Date** field is one of the ones I use the most. With this field, you can select how you would like your date formatted and choose your field options. Then, within the document, updating the field is easy: you simply hit the *F9* key or click on the **Update** button above the field:

Figure 5.24 – The Update button

From the ribbon, within the **Quick Parts** gallery, you will find **Building Blocks Organizer...**:

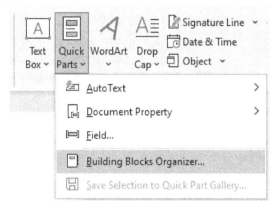

Figure 5.25 – Building Blocks Organizer...

Clicking on **Building Blocks Organizer...** will launch a large window, where you will find reusable content across a variety of Word galleries. If there is content inside a gallery that you would like to edit, for instance, to edit, delete, or insert properties into your document, here is where you could go to make those changes:

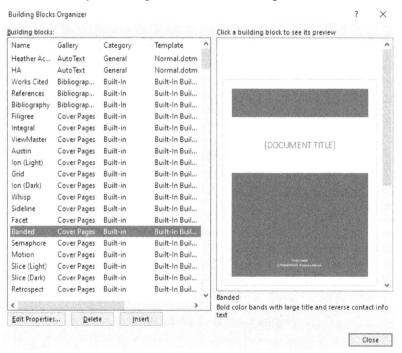

Figure 5.26 – Building Blocks Organizer

If there is a specific **cover page** that you would like to use, you could go to the **Insert** tab and click on **Cover Page** to open the gallery and view those cover pages there. Alternatively, you can view and insert them from this **Building Block Organizer** window, too. It is really the same thing, except in the **Building Block Organizer** window, you have access to all your Quick Parts and not just the ones from one specific category.

To learn more about building blocks, please refer to the following resource: `https://docs.microsoft.com/en-us/office/vba/word/concepts/working-with-word/working-with-building-blocks`.

Creating your own custom Quick Part

Perhaps the most useful part of Quick Parts, though, is the ability to create your own Quick Parts, specifically your own AutoText. Let's say that I write a lot of letters, and I would like to save my address information along with the recipient controls and date field together as a Quick Part:

Figure 5.27 – My letter in design mode

The preceding screenshot shows you what the top of my letter looks like in design mode. As you can see, my name appears as an **Author** document property, the date is a field, and the recipient information is a series of rich text content controls. What I want to do is to save this information to my Quick Parts gallery, specifically my AutoText gallery, so I can reuse this in a new document.

Saving to the Quick Parts gallery

To save text to the Quick Parts gallery, perform the following steps:

1. First, I will exit out of design mode and double-check to make sure my text appears the way that I want it to look:

    Heather Ackmann
    123 Fake St.
    Schaumburg, IL 60194
    555-123-4567

    3/21/2021

    Recipient Name
    Title
    Company Name
    Street Address
    City, ST Zip Code

    Figure 5.28 – My letter in normal view

2. Next, select the portion of the text that you want to create as your Quick Part AutoText.

3. Then, navigate to your **Insert** tab, click on the **Quick Parts** button, and select **Save Selection to Quick Part Gallery…**:

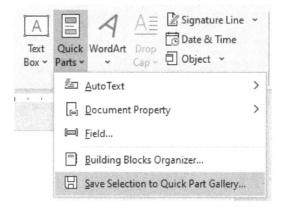

Figure 5.29 – Save Selection to Quick Part Gallery…

4. In the **Create New Building Block** window, give your Quick Part a name.

5. Select the gallery that you'd like to save the Quick Part to. In our example, we are saving it to the **AutoText** gallery:

Figure 5.30 – Selecting the Quick Part gallery: AutoText

6. You can create categories for your Quick Parts besides **General** if you anticipate making a lot of Quick Parts.

7. Give your Quick Part a meaningful description that helps you remember what the Quick Part is and why you created it.

8. Select which template you'd like to save the Quick Part to.

   Note that the Normal.dotm template contains all of Word's default styles and customizations. Any changes you make to this file will appear in future files and documents that you create in Word.

9. Next, select the options that you'd like for your content. For **AutoText**, more than likely, you will be selecting the **Insert content only** option, but you could also choose to insert the content as its own paragraph or even its own page.

10. Finally, click on **OK** to save your options and create the Quick Part.

Now that we've created a Quick Part, let's check whether what we did actually worked. To test it out, open a new blank Word document. Then, from that new blank document, navigate to the **Insert** tab and select the **Quick Parts** menu. Underneath **AutoText**, you should be able to view the Quick Part that you just created:

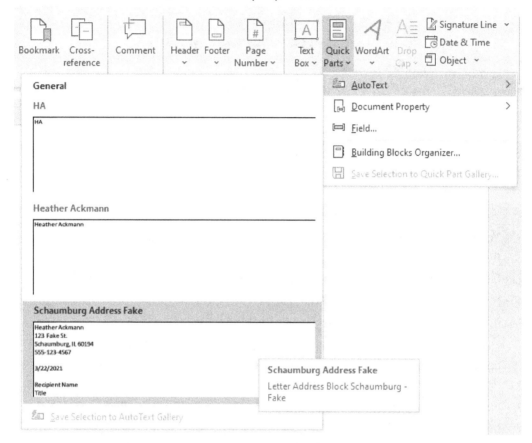

Figure 5.31 – The new AutoText Quick Part

Quick Parts are a great way in which to save time for short documents where pieces of the document tend to be reused. If you have more than just a little piece of content that is reusable, then consider making or modifying a template. The bottom line is that if the content is something you think you might use again, taking those few extra minutes now to save content and make it reusable will save a lot of time in the future when you are having to type and recreate content. Short documents can be deceiving. Trust me, all those minutes spent formatting and typing do add up over time.

Summary

In this chapter, you explored a number of different ways in which to improve your workflow when working with short documents such as letters and résumés. Whether you start from a Microsoft-supplied template and modify it for your own use, create your own custom template, or use or create your own custom Quick Part, there are many ways in which to save and reuse documents and document parts in Microsoft Word.

In the next chapter, we will be expanding upon these ideas and exploring ways in which to use tools within Microsoft Word to discuss how to create, navigate, and best format long documents such as multi-page reports and essays.

6
Lists and Characters

Working with lists in Word can be overwhelming at times. In this chapter, we will explore creating and working with bulleted, numbered, and multilevel lists. You will learn how to define bullet and number formatting and apply that formatting to a list. We will also look at how to define a multilevel list and apply it before learning how to change list indents and renumber a list.

We will then move on to viewing word and character counts in a document. Knowing the word and character count of a document can help you understand things such as the readability of the document and how much space you are using. We will learn how to use the Word Count tool to do this.

As you type a document in Word, many hidden formatting marks are created that you never see. Word also has what are known as special characters, which are regular text and formatting characters that are not on a standard keyboard. In this chapter, you will learn how to unhide hidden formatting marks and how to add those special characters.

In this chapter, we will cover the following main topics:

- Working with bulleted and numbered lists
- Viewing word and character counts
- Special characters

Working with bulleted and numbered lists

At the beginning of this chapter, a list of this chapter's topics was provided. This list has been bulleted to emphasize the items included so that you, the reader, will take notice of it without suggesting that the list belongs in a specific order. This is usually the purpose of a bulleted list. We could have also numbered the list because the items are being presented in that specific order. Typically, a numbered list is used to denote a sequence of things in a particular order, such as steps in a procedure. We will begin this section by showing you how to create a bulleted list. From there, you will learn how to create a numbered list and a multilevel list.

Creating a bulleted and numbered list

When you want to create a bulleted list, there are two ways to go about it in Word. You can either start by creating a bulleted list first and adding items to it, or you can create a list first and apply a bulleted list style afterward.

To create a bulleted list, you will need to be on the **Home** tab of the Ribbon. In the **Paragraph** section, you will find the **Bullets** button.

The following screenshot shows the **Bullets** button:

Figure 6.1 – The Bullets button

The **Bullets** button is made up of two parts; the left part shows a representation of a bulleted list, while the right section is a down arrow. To create a bulleted list, click on the left portion of the button. Your insertion point will indent **0.25"** from the left margin and a small black circle will appear. Your insertion point will then indent to **0.50"** from the left margin. At this point, you can begin adding text. After you type your first list item, use the *Enter* key to move down to the next line in the list. Another bullet will appear below the first, and you can continue to create your list in this manner. Remember that when you use the *Enter* key to create a new list item, you are creating a new paragraph. Each list item is its own paragraph.

> **Important Note**
>
> When you create either a bulleted or numbered list, it is important to know that the space between the bullet or number and the text is created by using a tab. If you turn on the **Show/Hide** feature to reveal the formatting marks, you will see the *Tab* character in the space. It is also important to remember that when you use the *Enter* key to create a new list item, it creates a new paragraph. Each list item is its own paragraph.

The following screenshot shows a default bulleted list and the ruler above for position:

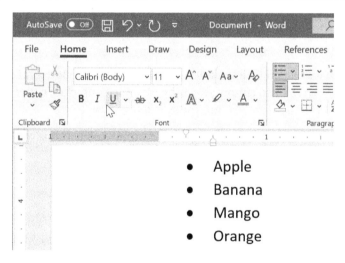

Figure 6.2 – A bulleted list

The second way to create a bulleted list is to type the list first. Once you have completed the list, you will need to select it, then go to the **Paragraph** section of the **Home** tab and click the **Bullets** button. The list will then be transformed into a bulleted list.

Numbered lists are created similarly to what I showed previously for creating a bulleted list, and likewise, there are two methods. On the **Home** tab, in the **Paragraphs** section, you will see the **Numbering** button:

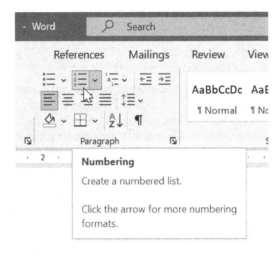

Figure 6.3 – The Numbering button

You can also convert a bulleted list into a numbered list, or a numbered list into a bulleted list at any time. To convert a list, simply select the entire list and click either the **Bullets** or **Numbering** button to change that list into the selected option.

Now that we understand how to create bulleted and numbered lists, we will explore multilevel lists in the next section.

Creating multilevel lists

Multilevel lists are used when you have a sequence of things that have a hierarchy, such as a policy or procedure. Typically, each level will have some indication that it is a subheading of the item above it, such as the alignment, indentation, bullet style, or number. This will be determined by the list's style. Multilevel lists can use bullets, numbers, or a combination of both. Any list, whether bulleted or numbered, can become a multilevel list. In Word, a multilevel list can have up to nine levels.

The following is an example of a multilevel list using the default multilevel list format:

1. Top level heading
   a. Level 2
      i. Level 3
         1. Level 4
            a. Level 5

Figure 6.4 – Multilevel list

To create a multilevel list, start with a standard list. To demote an item in the list by one level in the hierarchy, place your insertion point in front of the text of that item and press the *Tab* key once. To demote an item two levels, press the *Tab* key twice. If you want to promote a list item in the hierarchy, hold down the *Shift* key and press *Tab*. You can also demote and promote a list item by using the **Decrease Indent** and **Increase Indent** buttons, which are located on the Ribbon:

Figure 6.5 – The Decrease and Increase Indent buttons

Now that we have learned how to create lists, we can start to make changes to their appearance. We will begin by looking at how to change the type of bullet that's used.

Applying a bullet

By default, the bullet is a small black circle. However, several other choices are readily available. To apply a different bullet from **Bullet Library**, select the list or list item you wish to change and click the small down arrow to the right-hand side of the **Bullets** button.

The following screenshot shows the **Bullet Library** option:

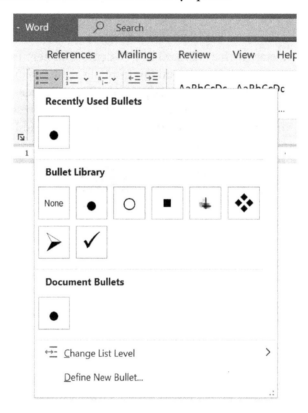

Figure 6.6 – Bullet Library

You will now see several other bullet options that you can apply. To see a live preview of the bullets, hover your mouse over a bullet style and your selected bullets will change to show that new bullet. To change the bullet, simply click on the desired bullet to change it.

The following is an example of a list with different bullets applied:

- ○ Apple
- ➢ Banana
- ❖ Mango
- ✓ Orange

Figure 6.7 – Different bullets

Now, let's look at how we can choose from hundreds of different symbols to define a new bullet.

Defining a bullet

The **Bullet Library** option in Word only shows a few different bullet types. However, hundreds of other symbols can be used as bullets if you know how to find them. To define a new bullet, you will need to click the down arrow to the right of the **Bullets** button. At the bottom of the **Bullets** window, you will see the **Define New Bullet** option. Click there and the **Define New Bullet** window will now appear.

The following screenshot shows the **Define New Bullet** window:

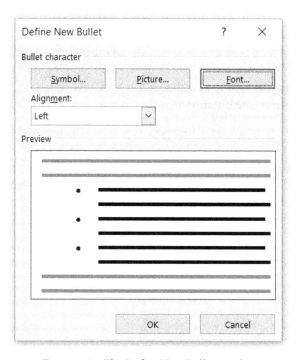

Figure 6.8 – The Define New Bullet window

To define a new bullet, click the **Symbol** button at the top. This will open the **Symbol** window.

The following screenshot shows the **Symbol** window:

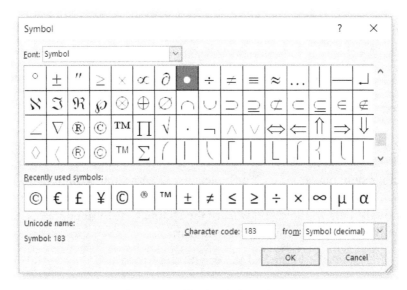

Figure 6.9 – The Symbol window

The **Symbol** window shows all the characters of the **Symbol** font. You can now scroll through and choose any of these characters to use as a bullet. Find and select the one you want, then click **OK**, and **OK** again. That new bullet will now appear in the bullet library for you to use at any place in the document.

At the top of the **Symbol** window is a drop-down font list. The **Symbol** font is displayed by default. You can click the drop-down list to see a list of all the installed fonts on that computer. Most fonts have symbols and other characters associated with them. If you select a particular font, you will see all the characters and can search through them to find even more options to use as bullets. One of my favorite fonts to find unusual bullets is **Webdings**. It contains things such as alien heads, lightning bolts, spider webs, and lots of other fun symbols.

The following screenshot shows the **Webdings** symbols page:

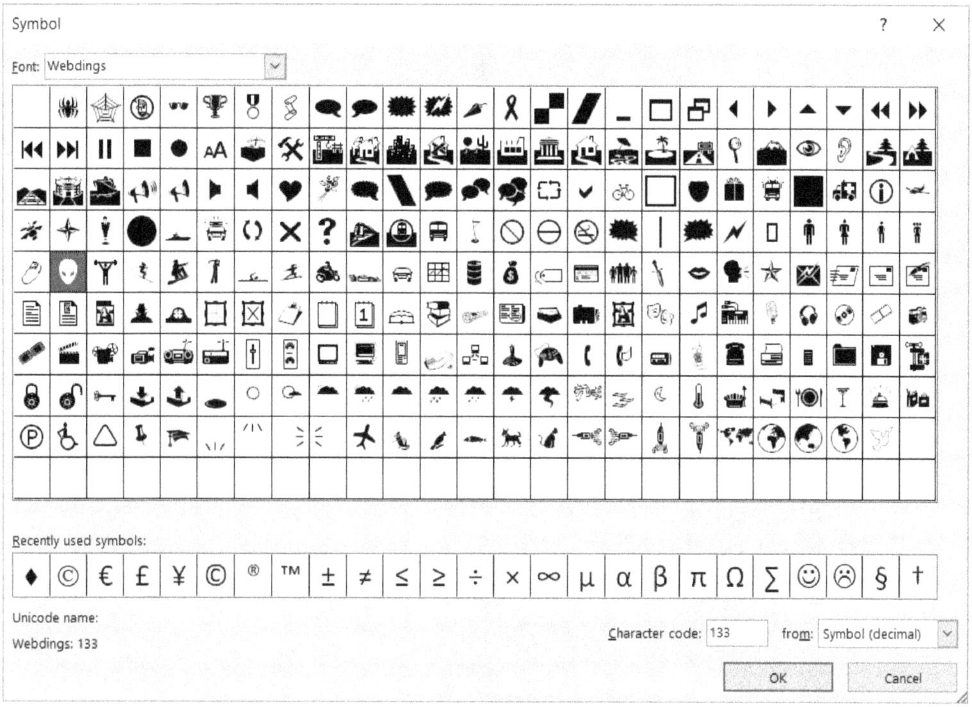

Figure 6.10 – Webdings

Next, let's see how to change the color of the bullet point.

Changing the bullet color

If you want to change the color of a bullet, before you click **OK** in the **Define New Bullet** window, select the **Font** button. This will bring up the **Font** window so that you can change the color. Near the middle of the window, you will see **Font color:** and below will be a box with a drop-down arrow to the right. Click that arrow and the **Theme Colors** window will be revealed.

The following screenshot shows the **Font** window:

Figure 6.11 – The Font window

You can now select a color from the choices shown or select the **More Colors** option at the bottom to see a full color palette of choices. Once you have selected the color you want, click **OK**, then **OK** again, and your bullet will now be the selected color.

The **Font** window also gives you options for changing the font style, size, effects, and underline style and color. Other than size, these options are seldom used with bullets.

Applying numbering

The default numbering for a list in Word is a number followed by a period, but there are several other formats you can use, including letters and Roman numerals.

To apply a numbering style, create your list and select it. Next, click the down arrow to the right of the **Numbering** button; you will see the **Numbering Library** option.

The following screenshot shows the **Numbering Library** option:

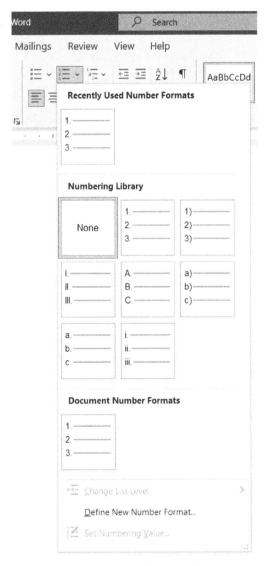

Figure 6.12 – Numbering Library

There are several formats to choose from and if you hover your mouse over them, you will see a live preview of the format applied to your list. Choose the format you want and click it to apply it to your list.

The following is an example of a numbered list using Roman numerals:

I.   Apple

II.   Banana

III.   Mango

IV.   Orange

Figure 6.13 – A numbered list

Defining a number format

To define a new number format, select the down arrow to the right of the **Numbering** button to reveal the **Numbering Library** option. Near the bottom, you will see **Define New Number Format**; click here. Once you've clicked that, the **Define New Number Format** window will appear.

The following screenshot shows the **Define New Number Format** window:

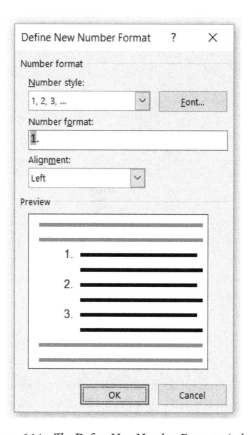

Figure 6.14 – The Define New Number Format window

At the top of this window is the **Number style** box. If you select the drop-down arrow on the right, you will see the list of choices with a scroll bar on the left. You can use that to scroll through multiple options.

The following screenshot shows the **Number style** list:

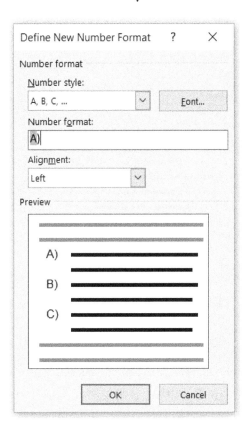

Figure 6.15 – The Number style list

You can make your selection from the list and you will see a preview of the number style in the preview window below.

Below the **Number style** menu is the **Number format** box. This is where you can decide to add or remove a period, a closed parenthesis symbol, a hyphen, or anything else to appear before or after the number style. You can simply type in the box to add whatever you wish. This will also be shown in the preview window below.

The following is the **Number Format** box with a closed parenthesis symbol after the letter:

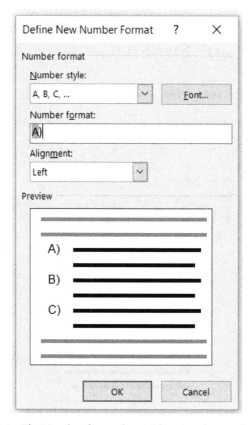

Figure 6.16 – The Number format box with a closed parenthesis added

Once the style and format are to your liking, click **OK** and the format will be added to **Numbering Library** for you to use anywhere in the document.

Modifying the number font's formatting

To modify the formatting of the font of your number style, you will need to click the **Font** button to the right of the **Number style** box. This will open the **Font** window. The **Font** window has options for changing the font, font style, size, font color, underline style, underline color, and font effects. You can choose to change any of these options as you would any text in Word by selecting the options from the specific lists. Once you have made your choices, click **OK** to apply them; your number font format will be changed accordingly.

The following screenshot shows the **Font** window:

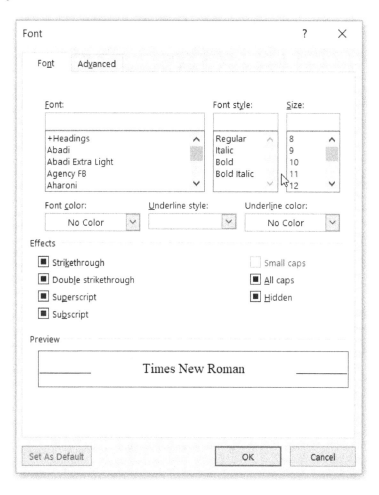

Figure 6.17 – The Font window

Now that we have worked with bulleted and numbered lists, it is time for us to learn about using multilevel lists. We will begin by learning how to apply one of the default multilevel list styles.

Applying a multilevel list

To apply a multilevel list style to a list, you will need to select the list and click the **Multilevel List** button.

The following screenshot shows the **Multilevel List** button:

Figure 6.18 – The Multilevel List button

Once you click the **Multilevel List** button, the **List Library** option will now appear, and you will have several list styles to choose from.

The following screenshot shows the **List Library** option:

Figure 6.19 – List Library

You can choose your desired list style and click to apply it to your list. Now, you can demote or promote the list items to achieve your desired level of hierarchy.

The following is an example of the default multilevel list with several levels:

1) Heading One
   a) Subheading 1a
      i) Subheading 1a section i
2) Heading Two
   a) Subheading 2a
   b) Subheading 2b
3) Heading Three
   a) Subheading 3a

Figure 6.20 – Multilevel list

Defining a new multilevel list

To define a new multilevel list, click the **Multilevel List** button and, near the bottom, select **Define New Multilevel List**. The **Define new Multilevel list** window will now appear.

The following screenshot shows the **Define new Multilevel list** window:

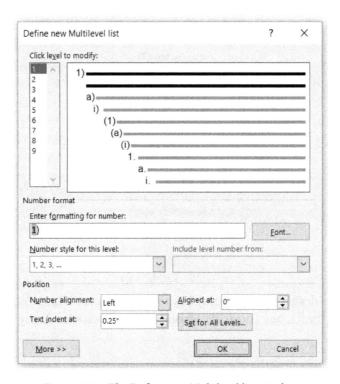

Figure 6.21 – The Define new Multilevel list window

Multilevel lists can have up to nine levels. On the left, you will see a column of numbers from 1 to 9. Each of these represents those levels and if you click on one, the corresponding level will become active in the box to the right. Begin by selecting the first level and define that level using the options in the **Number format** section. You have options for formatting the number, and the number style below that. These options are the same as for a numbered list.

The bottom section of the **Define new Multilevel list** window has a section for **Position**. Here, you can set the alignment, where it aligns to, and the text indentation for each level individually. You can also set it for all levels at once by using the **Set for All Levels** button on the right. Once you have made your choices and defined the new list, click **OK**. Your new list style will now appear in **List Library** for use throughout the document.

If you want to change the font formatting for your new list style, you can click the **Font…** button in the **Define new Multilevel list** window to open the **Font** window. The **Font** window has options for changing the font, font style, size, font color, underline style, underline color, and font effects. You can choose to change any of these options as you would any text in Word by selecting the options from the specific lists. Once you have made your choices, click **OK** to apply the changes, and your font format will be changed.

In the next section, we will explore how to change the indents in a list.

Changing list indents

As stated previously, both bullets and numbers are indented **0.25"** from the left margin in a list, and the text is then indented **0.50"** from the left margin. This is the default setting in Word, but we can change the position of these indents in a list. These skills can be very useful, especially if you receive a document in which a list has been modified several times. The appearance of the list can be altered greatly. It can also be useful if you just feel that you would like to change the indents or the spacing. There is no rule that you always need to use the Microsoft Word default settings. Knowing how to make changes like these can help tremendously. The following screenshot is an example of a list that has several problems with its text indents:

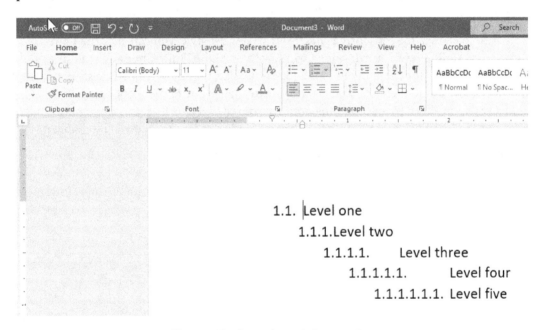

Figure 6.22 – Inconsistent indent spacing

To change the indents of a list, select the list and right-click, then select the **Adjust List Indents** option from the menu.

The following screenshot shows the **Adjust List Indents** window:

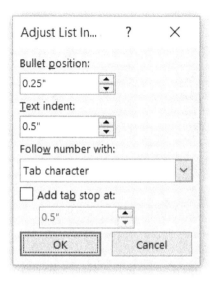

Figure 6.23 – The Adjust List Indents window

The **Adjust List Indents** window will open, and you will be presented with several options. The first is **Bullet (or Number) position**. By using the arrows on the right, you can change the amount of the indentation of the bullet or number from the left margin. The next option is **Text indent**. The arrows on the right can be used to change the amount that text is indented from the left margin.

The following screenshot shows the indent options of a numbered list being changed to **0.15"** and **0.75"**:

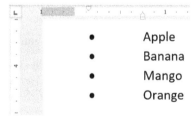

Figure 6.24 – Indents set to 0.15" and 0.75"

The third option in the **Adjust List Indents** window is **Follow bullet (or number) with**. The default option is **Tab character**, which adds a *Tab* to the text indentation. To the right is a drop-down arrow. If you click this, you will see a list of three choices.

The following screenshot shows the **Follow number with** options:

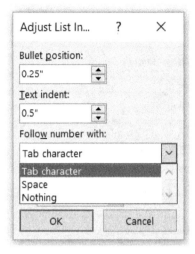

Figure 6.25 – The Follow number with options menu

The **Space** option will remove the Tab and simply insert a single space between the bullet or number and the text.

The following screenshot shows a list with the **Space** option selected:

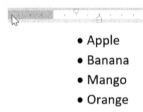

Figure 6.26 – A list using the Space option

The **Nothing** option will remove all space between the bullet or number and the text.

The following screenshot shows a list with the **Nothing** option selected:

Figure 6.27 – A list using the Nothing option

Once you have made your choices, click **OK** to apply them.

You can also change the spacing on an individual list item by choosing just that item, and from the **Adjust Line Indents** window, make any changes desired.

Renumbering a list

By default, numbered lists begin with the number 1, but that may not always be appropriate. You may also, at times, need to divide a list into smaller lists. By default, the list numbering will continue sequentially. In this section, you will learn how to renumber a list.

To begin a list with a number other than 1, select the list first, then click the small down arrow next to the **Numbering** button on the **Home** tab. The **Numbering Library** window will now open and at the very bottom, you will see **Set Numbering Value**.

The following screenshot shows the **Numbering Library** option:

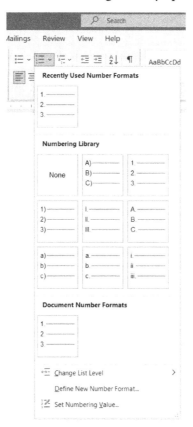

Figure 6.28 – Numbering Library

Click **Set Numbering Value** and the **Set Numbering Value** window will open.

The following screenshot shows the **Set Numbering Value** window:

Figure 6.29 – The Set Numbering Value window

By default, the **Start new list** option is selected at the top and near the bottom, **Set value to** is set to **1**. To begin the list with another number, you need to change the number in the **Set value to** box to the desired number. You can either type the number in the box or click the small up and down arrows to the right, to change the number incrementally. Once you have the desired number, click **OK** and your list will begin with the chosen number.

In this next scenario, we have two lists that both begin with the number 1. We would prefer that the numbering continues in the second list.

The following is an example of two lists beginning with the number 1:

Directors

1. Ashley
2. Tucker

Managers

1. Dave
2. Lucia

Figure 6.30 – Two lists beginning with 1

To continue the numbering in the second list, we will need to select it first. We then need to click the down arrow to the right of the **Numbering** button on the **Home** tab to open **Numbering Library**. At the bottom of that window, select the **Set Numbering Value** option to open that window. In the **Set Numbering Value** window, check the **Continue from previous list** radio button.

The following screenshot shows the **Set Numbering Value** window with **Continue from previous list** checked:

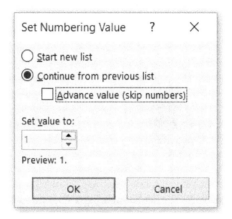

Figure 6.31 – Continue from previous list

Once you click **OK**, your list will continue the numbering from the previous list.

The following example shows the previous list with the numbering continued:

Directors

1. Ashley
2. Tucker

Managers

3. Dave
4. Lucia

Figure 6.32 – Two lists with numbering – continued

You will notice that once **Continue from previous list** is checked, the **Advance value (skip numbers)** option is now available. Also, notice that the **Set value to** box is now grayed out. If you check the **Advance value** box, the **Set value to** box will become available and you can continue the numbering, but it will start with a different value.

The following screenshot shows the **Set Numbering Value** window with **Continue from previous list** and **Advance value (skip numbers)** selected:

Figure 6.33– The Set Numbering Value window

You can now choose which number you would like the list to continue with by either typing the value into the **Set value to** box, or by using the small up and down arrows to the right to change the number incrementally. In this example, I have chosen to set the number to 6. Now, click **OK** and the numbering will be set to what you have chosen.

The following screenshot shows an example of the previous list with the numbering continued and starting with the number 6:

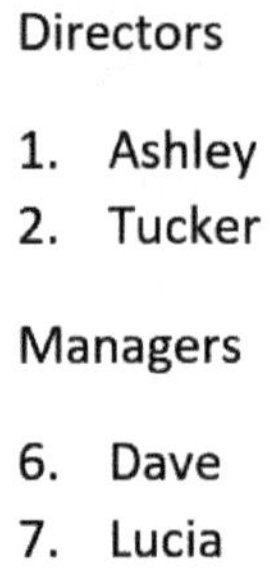

Directors

1. Ashley
2. Tucker

Managers

6. Dave
7. Lucia

Figure 6.34 – Two lists, the second one starting with 6

The automatic numbering of a list in Word is a great feature and one that you will probably use often. However, being able to renumber a list can also be very useful in many situations. It is often the uncommon features and capabilities that are the most useful.

In this section, we explored bulleted, numbered, and multilevel lists. We learned how to create them, and how to define, format, and apply them in multiple ways. A list is simply a series of items, but in Word, you have all the tools you need to transform that list into whatever you and your document require.

Knowing the character count can help you better understand the length of your writing. In the next section, we will look at how to determine word and character counts in a document.

Viewing word and character counts

Knowing the word and character count of a document can help you better understand things such as the readability of the document and how much space you are using in a document. You can use word length and word count in a sentence to help determine readability. Knowing these things can also be very helpful in publishing and typesetting. Word has an excellent word and character count tool that we will explore in this section.

The **Word Count** tool is located in the lower left of the Status Bar in Word. The Status Bar is at the bottom of the document and just above the Windows Start button and search box. It is between the page number and the **Editor** button.

The following screenshot shows the **Word Count** tool:

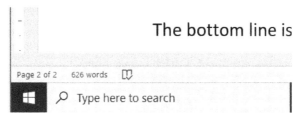

Figure 6.35 – The Word Count tool

By default, **Word Count** is set to display the word count in the document, but it also keeps track of several other statistics. To see those statistics, click on the word count and the **Word Count** window will appear. You can also find the **Word Count** window on the **Review** tab:

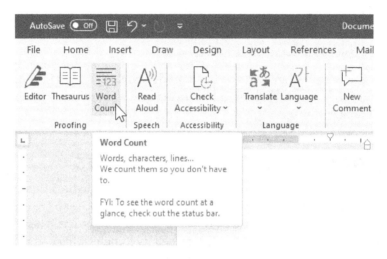

Figure 6.36 – The Word Count button on the Review tab

The following screenshot shows the **Word Count** window:

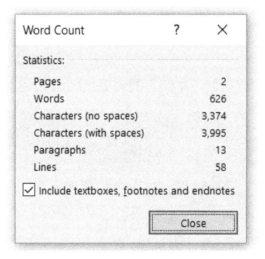

Figure 6.37 – The Word Count window

The **Word Count** window displays a list of these statistics:

- **Pages**: The count of pages in the document.

- **Words**: A count of how many words are in the document.

- **Characters (no spaces)**: A count of the characters in the document. This includes punctuation but not spaces.

- **Characters (with spaces)**: A count of characters in the document, including punctuation and spaces.

- **Paragraphs**: A count of paragraphs in the document.

- **Lines**: A count of lines in the document. This includes lines with no text.

At the bottom of the window is a checkbox that, when checked, will include textboxes, footnotes, and endnotes in the counts. This box is checked by default. If unchecked, it will exclude those items from the count.

It is also possible to display the **Character Count (with spaces)** option on the Status Bar. To do so, you will need to customize the Status Bar. Bring your mouse down to the word count on the Status Bar and right-click. The **Customize Status Bar** menu will open.

The following screenshot shows the **Customize Status Bar** menu:

Customize Status Bar	
Customize Status Bar	
Formatted Page Number	2
Section	1
✓ Page Number	Page 2 of 2
Vertical Page Position	
Line Number	
Column	
✓ Word Count	626 words
Character Count (with spaces)	3995 characters
✓ Spelling and Grammar Check	No Errors
✓ Language	
✓ Label	
✓ Signatures	Off
Information Management Policy	Off
Permissions	Off
Track Changes	Off
Caps Lock	Off
Overtype	Insert
Selection Mode	
Macro Recording	Not Recording
Accessibility Checker	
✓ Upload Status	
✓ Document Updates Available	
✓ Focus	
✓ View Shortcuts	
✓ Zoom Slider	
✓ Zoom	160%

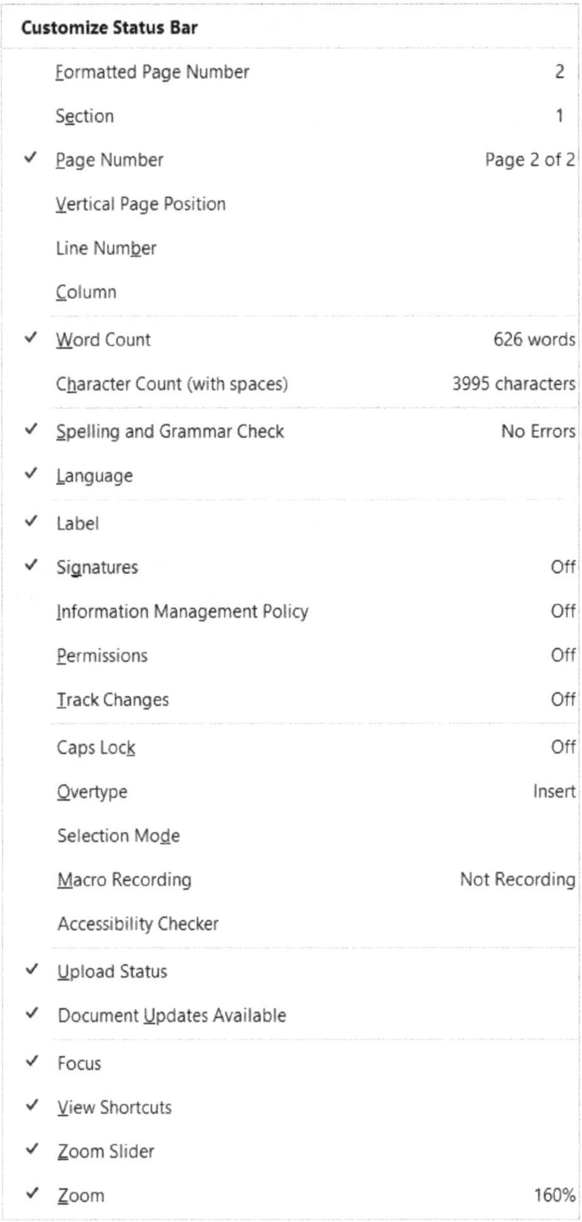

Figure 6.38 – The Customize Status Bar menu

There are many options in this menu but the ones we will focus on can be found in the second section from the top, where you will see **Word Count** and **Character Count (with spaces)**. To the left of the **Word Count** option, you will see a small checkmark. This indicates that **Word Count** will appear on the Status Bar. You can click in the space to the left of the **Character Count (with spaces)** option to add the checkmark and display that option on the Status Bar.

The following screenshot shows the **Character Count (with spaces)** option checked:

Figure 6.39 – The Character Count (with spaces) option

Both options will now appear on the Status Bar.

The following screenshot shows the Status Bar with the **Word Count** and **Character Count (with spaces)** statistics shown:

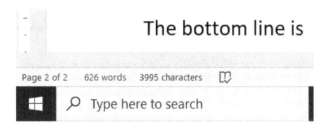

Figure 6.40 – Status Bar

At any time, you can go back to the **Customize Status Bar** window and uncheck either or both options to display or not display them on the Status Bar.

The information that is kept in the **Word Count** window can be helpful in countless ways. We saw how to access the **Word Count** window to view those statistics and how we could continually display the word and character count on the Status Bar. However, when using these statistics, I am sure you can agree that Word being able to keep track of these statistics is a great deal easier than counting them manually.

In the next section, we will learn how to show and hide paragraphs and other formatting marks in a document, and how to insert special characters.

Special characters

As you type a document in Word, many hidden formatting marks are created that you never see unless you choose to unhide them. Word also has what are known as special characters. These are regular text and formatting characters that are not on a standard keyboard. These text special characters belong to fonts and may appear differently in different fonts. Some characters may not be available in all fonts either. The special formatting characters in Word affect the layout of a document.

In this section, we will learn how to show and hide hidden formatting marks and what those marks indicate. We will also learn how to insert those special characters that do not appear on standard keyboards into a document.

The **Show/Hide** button appears on the **Home** tab of the Ribbon in the **Paragraph** section. The button looks somewhat like a backward letter **P**. It represents the paragraph formatting mark.

The following screenshot shows the **Show/Hide ¶** button:

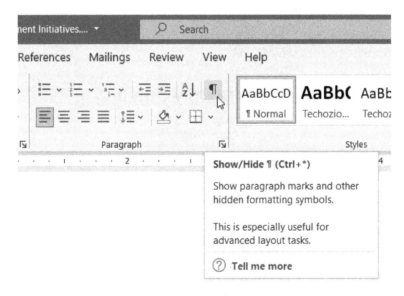

Figure 6.41 – The Show/Hide ¶ button

Once clicked, it will reveal all the hidden formatting marks in the document.

The following screenshot shows a section of a document with the hidden formatting marks revealed:

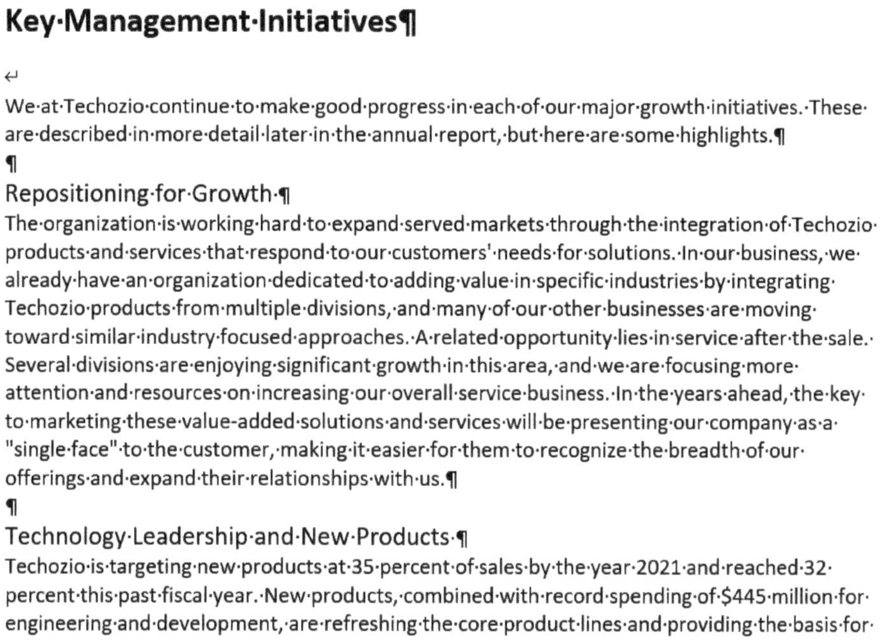

Key·Management·Initiatives¶

↵
We·at·Techozio·continue·to·make·good·progress·in·each·of·our·major·growth·initiatives.·These·are·described·in·more·detail·later·in·the·annual·report,·but·here·are·some·highlights.¶
¶
Repositioning·for·Growth·¶
The·organization·is·working·hard·to·expand·served·markets·through·the·integration·of·Techozio·products·and·services·that·respond·to·our·customers'·needs·for·solutions.·In·our·business,·we·already·have·an·organization·dedicated·to·adding·value·in·specific·industries·by·integrating·Techozio·products·from·multiple·divisions,·and·many·of·our·other·businesses·are·moving·toward·similar·industry·focused·approaches.·A·related·opportunity·lies·in·service·after·the·sale.·Several·divisions·are·enjoying·significant·growth·in·this·area,·and·we·are·focusing·more·attention·and·resources·on·increasing·our·overall·service·business.·In·the·years·ahead,·the·key·to·marketing·these·value-added·solutions·and·services·will·be·presenting·our·company·as·a·"single·face"·to·the·customer,·making·it·easier·for·them·to·recognize·the·breadth·of·our·offerings·and·expand·their·relationships·with·us.¶
¶
Technology·Leadership·and·New·Products·¶
Techozio·is·targeting·new·products·at·35·percent·of·sales·by·the·year·2021·and·reached·32·percent·this·past·fiscal·year.·New·products,·combined·with·record·spending·of·$445·million·for·engineering·and·development,·are·refreshing·the·core·product·lines·and·providing·the·basis·for·

Figure 6.42 – The hidden formatting marks revealed

Being able to see these formatting marks can be especially helpful for document layout. In the past, formatting marks were referred to as non-printing characters because they would not be printed, even if they were unhidden. Let's look at some examples of the more common formatting marks in Word.

The following screenshot shows the paragraph return mark highlighted in red:

"single·face"·to·the·customer,·making·it·easier·for·the
offerings·and·expand·their·relationships·with·us.¶
¶
Technology·Leadership·and·New·Products·¶
Techozio·is·targeting·new·products·at·35·percent·of·sal

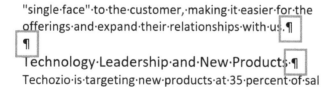

Figure 6.43 – The paragraph return mark

The following screenshot shows the line break mark highlighted in red:

Key·Management·Initiatives¶

↵

We·at·Techozio·continue·to·make·good·progre
are·described·in·more·detail·later·in·the·annua

Figure 6.44 – The line break mark

The following screenshot shows the tab mark highlighted in red:

→   Řepositioning·for·Growth·¶
The·organization·is·working·hard·to·expan
products·and·services·that·respond·to·ou

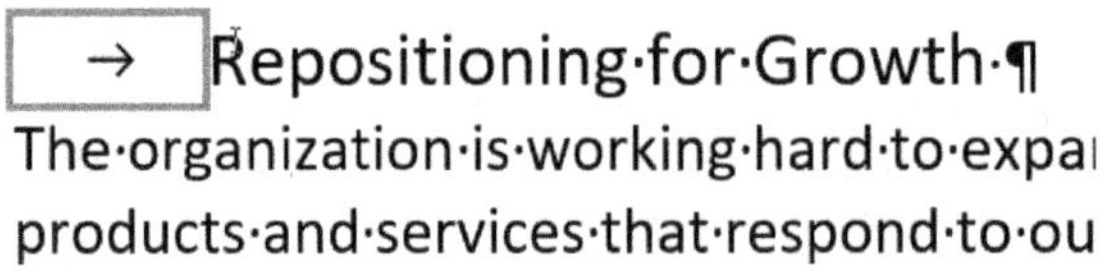

Figure 6.45 – The tab mark

The following screenshot shows the spaces mark with a red arrow:

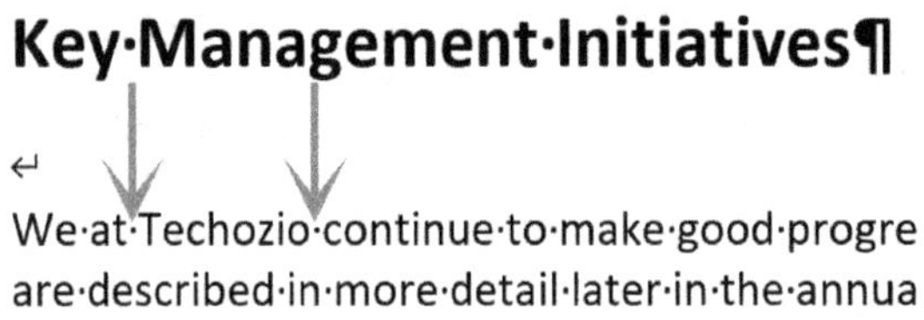

Key·Management·Initiatives¶

↵

We·at·Techozio·continue·to·make·good·progre
are·described·in·more·detail·later·in·the·annua

Figure 6.46 – Spaces marks

These hidden formatting marks can be especially helpful when you receive a document and need to adjust the layout. Being able to see exactly how the document is formatted can save you a lot of headaches. In the next section, we will look at adding special characters to a document.

Inserting special characters

Word has 12 special text characters that are typically not found on a standard keyboard. These text characters include things such as the en dash and the em dash. The en dash (–) is approximately the width of the letter *n* and is used to connect things that are related by distance. The em dash (—) is approximately the width of the letter *m* and can be used as a break in a sentence. There are also 15 special formatting characters, such as a non-breaking space. In this section, we will learn how to insert those characters into a document.

As we have mentioned previously, these special characters do not appear on a standard keyboard. So, the question is, how do we add them to a document? Well, there are keyboard shortcuts for some of them, but not all, and a few of them can be added using **AutoCorrect**. The best method for inserting special characters is right there on the **Insert** tab of the Ribbon.

To find the special characters and insert them into a document, you need to be on the **Insert** tab. At the far right, you will find the **Symbols** section. Click the **Symbol** button and a small window of symbols will appear.

The following screenshot shows the **Symbol** button and a window of symbols:

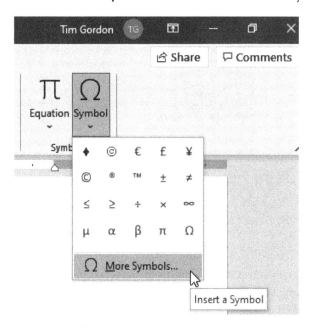

Figure 6.47 – The Symbol button and More Symbols window

At the bottom of this window is the **Ω More Symbols** option. Click this to reveal the **Symbol** window. When the **Symbol** window opens, there will be two tabs at the top: **Symbols** and **Special Characters**. Click on the **Special Characters** tab.

The following screenshot shows the **Special Characters** window:

Figure 6.48 – The Special Characters window

From this window, you can select and insert all the special characters in Word. To insert any of these special characters, click to select one, and then click the **Insert** button at the lower right. The special character will then be inserted into your document at the place of your insertion point. Click the **Close** button when you are finished.

You will also notice that several of the special characters have keyboard shortcut sequences listed in the **Shortcut key** column to the right. These shortcuts can also be used to insert specific special characters.

Now, let's look at the special text characters.

The following screenshot shows the **Special Characters** tab of the **Symbol** window with the special text characters highlighted in red boxes:

Figure 6.49 – The special text characters

Here is a list of the special text characters:

- **Em dash**: Used to mark a break in a sentence.
- **En dash**: Used to mark ranges.
- **Copyright**: Used to indicate a copyrighted work.
- **Registered**: Used to indicate a registered phrase or logo.
- **Trademark**: Used to indicate a phrase or logo is intended to be an identifier.
- **Section**: This is a section break symbol. It does not insert a section break.
- **Paragraph**: This is a paragraph symbol. It does not insert a new paragraph.
- **Ellipsis**: A set of three dots used to indicate that text has been omitted.
- **Single opening quote**: The same as this quote being inserted from the keyboard.
- **Single closing quote**: The same as this quote being inserted from the keyboard.
- **Double opening quote**: The same as this quote being inserted from the keyboard.
- **Double closing quote**: The same as this quote being inserted from the keyboard.

Now, let's look at the special formatting characters.

The following screenshot shows the **Special Characters** tab of the **Symbol** window with the special formatting characters highlighted in red boxes:

Figure 6.50 – Special formatting characters

Here is a list of the special formatting characters:

- **Nonbreaking Hyphen**: Prevents hyphenated words, numbers, or text strings from breaking at the end of a line.

- **Optional Hyphen**: Only appears if a word or text string needs to be hyphenated at the end of a line.

- **Em Space**: A space that is of equal length to an em dash from the same font.

- **En Space**: A space that is of equal length to an en dash from the same font.

- **¼ Em Space**: An em space that is ¼ of the length of an em dash from the same font.

- **No-Width Optional Break**: Used to control where a word or text string breaks at the end of a line.

- **No-Width Non Break**: Prevents a word, number, or text string from breaking at the end of a line.

- **Left-to-Right Mark**: An invisible control character used in documents that combines left-to-right languages, such as English or Spanish, with right-to-left languages, such as Arabic or Hebrew.

- **Right-to-Left Mark**: An invisible control character used in documents that combines left-to-right languages, such as English or Spanish, with right-to-left languages, such as Arabic or Hebrew.

- **Left-to-Right Embedding**: An invisible control character used in documents that combines left-to-right languages, such as English or Spanish, with right-to-left languages, such as Arabic or Hebrew.

- **Right-to-Left Embedding**: An invisible control character used in documents that combine left-to-right languages, such as English or Spanish, with right-to-left languages, such as Arabic or Hebrew.

- **Left-to-Right Override**: An invisible control character used in documents that combines left-to-right languages, such as English or Spanish, with right-to-left languages, such as Arabic or Hebrew.

- **Right-to-Left Override**: An invisible control character used in documents that combines left-to-right languages, such as English or Spanish, with right-to-left languages, such as Arabic or Hebrew.

- **Pop Directional Formatting**: An invisible control character used in documents that combines left-to-right languages, such as English or Spanish, with right-to-left languages, such as Arabic or Hebrew.

Special text characters can be useful in many obvious ways, but the special formatting characters can be invaluable when you're on the document's layout. Knowing what these special characters are and how to add them to a document can be very beneficial.

Summary

In this chapter, we spent a great deal of time learning about lists in Word. We saw how to create bulleted, numbered, and multilevel lists. Then, we looked at how to apply different bullets or numbers to a list, and how to define new bullets and numbers. We also explored how to define a new multilevel list and how to change its number style and format. Next, we explored how to change the indents in a list, as well as how to continue list numbering or change the numbering value in a list.

In the next section, we learned how to display the word count in a document and how we could view other statistics kept by Word. This included statistics such as the number of characters, with or without spaces, how many paragraphs, and how many lines are in the document.

Every Word document contains hidden formatting characters and in the next section, we showed you how to reveal those hidden characters by using the **Show/Hide** button. We also saw examples of some of the most common formatting marks.

Lastly, we explained Word's special characters and how we could add them to a document. There are two types of special characters: text and formatting. Text special characters such as en dashes and em dashes are just regular text characters that are not found on a standard keyboard. Formatting special characters assist with the document's layout and are not printed. We learned how to find these special characters and insert them into a document.

This chapter dealt with a lot of features that can affect document layout and how we can manipulate and view these things. These are all especially useful tools when creating long documents in Word.

In the next chapter, we will learn about structuring long documents for better organization. We will cover how to create sections and work with page orientation. We will also learn about numbering pages and sections, as well as how to work with headers and footers.

7
Structuring Long Documents for Better Organization

The longer a document becomes, the harder it can be for people to read and understand the information contained within the document. Adding simple, visually different elements such as a simple list can do wonders to help break up long paragraphs, making it easier for people to read information and scan documents for what it is important. But that is certainly not all you can do to break up long documents by organizing the document into sections, both for you, your readers, and for special Microsoft Word features.

In this chapter, we are going to explore some tools to help you create different looks and labels for the various sections and parts of your document. We will cover the following key topics to help you create a more readable and scannable document with Microsoft Word:

- Creating breaks
- Creating different page orientations
- Numbering sections and pages
- Customizing the header and footer

These various elements, combined with other important Word features such as headings and styles (see *Chapter 8*, *Saving Time and Ensuring Consistency with Styles*) will help your coworkers and clients sift through longer business documents to find exactly what they are looking for. The key to getting started with organizing a Microsoft Word document is to create sections.

Creating breaks

Beginners to Microsoft Word and other word processing programs frequently make the mistake of creating new sections or pages by simply hitting the *Return* or *Enter* key repeatedly on their keyboard to create the appearance of a new page or a new section within their document. The problem with this method is that if you ever go back and edit a previous paragraph in your document or insert a picture or resize anything that appears before all those carriage returns, all that space may shift to an unintended place within your document.

A break is different from hitting the *Enter* key on your keyboard. In fact, if you open any Word document and click on the **Show/Hide Paragraph Marks** toggle button, you can view all of the hidden formatting marks in any Word document to view all the spaces, paragraph marks, or even section breaks that appear within that document. You can find this option in the **Home** tab, as you can see in the following screenshot:

Figure 7.1 – Showing/hiding formatting marks

With formatting marks visible, all spaces will appear as tiny little dots between each word. Section breaks, however, will appear inside dotted lines with the words **Section Break** and then the kind of break following in parentheses, as you can see in the following screenshot:

Figure 7.2 – Section Break (Continuous)

The preceding screenshot shows a continuous section break. With formatting marks toggled off, readers would never know a section break appears here because the text continues or flows directly beneath on the same page. But there are several other types of section breaks you can choose from, depending on your needs. Let's look at them in the next section.

Types of breaks

There are two basic types of breaks you can create in Microsoft Word: page breaks and section breaks. Page breaks are usually the kind that most people are familiar with, and they are certainly the most popular. But there are other kinds of page breaks: column and text wrapping. A column break is used to stop the text in one column and continue text in the beginning of the next column. A text wrapping break separates text around objects on web pages (yes, you can technically use Word to create web pages, though these authors believe there are other tools better suited for building web pages). Those three breaks are the kinds of page breaks you will find in Word. As for creating a page break, that we will cover next.

Creating a page break

Once you have decided which type of break is appropriate for your document, save your document and then follow these steps:

1. To create a break, you will first need to move your insertion point to where you want the break to begin.

2. Next, navigate to the **Layout** tab and click on **Breaks**. This will open the **Breaks** menu:

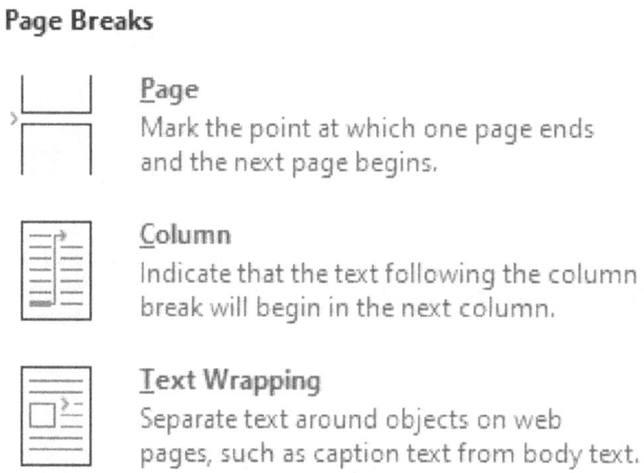

Page Breaks

Page
Mark the point at which one page ends and the next page begins.

Column
Indicate that the text following the column break will begin in the next column.

Text Wrapping
Separate text around objects on web pages, such as caption text from body text.

Figure 7.3 – Types of page breaks

3. Toward the very top, you will see **Page**; click on that to insert a page break.

Now that you know how to create a page break, in the next section, we will see how to create a section break.

Creating section breaks

In addition to page breaks, there is another category of breaks called section breaks. In addition to the continuous section break you saw earlier, which creates a new section and continues the text on the same page, there are several other kinds of section breaks, including a next page section break, an even page section break, and an odd page section break:

Figure 7.4 – Section breaks

You might be wondering why all these section breaks are necessary, especially the next page section break. Well, section breaks are useful in times when you want a part of your document to look different from the rest of your document. Sections, in Microsoft Word, can have their own look, including their own page orientations, layouts, and even their own headers and footers and other formatting too. We will cover how to format these kinds of sections in the next few sections.

Creating different page orientations

Sometimes, you might find it necessary to create different layouts or page orientations for a select page range within a document. For example, let's say you'd like the first page in your document to be oriented as portrait, but the second page to appear as landscape:

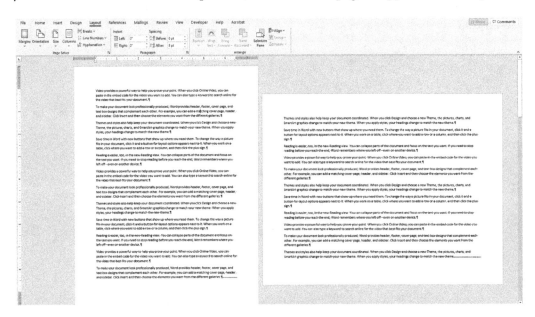

Figure 7.5 – Different page orientations

The preceding example is only possible with sections. In fact, if you've ever attempted to select a page range and change the layout in a document without first creating sections in your document, then you may have already discovered that the orientation for your entire document will change rather than just one select area of the document. Section breaks are necessary if you want to change part of a document's layout. This is especially true for the page orientation.

Changing the page orientation

If you would like to change the page orientation like I have done in the preceding example, you will need to insert a section break at the start and at the end where you would like that page to change layout. In the preceding example, page 1 is portrait, page 2 is landscape, and then the rest of the document returns to portrait. So, at the start of page 2, I have inserted a continuous section break and at the end of page 2, I have another continuous section break as well.

> **Tip**
>
> If you would like to practice and recreate the preceding example yourself, just open a blank Microsoft Word document and type =random(). Then press the *Enter* key to insert some random fake text. Repeat as often as you like until you have several pages to work with.

In order to change the page orientation, you must insert a section break.

Inserting a section break

To insert a section break, follow these steps:

1. Move your insertion point to where you want the break to begin.

2. Next, from the **Layout** tab, click **Breaks**. This will open the **Breaks** menu. Toward the middle of the menu, you will see **Section Breaks**:

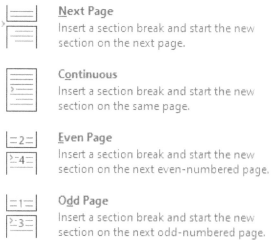

Figure 7.6 – Section breaks

3. Click on **Continuous** to insert a continuous section break.

Once you have inserted the section breaks, you can now change the page orientation of any of the sections individually without affecting the layout of any of the other sections. So, you can now move your insertion point to section 2 and change the page orientation.

Changing the page orientation

To change the page orientation, follow these steps:

1. Select the **Layout** tab and click on **Orientation**. That will open a menu with two options: **Portrait** and **Landscape**:

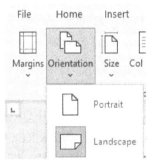

Figure 7.7 – Portrait and Landscape

2. Select **Landscape**.

    Section 2 should appear in landscape whereas the rest of the document should remain in portrait:

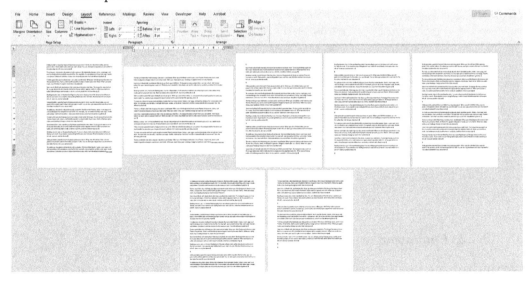

Figure 7.8 – Section 2 in landscape

And that is how you can use sections to change the orientation or the layout of your Word documents. This is just one very simple example of what you can do with sections.

Sometimes, Microsoft Word will insert section breaks automatically, perhaps without you realizing it, as is the case when you insert columns. If you select any text in your document, go to **Layout | Columns | Two**, Microsoft Word will automatically create continuous section breaks before and after the area you selected:

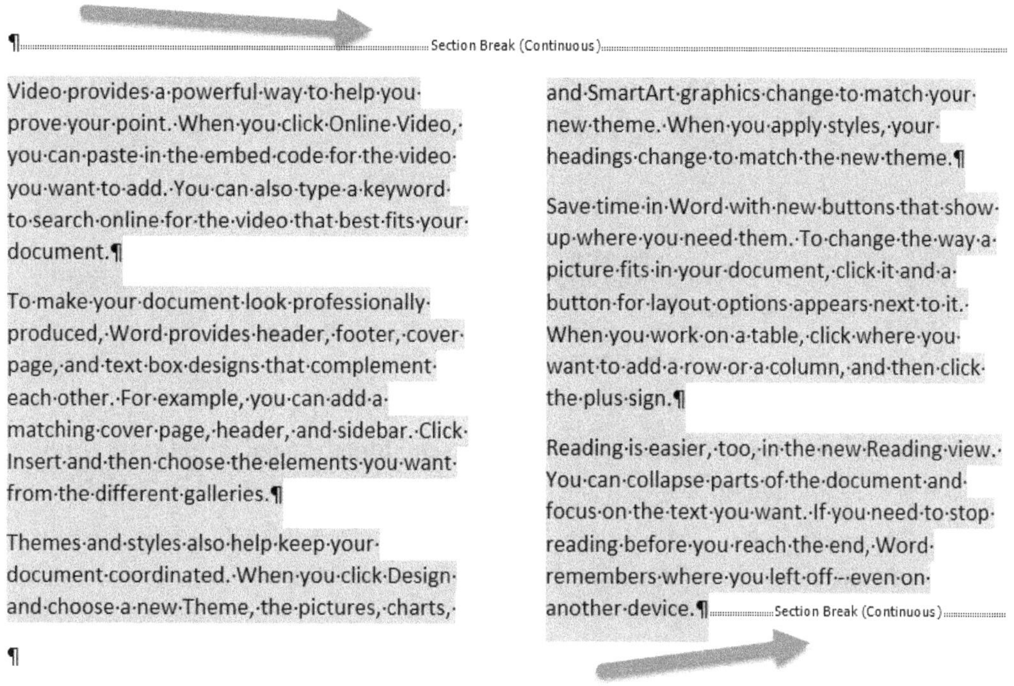
¶ Section Break (Continuous)

Video·provides·a·powerful·way·to·help·you·prove·your·point.·When·you·click·Online·Video,·you·can·paste·in·the·embed·code·for·the·video·you·want·to·add.·You·can·also·type·a·keyword·to·search·online·for·the·video·that·best·fits·your·document.¶

To·make·your·document·look·professionally·produced,·Word·provides·header,·footer,·cover·page,·and·text·box·designs·that·complement·each·other.·For·example,·you·can·add·a·matching·cover·page,·header,·and·sidebar.·Click·Insert·and·then·choose·the·elements·you·want·from·the·different·galleries.¶

Themes·and·styles·also·help·keep·your·document·coordinated.·When·you·click·Design·and·choose·a·new·Theme,·the·pictures,·charts,·and·SmartArt·graphics·change·to·match·your·new·theme.·When·you·apply·styles,·your·headings·change·to·match·the·new·theme.¶

Save·time·in·Word·with·new·buttons·that·show·up·where·you·need·them.·To·change·the·way·a·picture·fits·in·your·document,·click·it·and·a·button·for·layout·options·appears·next·to·it.·When·you·work·on·a·table,·click·where·you·want·to·add·a·row·or·a·column,·and·then·click·the·plus·sign.¶

Reading·is·easier,·too,·in·the·new·Reading·view.·You·can·collapse·parts·of·the·document·and·focus·on·the·text·you·want.·If·you·need·to·stop·reading·before·you·reach·the·end,·Word·remembers·where·you·left·off·--·even·on·another·device.¶ Section Break (Continuous)

¶

Figure 7.9 – Section breaks around columns

So, sometimes, when adding certain formatting features in Word, you may not be aware that Word is inserting sections on your behalf. This may not seem like a big deal, but if you use section numbers and start to notice randomly that your numbering appears "off," this may be why. You may have used a feature in Word that has added a section break. When in doubt, toggle on your hidden formatting marks:

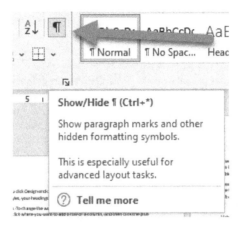

Figure 7.10 – Hidden formatting marks

Just like the note says, those symbols are especially useful for advanced layout tasks. And anything that uses section and page breaks certainly counts as an advanced layout task.

Changing page orientation is useful to know when you have charts or tables that don't quite fit in portrait mode. But still, you probably won't be using this formatting trick as frequently as our next tip: numbering sections and pages.

Numbering sections and pages

One question I am frequently asked regarding sections and page breaks is *"What is the difference between a page break and a next page section break?"*:

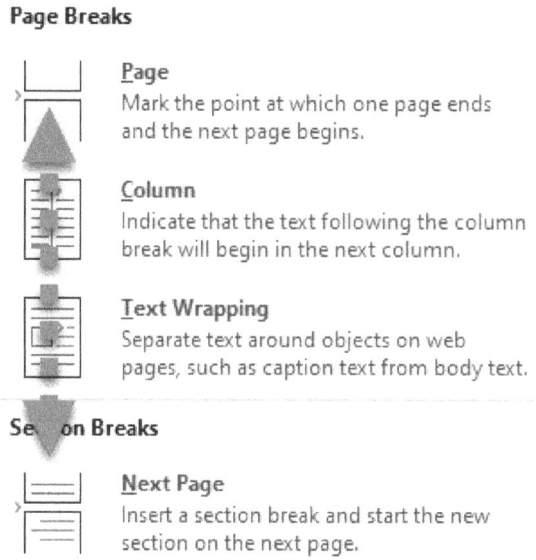

Page Breaks

Page
Mark the point at which one page ends
and the next page begins.

Column
Indicate that the text following the column
break will begin in the next column.

Text Wrapping
Separate text around objects on web
pages, such as caption text from body text.

Section Breaks

Next Page
Insert a section break and start the new
section on the next page.

Figure 7.11 – Page break versus next page section break

The simple answer I gave you earlier is that the first one is merely a page break and the latter allows for more complex formatting. This will become even clearer now when we begin working with numbering sections and pages.

In *Figure 7.12*, I have pictured a table of contents for a 121-page document. I have the formatting marks shown so you can see where all breaks and paragraph marks appear as well:

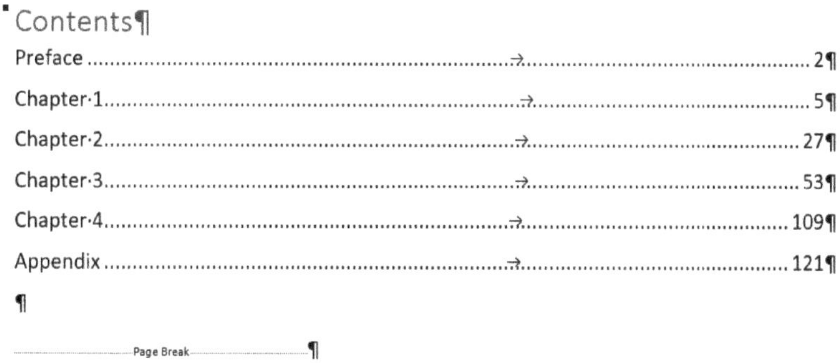

Contents¶

Preface ....→... 2¶

Chapter·1..→.. 5¶

Chapter·2..→.. 27¶

Chapter·3..→.. 53¶

Chapter·4..→.. 109¶

Appendix..→.. 121¶

¶

------------Page Break------------¶

Figure 7.12 – Table of contents

As you can see on the right of the table of contents, the page numbers for the preface and the appendix are styled the same as the rest of the chapters. Let's say we want them to appear differently. Perhaps as Roman numerals, for example.

For this to work, I would need to first section off or chunk up my document, so Word knows how I want to organize it by sections – by creating next page section breaks instead of regular page breaks to break up the chapters:

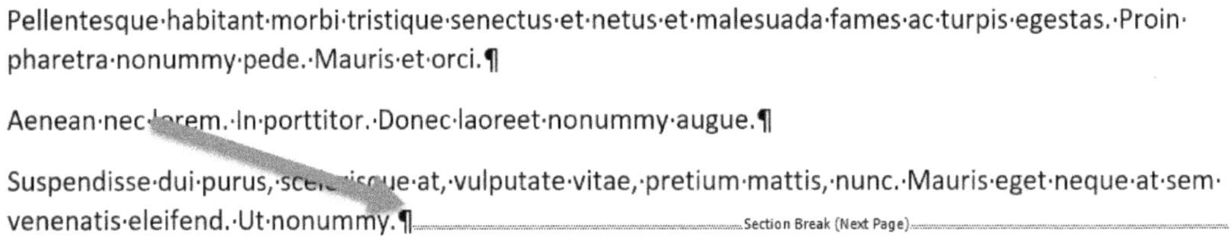

Pellentesque·habitant·morbi·tristique·senectus·et·netus·et·malesuada·fames·ac·turpis·egestas.·Proin· pharetra·nonummy·pede.·Mauris·et·orci.¶

Aenean·nec·lorem.·In·porttitor.·Donec·laoreet·nonummy·augue.¶

Suspendisse·dui·purus,·scelerisque·at,·vulputate·vitae,·pretium·mattis,·nunc.·Mauris·eget·neque·at·sem· venenatis·eleifend.·Ut·nonummy.¶————————————Section Break (Next Page)————————————

Figure 7.13 – Swap out page breaks for next page section breaks

Once I have swapped out all the page breaks and placed in next page section breaks, I am now ready to customize my page numbers.

In the next section, we will learn how to customize the headers to make our page numbers appear the way we want them to appear.

Customizing the header and footer

When working with a table of contents in Microsoft Word and if folks decide they want to customize something such as page numbers, navigating to the header and footer area is the last place most people will think to look. So, naturally, many get confused here. Working with Word's automatic table of contents feature is not the most intuitive feature or process if you are not accustomed to working with Microsoft Word documents and features.

If you have used one of Microsoft Word's automatic table of contents (like I have), content such as the names of chapters and the page numbers will be pulled from your document headings (see *Chapter 8, Saving Time and Ensuring Consistency with Styles*) and automatically be updated when you click the **Update Table** button:

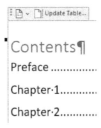

Figure 7.14 – Update Table button

So, if you want to change the appearance of something such as page numbers, knowing where to go to format them isn't very intuitive at first glance. Just remember, ultimately you want to insert page numbers, and that will help you remember where you have to go in Microsoft Word to customize your page numbers in **Table of Contents** (**TOC**) or in a header or footer – go to your **Insert** tab.

Adding page numbers to your footer

Follow these steps to add page numbers to a footer:

1. Navigate to your **Insert** tab and look for the **Header & Footer** group. In that, you will find the **Page Number** button; click on that.

    This will open a menu with a variety of options where you can insert page numbers into your document:

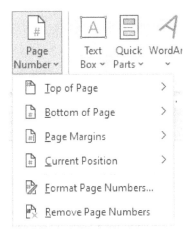

Figure 7.15 – Inserting page numbers

2. Click on **Bottom of Page**.
3. Select **Plain Number 2** to insert a page number in the center of your footer area.

Currently, however, our page numbers still aren't formatted the way we want. They still all appear as Arabic numerals. To customize the number by each section, we will need to navigate to each section and tell Microsoft Word how to format page numbers for each section.

Navigating Microsoft Word by section

One great feature and shortcut in Word if you have already created section breaks in your document is to use the **Go To...** command to navigate your long documents by section:

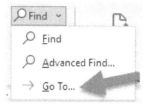

Figure 7.16 – Go To (Ctrl + G)

From the **Home** tab, in the **Editing** group, click on **Find | Go To** (or press *Ctrl + G* on your keyboard). That will open your **Find and Replace** window directly to the **Go To** tab:

Figure 7.17 – Find and Replace, Go To tab

There, in the **Go to what** window, you can select **Section** and click the **Next** button to navigation your document by section. If you have very long, 100+ page documents, this makes navigating to these sections very fast and easy, especially for page numbering tasks like this.

So, using the **Go To** box, I navigated to my preface section:

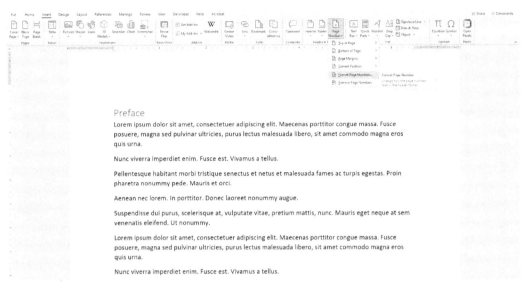

Figure 7.18 – Preface section

With my insertion point placed in this section, now I need to format the page numbers in this section.

Formatting page numbers

To format the page numbers, follow these steps:

1. Go to the **Insert** tab, to the **Header & Footer** group, and click on the **Page Number** button.

2. Inside the menu, click on the **Format Page Numbers** option. This will open the **Page Number Format** window:

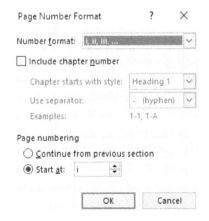

Figure 7.19 – Page Number Format window

3. Select the Roman numeral number format.

4. Choose Start at **i**.

5. Click **OK**.

6. Return to the table of contents and click **Update Table | Update page numbers only | OK**:

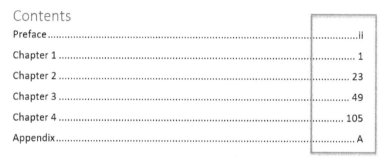

Contents

Figure 7.20 – Finished table of contents

So, as you can see in the preceding screenshot, the next page section break allows a bit more flexibility when used in combination with other Microsoft Word features such as the table of contents and page numbers.

Summary

In this chapter, we learned ways to break up a chapter into a variety of different kinds of sections so that we can use other tools and features in Microsoft Word to visually break up documents and communicate to our readers where they are within longer documents.

We learned about the different types of breaks you can create in Microsoft Word (both page and section breaks), and why section breaks are useful and necessary for formatting. We then discussed how and when you need to insert your own section breaks into a Word document. We explored several scenarios when section breaks are useful, including when changing the page orientation and when changing page numbers across different sections or chapters in a longer document. These certainly aren't the only times when breaks are handy, but they do remain some of the most frequently asked questions we receive.

In the next chapter, we will continue discussing ways to structure and organize documents to make them easier for your readers to read, for you to edit, and for you to use the tools we've discussed here with other tools and features within Microsoft Word.

8
Saving Time and Ensuring Consistency with Styles

From the moment you open a Microsoft Word document and begin to format text, from the **Home** tab, you will find several groups of options designed to help you quickly do just that. Many people choose options in the **Font** and **Paragraph** groups to change the appearance of text, but fewer will notice the far more useful options in the **Styles** group.

You can use Word styles to not only format your document faster but to create a more consistent look throughout. Styles are also helpful for using other features in Word, such as the Table of Contents, and even for navigating long documents via the **Navigation** pane. Styles are essential for people who read documents with screen readers too. So, knowing how best to incorporate and apply styles to your documents is a must-have skill.

In this chapter, we will cover the following main topics:

- What is a style?
- Applying Quick Styles
- Understanding how themes affect styles
- Creating and applying custom styles

What is a style?

A style in Word is a set of preset formatting options such as font, size, spacing, color, and other effects. You can apply these styles to any text in your document, which can make it easier to give your document a consistent look. Word comes with several already created styles, but you can also create custom styles that you can use again and again to give all your documents a consistent look.

There are many styles in Word but the ones we are probably most familiar with are found on the **Home** tab in the **Styles** section. This is referred to as the **Quick Styles** gallery:

Figure 8.1 – The Quick Styles gallery

There are three basic types of styles (paragraph, character, and linked styles). Later, in the *Telling the difference between style types* section, we will learn how to find a list of all the styles and how to discern what type of style each one is. There are many other styles in Word that are specific to different objects, such as tables and pictures.

The following screenshot shows the **Table Design** gallery:

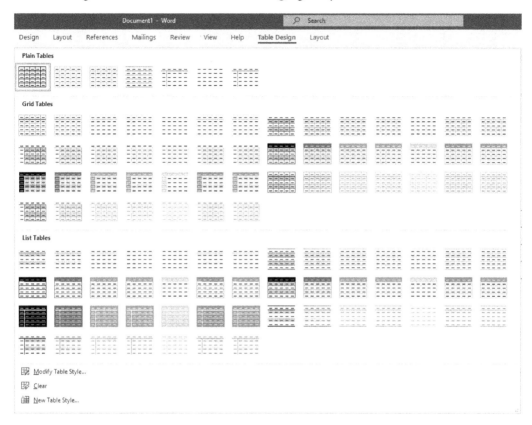

Figure 8.2 – The Table Design gallery

Style galleries like this and others, such as those for pictures, are contextual and will only be available if the specific object is selected.

The techniques we will be showing you throughout the rest of this chapter will focus on character, paragraph, and linked styles, but they will be similar for other types of styles as well.

In the following section, we will show you how to apply Quick Styles to your documents.

Applying Quick Styles

When you open a new blank Word document, on your **Home** tab, in your **Styles** group, you will see a set of predefined **Styles** ready for you to use:

Figure 8.3 – Quick Styles pane

To preview what a style will look like applied to your text or paragraph, simply move your cursor to where you would like the style applied and hover your mouse over a style in the **Styles** gallery:

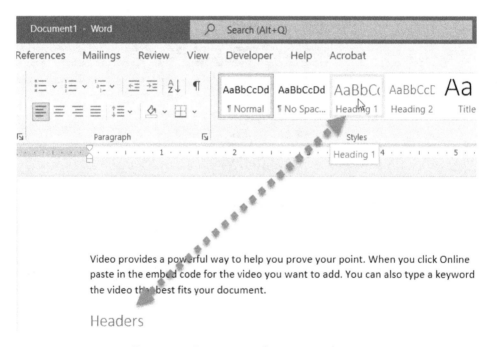

Figure 8.4 – Previewing styles on mouse hover

If you would like to view more styles, click on the **More** button to open the **Styles** gallery:

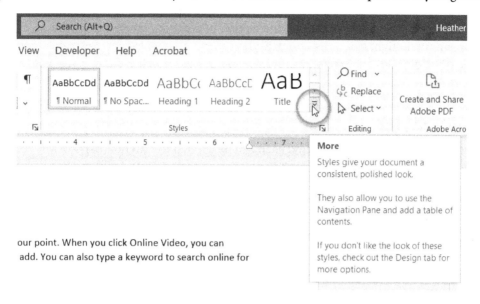

Figure 8.5 – More styles

When you click on the **More** button, the **Styles** gallery will expand and display the complete list of styles available in your Word document, along with additional options for creating new styles and clearing formatting:

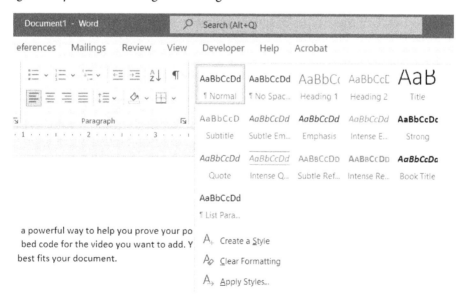

Figure 8.6 – The Styles gallery

To apply the style, click or tap on any style in the **Styles** gallery. That will apply the style to either the selected text or the entire paragraph, depending on the type of style and what you have selected. Knowing what kind or type of style you are working with isn't always apparent, though, from this **Quick Styles** gallery. The next section explains more about the types of styles and offers tips for how you can tell which types of styles you are working with.

Types of styles

There are three basic types of styles and each can be applied to different parts of a document. In this section, we are going to focus our attention on the following three types of styles:

- **Paragraph styles**: These can be applied to an entire paragraph and can include things such as line spacing, alignment, and indentation. An example of a paragraph style is the **Normal** style.

- **Character styles**: These can be applied to words or even characters and can include character formatting such as font, font size, color, and other effects. An example of a character style is the **Subtle Emphasis** style.

- **Linked styles**: These can behave like a paragraph style if an entire paragraph is selected, or like a character style if a character, word, or group of words is selected. An example of a linked style is **Heading 1**.

Next, let's explore each of these types of styles a bit more, starting with the most popular: paragraph styles.

Paragraph styles

Since a paragraph style is applied to the entire paragraph, this type of style should be thought of as more than just mere decoration. In addition to helping keep formatting consistent across your document, paragraph styles can be utilized to help organize and structure your documents, help define and clarify purpose, and help make navigating, reading, and editing simpler for others.

In the previous chapters, you saw how the **Navigation** pane can be used to navigate by page or search results. With **Styles** present, the **Navigation** pane is even more powerful as you can navigate your document by **Headings**, which is a specific kind of paragraph style in Word:

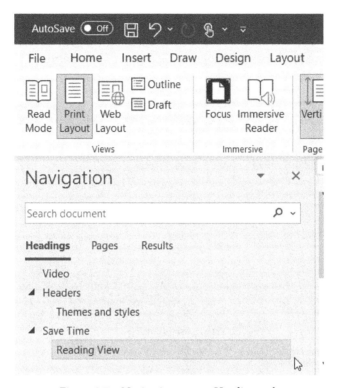

Figure 8.7 – Navigation pane – Headings tab

Inside the **Navigation** pane, your **headings** will appear organized by their **heading level**, allowing viewers to expand and collapse **headings**, making it easy to navigate long documents with many headings, sections, and subsections. Headings are helpful for everyone, especially those who use special equipment to read and navigate Microsoft Word.

Headings for people who use screen readers

For longer documents, many users of Word will often visually scan a document's headers to get the gist of what a document is all about before reading the whole document. Or, if pressed for time, they will use these headers to skip to the part of the document that pertains to them.

For people who rely on screen readers, headers function the same way and are just as important for navigation. But what's more important is how these headers are created in Word. Screen readers need Word to recognize the header as **Heading 1**, not just *Calibri, Size 18 pt, Bold*:

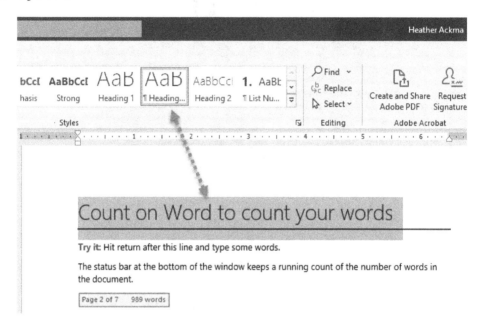

Figure 8.8 – Applying a style for accessibility

If you take anything at all away from this chapter, be sure to create headings by using the **Heading** styles in your **Styles** gallery or the **Styles** pane to help ensure document accessibility.

Heading styles and the Outline view

One great built-in feature to help you organize and view the structure of your document, as well as manage heading styles, is the **Outline** view.

To switch to the **Outline** view, navigate to the **View** tab and click the **Outline** button:

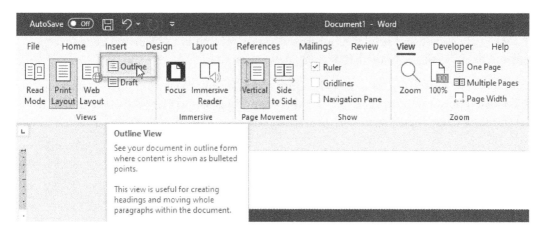

Figure 8.9 – The Outline View button

Your view will change from your **Normal** view to your **Outline** view, which will include an **Outlining** contextual tab in the Ribbon with special commands specific to this view:

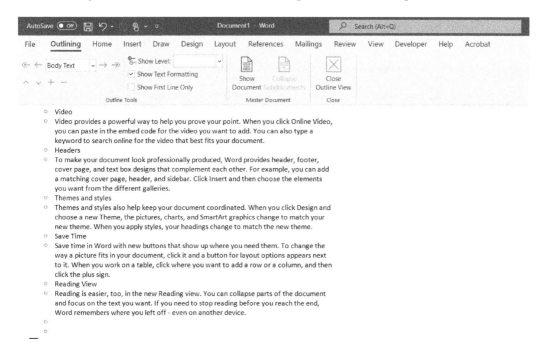

Figure 8.10 – The Outlining view with only body text

If you haven't added any styles or headings, as shown in *Figure 8.9*, your **Outline** view will look fairly simple and similar to what you have displayed in the **Normal** view (except there will be open circles to the left of every new paragraph).

To use this view to organize and apply heading styles, simply move your cursor to where you'd like to apply a heading, and click on the **Promote** arrow to promote the text up one level from the current position:

Figure 8.11 – Promote

Alternatively, you can use the keyboard shortcut *Alt + Shift + Left*.

Or, if you would like to promote the text to the highest level, **Heading 1**, you can click on the double arrow to **Promote to Heading 1**:

Figure 8.12 – Promote to Heading 1

Similarly, you can use the right-facing arrow to **Demote** headings as necessary. Clicking on the single right arrow will **Demote** a heading style one level at a time:

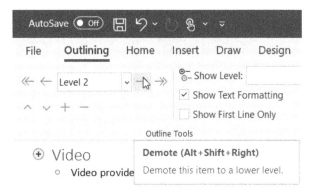

Figure 8.13 – Demote (Alt + Shift + Right)

On the other hand, clicking the double-right arrow will **Demote** a level to body text:

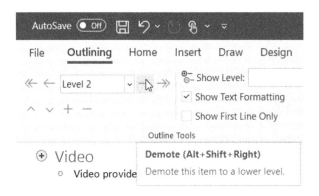

Figure 8.14 – Demote to body text

Promoting and demoting headings from this view is a personal preference. Some find it to be slightly faster and a more compact way of viewing the structure of a document all at once, as shown here:

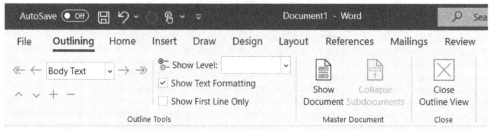

⊕ Video

　○ Video provides a powerful way to help you prove your point. When you click Online Video, you can paste in the embed code for the video you want to add. You can also type a keyword to search online for the video that best fits your document.

⊕ Headers

　○ To make your document look professionally produced, Word provides header, footer, cover page, and text box designs that complement each other. For example, you can add a matching cover page, header, and sidebar. Click Insert and then choose the elements you want from the different galleries.

　　⊕ Themes and styles

　　　○ Themes and styles also help keep your document coordinated. When you click Design and choose a new Theme, the pictures, charts, and SmartArt graphics change to match your new theme. When you apply styles, your headings change to match the new theme.

⊕ Save Time

　○ Save time in Word with new buttons that show up where you need them. To change the way a picture fits in your document, click it and a button for layout options appears next to it. When you work on a table, click where you want to add a row or a column, and then click the plus sign.

　　⊕ Reading View

　　　○ Reading is easier, too, in the new Reading view. You can collapse parts of the document and focus on the text you want. If you need to stop reading before you reach the end, Word remembers where you left off - even on another device.

Figure 8.15 – Outline structure

You can click on the plus and minus symbols next to each heading to collapse and expand any paragraph in the **Outline** view to make viewing and navigating content simpler. Of course, in newer versions of Microsoft Word, once a heading has been applied, you can collapse and expand paragraphs in the **Normal** view too:

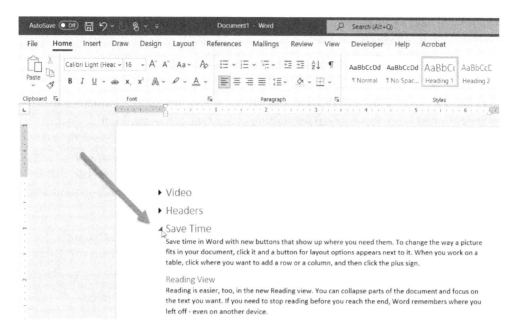

Figure 8.16 – Expanding and collapsing heading styles in the Normal view

So, to use this particular feature, you don't have to jump over to the **Outline** view anymore. All you need are heading styles, such as **Heading 1** or the other styles mentioned earlier:

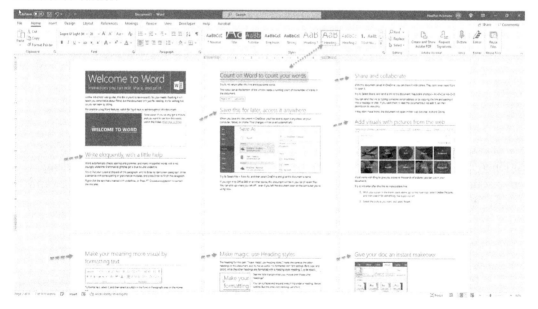

Figure 8.17 – Bird's-eye view of the headings in a document

These styles will help focus your attention and make sifting through longer documents easier, regardless of the view you are in.

Character styles

Because character styles can be applied to just words or even just a few characters, this type of style is great – not just to keep formatting consistent across your entire document, but to quickly apply multiple formatting effects to a word or a few characters with just one click of a button. What's more, rather than remembering your company's propriety font, color, size, and other specific styles, you can create a character style and use that style whenever you need it to save time and keep your professional documents consistent and on brand.

The tricky part in Word, however, is telling the difference between a character and a paragraph style. For that, when working with character styles, I like to open my **Styles** pane.

Telling the difference between style types

To quickly tell the difference between styles, we are going to use our **Styles** pane so that we can compare styles at a glance. From the **Home** tab, in the **Styles** group, click the **Styles** button in the lower right-hand corner to open the **Styles** pane:

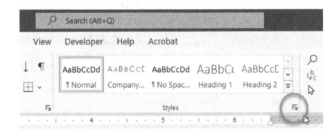

Figure 8.18 – The Styles button

Upon clicking the **Styles** button, the **Styles** pane will open. Depending on where it was positioned last, it may appear docked to the far right-hand side of the screen or floating over your document. I prefer to keep my **Styles** pane docked to the right of my screen and out of the way:

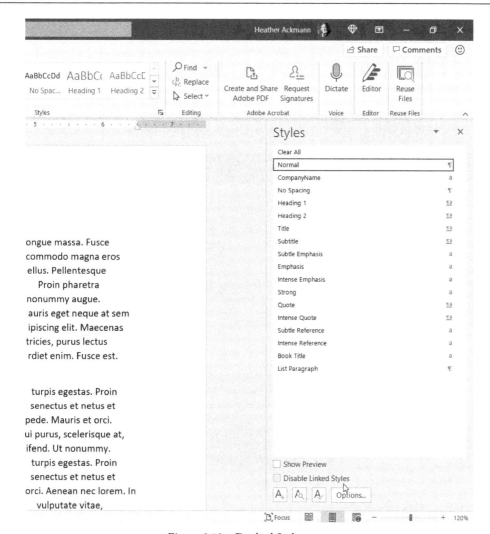

Figure 8.19 – Docked Styles pane

If you would like your pane docked to the right, simply click and hold the top of the pane and drag the pane to the right until it snaps into place.

Now, let's take a deeper look at the **Styles** pane so that we have a better understanding of the options there.

Using the Styles pane

The **Styles** pane gives you a list of all the available styles and shows you which type of style each one is. The **Styles** pane is also home to **Style Inspector**, the **Manage Styles** window, and the **Styles Pane Options** window.

To open the **Styles** pane, you will need to go to the **Home** tab. Then, in the lower-right corner of the **Styles** section, click on the expand dialogue box button:

Figure 8.20 – The Styles dialogue box button

Once clicked, the **Styles** pane will open:

Figure 8.21 – The Styles pane

The **Styles** pane can be resized by clicking and dragging the sides or corners. In the preceding screenshot, I have resized the **Styles** pane to show the list of recommended styles.

By default, the **Styles** pane shows a list of recommended styles. You will see a list of the style names on the left. To the right, you will see a corresponding list of symbols or markers. There are three markers, and each one represents a style type:

- **a** indicates a character style

- ¶ indicates a paragraph style

- ¶a indicates a linked style

At the bottom of the **Styles** pane are two checkboxes. The first is **Show Preview**, which will show you a preview of each style in the list if checked. The second is **Disable Linked Styles**, which will prevent linked styles from being able to act as character styles when applied to individual characters or words.

There are four buttons along the bottom of the **Styles** pane. The first button is the **New Style** button. This will bring up the **Create New Style from Formatting** window, where you can create a new style, as described previously in this chapter.

The second button is for **Style Inspector**. This will bring up the **Style Inspector** panel:

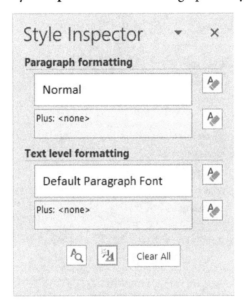

Figure 8.22 – The Style Inspector pane

The **Style Inspector** panel gives you options to clear and reset individual formatting options in a style and create a new style using the **New Style** button at the bottom.

The third button at the bottom of the **Styles** pane will open the **Manage Styles** window:

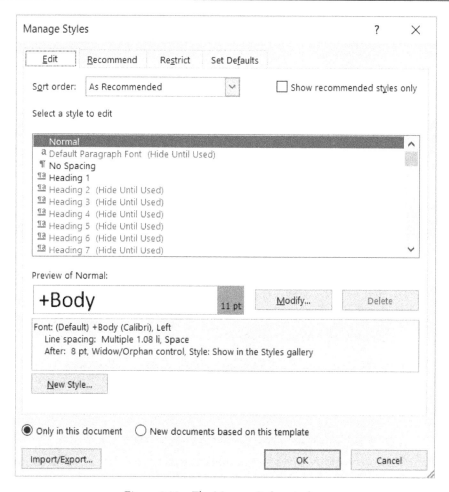

Figure 8.23 – The Manage Styles window

The **Manage Styles** window is yet another place to see all styles and modify them from the **Edit** tab. You can also choose which styles are assigned to the **Recommended** styles list from the **Recommend** tab. You can restrict the availability of styles in a protected document on the **Restrict** tab. Lastly, you can set defaults for things such as the font, font size, paragraph position, spacing, and several other options for the entire document.

The final button on the **Styles** pane is the **Options** button. This will open the **Style Pane Options** window:

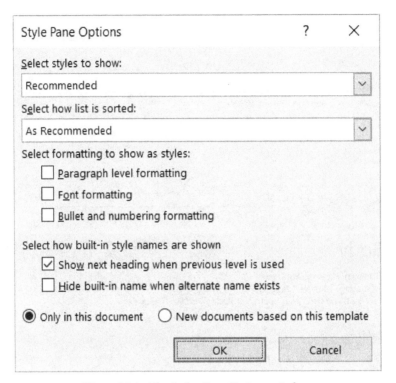

Figure 8.24 – The Styles Pane Options window

The **Style Pane Options** window gives you options as to what will be shown in the **Styles** pane. The first dropdown allows you to select which styles are shown:

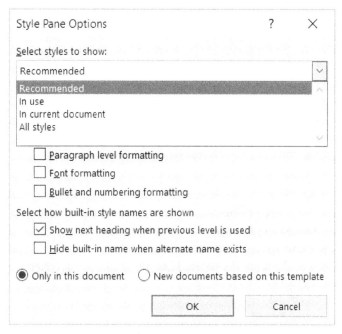

Figure 8.25 – The Select styles to show menu

The second dropdown allows you to choose how the list is sorted:

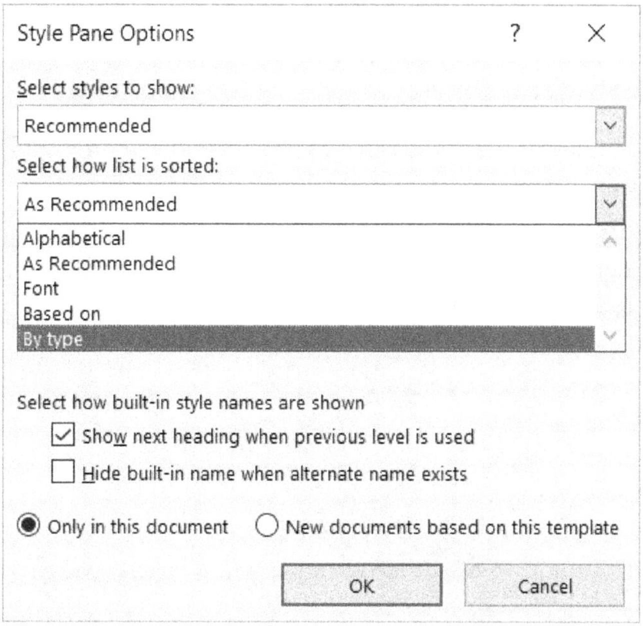

Figure 8.26 – The Select how list is sorted menu

Below these drop-down lists are three checkboxes, of which if any are checked, they will add those specific types of formatting to the **Styles** pane as styles. This can be particularly useful if you have formatting choices that you wish to reuse in a document:

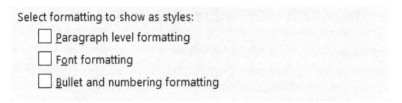

Figure 8.27 – Select formatting to show as styles options

The next set of two checkboxes give you the option to **Select how built-in style names are shown**, either via **Show next heading when previous level is used** or **Hide built-in name when alternate name exists**. In the **Styles** pane, Word will only list **Heading 1** and **Heading 2**. With this box checked, if you use **Heading 2** in the document, Word will display **Heading 3** and so on:

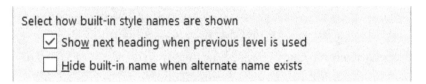

Figure 8.28 – Select how built-in style names are shown options

At the bottom of the **Style Pane Options** window are two radio buttons:

- **Only in this document**: This is selected by default and will only apply these options to this specific document.

- **New documents based on this template**: This is not selected by default but should be used if the current document is going to be used as a template, and you also want these choices to be included in any document that's created by that template.

Now that we have a better understanding of paragraph and character styles, in the next section, we will talk a bit about linked styles.

Linked styles

At this point, you may be wondering what the point is of linked styles. Well, don't lose too much sleep over it. It has to do with how users created a Table of Contents in legacy versions of Word.

In older versions of Word (before 2002), all paragraph styles were linked styles. With the introduction of Word 2007, developers introduced the **Disable Linked Styles** option. And now, we can simply create linked styles and disable those linked styles when we don't want people to use them as character styles. We can apply them quickly to, say, a Table of Contents, and then disable them, forcing people to use them like regular paragraph styles thereafter.

If you are curious and would like to learn more about how styles used to work in Word, here is the old help article at Microsoft called *How to use style separators with headings*: `https://support.microsoft.com/en-us/office/how-to-use-style-separators-with-heading-style-to-generate-a-toc-in-word-48af64fa-9b3c-4232-be20-cf244cef7fea?ui=en-us&rs=en-us&ad=us`.

But moving back to how things work now, if you want to change the appearance of your entire document in one fell swoop after you have applied styles, this is simple to do with themes.

Understanding how themes affect styles

Every time you open a brand new Word document, you are using a Word theme. It's called the Office theme and that theme affects the default font, colors, and effects that you see in Word. For example, from the **Home** tab, in the **Font** group, if you were to click on the **Font Color** menu button, you would see a variety of familiar **Theme Colors**:

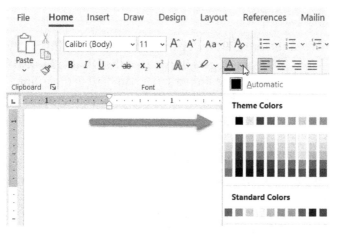

Figure 8.29 – Office Theme Colors | Font

You can also find these **Theme Colors** in other color galleries, such as when you insert a shape or insert a chart:

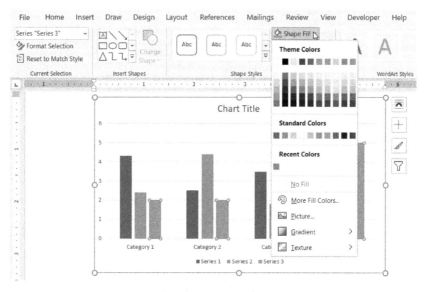

Figure 8.30 – Office Theme Colors | shapes and charts

Even **Styles** will be affected by the document's theme. From the **Home** tab, if you open the **Styles** gallery, you may notice that some styles will have colors applied to them:

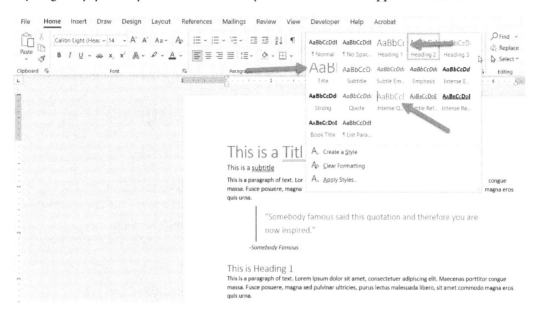

Figure 8.31 – Styles and theme colors

For example, in *Figure 8.31*, several styles use a theme color; **Heading 1**, **Title**, and **Intense Quote** all use the Office theme's **Blue, Accent 1** color.

If, however, you have a set of colors that you would rather use instead of these Office colors, you can simply change your **Theme Colors** or the theme itself rather than changing every individual instance of color across your document or by modifying the style.

Changing the theme

If you would like to change the colors that are used across all your styles and the rest of your document, the simplest and fastest way is to change your document theme:

1. Click on the **Design** tab and click on the **Themes** button.

    This will open the **Theme** gallery. The theme that has been applied will be selected (have a box around it).

2. To preview what another theme will look like, once applied to your document, simply hover your mouse over another theme.

3. To apply a new theme, click on a new theme.

And that is the fastest way to change a document's theme. But remember, a theme is a collection of colors, fonts, and effects for a document. When you change the theme, you will be changing many aspects of the document according to that theme.

Changing theme colors

Since **Themes** control more than just colors, you may notice other aspects of your document's appearance change when you apply a new or different theme – things such as the font, for example. If you just want to change a theme's colors but keep the other aspects of that theme intact, you can change just the theme colors:

1. Click on the **Design** tab and click on the **Colors** button to open the **Theme Colors** menu.

    From the **Theme Colors** menu, you will see a set of standard **Office** color sets:

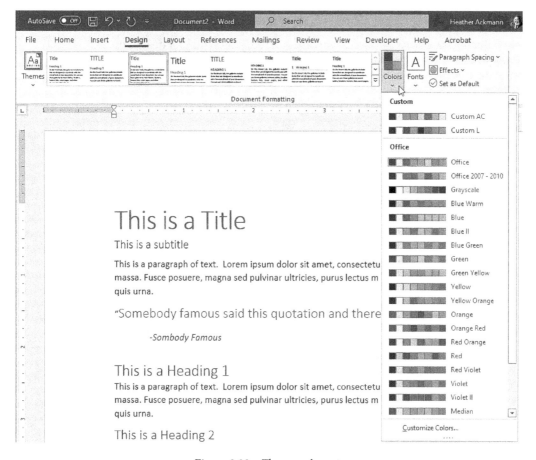

Figure 8.32 – Theme color sets

2. To preview what a color looks like, hover your mouse over one of the theme color sets. The theme colors in your document will update to reflect the new colors.

3. To apply a new theme color, simply click on a new theme and that theme will be applied to your entire document.

Now that we know how to quickly change and apply a theme color, let's talk about those times when theme colors work, and some of the times when they don't (and why and how themes work).

Working with theme colors – the tricky part

These color sets are great options if you are not working with any design guidelines and just want to make a quick overall change. If that is the case, simply clicking on a built-in color set is a lightning-fast way to change or update your document's colors – or at least every place where you've used a theme color, like so:

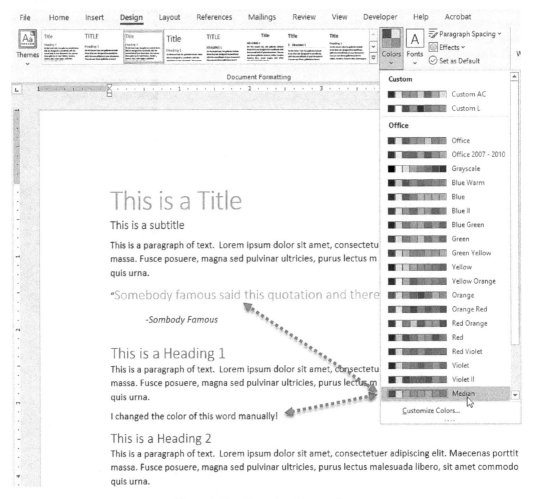

Figure 8.33 – Changing theme colors

In *Figure 8.33*, I changed the theme color set to **Median**. Every place in the document that used a theme color was instantly updated, except for one word where I had manually chosen a specific color for that one word, rather than choosing a theme color. In other words, updating a document's theme colors will only change the colors in your document if you have used or chosen colors from that theme's palette. If you have manually changed or used a custom color, those colors will remain.

The same will be true for how styles are applied, modified, and created. If the style uses a theme color, then updating the theme will update the style. If you have changed or modified the style at any point away from a chosen theme color, then changing the theme will not update the style.

Now that we understand how to make Word's built-in styles work and look a little better, let's talk about creating new styles.

Creating a new style by modifying an existing style

As we have seen, Word comes with several Quick Styles that we can apply easily to our documents. We have also learned how styles can be affected by themes. In this section, we want to explore how to create custom styles and add them to the **Styles** gallery.

We already know that using styles can help us create a consistent look in our documents. Being able to create custom styles gives us the freedom to create styles for any situation or look that we want in a document. Custom styles can also be copied to other documents or saved in a template so that all your documents can use them and have that consistency.

Like many things in Word, there is more than one way to create a custom style. For example, you can modify an existing style or you can create a style from formatting. We will begin by formatting text in our document in a specific way so that we can save it as our new style.

Creating a style from formatting

In the following example, I have formatted the heading of this document. I have made it bold, increased the size of the font to 18 points, and added 12 points of space after the paragraph:

Figure 8.34 – Formatted text

To turn this simple formatting into a style that will be added to the **Style** gallery, and that I can use again, I will need to select the text and click the **More** button in the right-hand corner of the **Styles** gallery window:

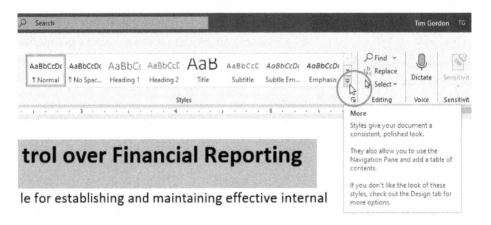

Figure 8.35 – The More arrow

The **Styles** gallery will now open, and you will see the **Create a Style** option:

Figure 8.36 – Create a Style

Once you click on **Create a Style**, the **Create New Style from Formatting** window will open. In this window, you are prompted to give this new style a name by typing it into the **Name** box. Its **Name** and a **Paragraph style preview** will be shown. In this example, I have named the new style Company Heading 2:

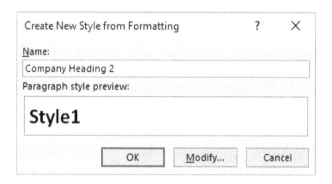

Figure 8.37 – The Create New Style from Formatting window

The new style will be added to the **Styles** gallery, where you will see a preview of the style and be able to use it anywhere in the document:

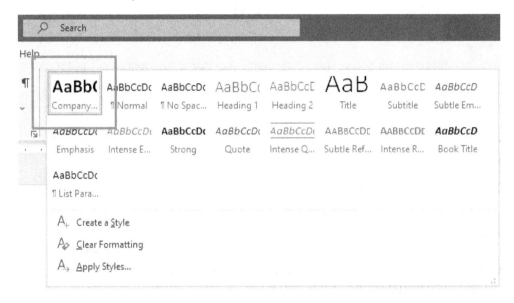

Figure 8.38 – A new custom style

This is a very quick method to create a simple custom style and a great way to get started. We will now learn how to create a new style by modifying an existing style.

Creating a new style by modifying an existing style

To modify an existing style, you need to select the style from the **Styles** gallery. Depending on where the style is in the gallery, you may need to open it first by clicking the **More** button in the lower-right corner of the gallery window. Once the style is selected, right-click and select **Modify...** from the list:

Figure 8.39 – The Modify… option

The **Modify Style** window will now open:

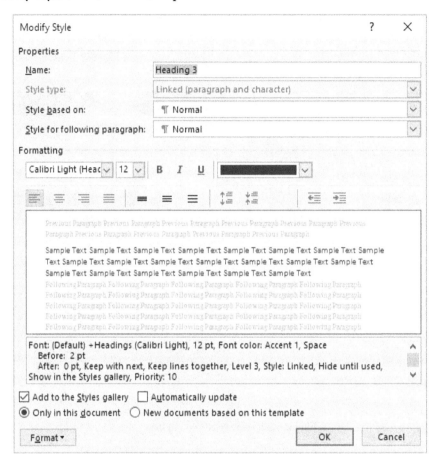

Figure 8.40 – The Modify Style window

The **Modify Style** window shows you all the attributes of the style you selected, along with a preview of the style. You can now modify the current style to suit your needs, or you can create a new style by changing the name in the **Name** box at the top of the window. I recommend that you don't modify any of the default styles in Word but create a new style instead.

Text formatting options appear near the top of the window in the **Formatting** section. For additional formatting options such as tabs, border, and text effects, you will need to click on the **Format** button in the lower-left corner of the window. This will reveal a list of other formatting selections, each of which will bring up a window for those specific options:

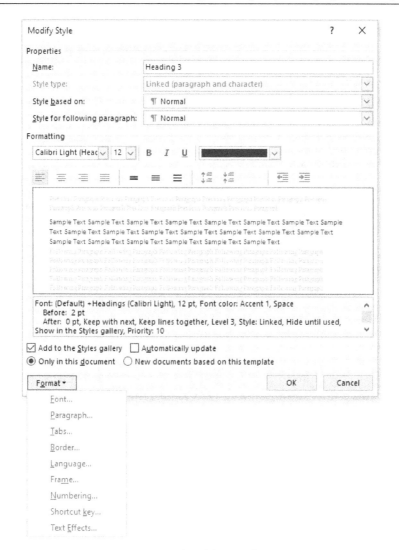

Figure 8.41 – Menu for additional format options

Once you have named your new style and made all your formatting and style choices, there are some options at the bottom of the window that you should also be aware of:

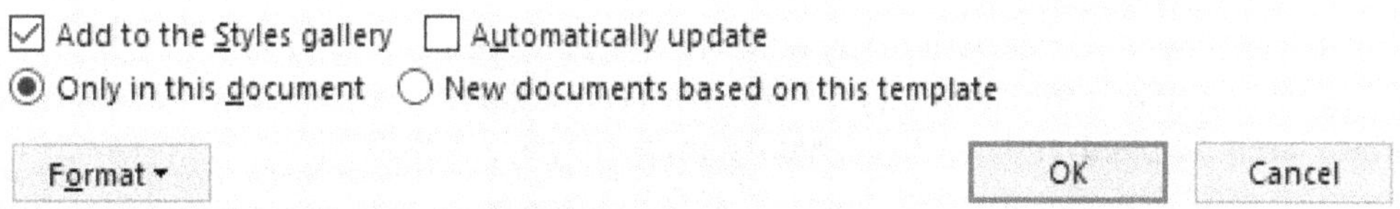

Figure 8.42 – New style options

These options are as follows:

- **Add to the Styles gallery**: This is checked by default and will automatically add the new style to the **Styles** gallery.

- **Automatically update**: This is not checked by default, but if checked, this will update anywhere the style is applied if you modify that style.

- **Only in this document**: This is selected by default and will only add the new style to this specific document.

- **New documents based on this template**: This is not selected by default, but it should be used if the current document is going to be used as a template and you want the new style to be included in any document that's created by that template.

To apply your changes, click **OK** at the lower right; your new style will be created and added to the **Styles** gallery.

So far in this chapter, we have focused on applying and creating styles, and how styles are affected by themes. Now, we want to look at how to find a list of all styles in a document how to determine what type of style it is, plus some other options that are available in the **Styles** pane.

In this section, we learned how to create custom styles either from formatting or by modifying a selected style. Creating styles gives you flexibility and control by making it easy for you to reuse the style throughout your document. This will help give your documents a consistent look and feel.

Summary

Styles are an essential part of creating a consistently formatted and accessible document. In this chapter, we explained what styles are, the main types of styles, how themes affect styles, and how to create custom styles.

We examined different types of styles and learned how styles can help us apply consistent formatting throughout a document. Styles are especially useful when we're creating longer documents or sets of similar documents. That way, documents across an organization will have the same look and feel.

We learned that Word comes with many built-in styles that you can begin using right away. We also discussed the different types of styles (paragraph, character, and linked), how they can be applied, and in what circumstances they are useful.

Styles control more than just character formatting. Styles can be used to apply color and change fonts, text size, and spacing. Styles are also affected by Word themes. Theme changes can alter the appearance of styles and we explored that relationship.

One of the most incredible features of Word is that you can create custom styles. In this chapter, we learned how to create a style from formatting, and how to create a style by modifying an existing style. We also opened the **Styles** pane and examined the options therein.

Now that we have explored how to style our document quickly, next, we'll explore how to automate other tasks in Word to make other workflows and common tasks even faster. Word has several tools to help you create documents more quickly, including keyboard shortcuts, autocorrect, and auto format. In the next chapter, we will learn how to use some common keyboard shortcuts, create custom keyboard shortcuts, and use autocorrect to maximize our efficiency and productivity.

9
Working Faster with Automation

When people think of how to automate Word documents, they typically think of macros (a set of grouped commands and instructions run together as a single command) or **Visual Basic for Applications (VBA)** code. Both have a few disadvantages. For one, they are a bit more complicated to write, especially VBA. And two, not all end users can open macro-enabled files at work. Because these types of files have the potential to be embedded with malicious code (or even potentially damaging human errors), some companies and IT departments have simply chosen to disable all macros and code contained within these types of files. So, even if you have successfully written a perfect macro-enabled, fully automated Word document or template for someone to use, they may not be able to utilize the automation within because their company has locked down those types of files for security reasons.

So, this chapter thinks a bit outside the box and focuses on preparation, as well as tips and tricks with Word's lesser-known built-in tools and other no-code methods that aren't typically used for automation, in addition to what people typically think of when they think of automation in Word: macros.

In this chapter, we will cover the following topics:

- Preparing for automation
- Keyboard shortcuts
- AutoCorrect and AutoFormat
- Creating custom Quick Parts
- Creating and running a macro

Preparing for automation

Before we start talking about how to automate in Word, let's take a moment to discuss why and how to prepare for automating tasks, or the work you do. This requires thinking about how often you repeatedly perform the same actions or tasks. You must work to prioritize tasks and develop a system to cut down on the amount of time you spend doing repetitive work.

Why automate?

When working in Word, you may find yourself repeating certain actions again and again. These can be things such as writing the same text at the top of a letter, your signature, legalese, a company slogan, an address block – anything. You are looking for any repetitive task that you do in Word. Those tasks are all great candidates for automation. How often you do them and how much time they take to type out will determine which ones you automate.

Identifying tasks for automation

To identify potential tasks for automation, I suggest blocking out time on your calendar specifically for this. Attempting to reorganize anything to save time to be more productive, oddly enough, takes time, and if you don't plan to take that time, you never will. So, I strongly suggest making time to identify the tasks in Word that you repeat frequently. This will possibly involve you going through your old Word documents over the past year and studying them, looking for anything within them that gets reused – phrases, language, design elements, or even things that you do in Word with your mouse. Every time you take your hands off your keyboard, move your hand to the mouse, to a different area of the screen, point and click, and then move your hands back to your keyboard – that takes time. And that time adds up over a day, a week, and a year to a substantial amount of time. So, be sure to also make note of any task that you do regularly on the Ribbon, whether it is spellcheck, inserting a symbol, or Accept Changes.

Prioritizing the list of tasks

Next, take the list of tasks you've identified and estimate the importance or the priority of each task. If the task is something that you do daily but doesn't take that long in Word to do, compare that to a task that's done twice a week but takes a long time to do in Word. Overall, which task takes up more of your time if you add it all up? If it is the second task, then that should be the priority, even if you perform that task only twice a week. Remember, this is about optimizing your total overall time.

Identifying the best automation system

Once you have prioritized your tasks, the next step is to figure out the best way to automate them in Word. If your organization blocks macros and VBA code through a Group Policy, you may need to think outside the box for how to automate some of these tasks, depending on what they are.

In the next section, we will discuss a few unconventional ways to automate, if this is your situation.

Keyboard shortcuts

The first method for automation we will discuss is to assign a keyboard shortcut to your task. Keyboard shortcuts are a combination of keystrokes on your keyboard that, when pressed, will perform some assigned Word command. Keyboard shortcuts are faster than using your mouse. As I mentioned earlier, every time you take your hands off your keyboard to move to your mouse, you are adding valuable seconds to your workflow. Keyboard shortcuts keep your hands on your keyboard and allow you to stay close to where you need to be for many Word processing tasks.

Word comes preloaded with common keyboard shortcuts already. For example, *Ctrl + S* will save your document, *Ctrl + C* will copy selected text, and *Ctrl + V* will paste the copied text. However, what many users of Word do not know is how to customize their keyboard shortcuts.

To customize keyboard shortcuts, there are several places in Word you can go, depending on what kind of keyboard shortcut you are assigning. But if you want to see the master list, the easiest place to go is to your **Word Options** window.

Viewing and customizing keyboard shortcuts

To view and customize keyboard shortcuts, follow these steps:

1. From an open Word document, go to the **File** menu and click on **Options**.

   This will open the **Word Options** window on the **General** tab:

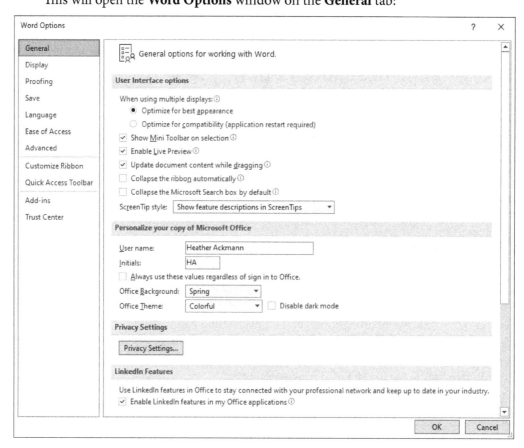

Figure 9.1 – Word Options | General

2. On the left-hand side, click the **Customize Ribbon** option to view the commands available in Microsoft Word:

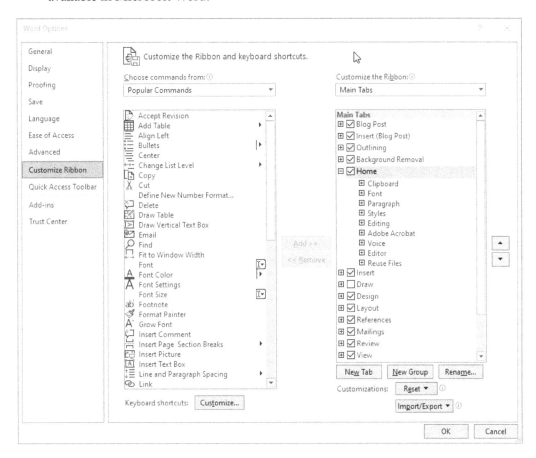

Figure 9.2 – Word Options | Customize Ribbon

Commands will be organized into various views, starting with **Popular Commands**. If you'd like to arrange commands by another view, click the drop-down menu underneath **Choose commands from** and select a different option.

3.   Click the **Customize...** button in the bottom-left corner of the window:

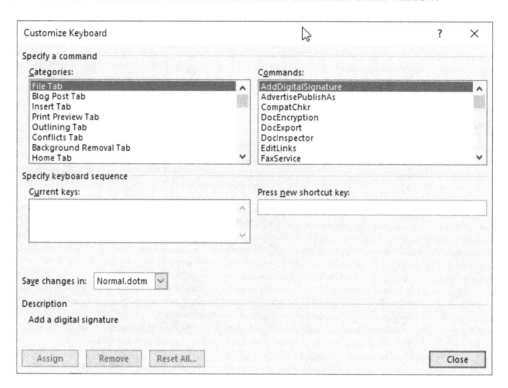

Figure 9.3 – Customize Keyboard

This will open the **Customize Keyboard** window. Here, you can view keyboard shortcuts by where they are located based on the Ribbon. In other words, if you were to repeatedly use any action or command on the Ribbon, you can locate that command here by its corresponding tab. Commands on the **Home** tab will be located in the **Categories** section labeled **Home Tab**. So, let's say you use the button on the **Home** tab for **Clear All Formatting** a lot:

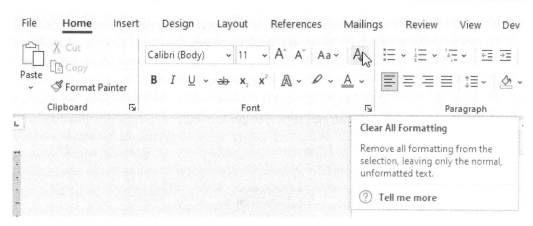

Figure 9.4 – The Clear All Formatting button on the Home tab

4.   Click **Home Tab** from the **Categories** area and, in the **Commands** area, scroll until you find the **ClearAllFormatting** command:

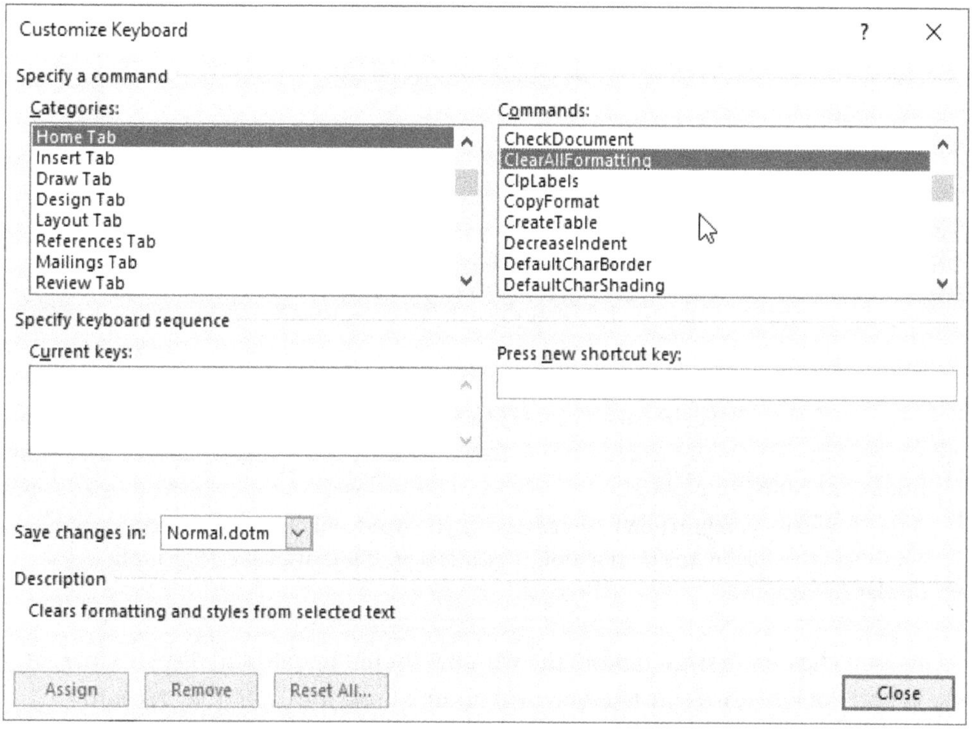

Figure 9.5 – Customize Keyboard | Home Tab | ClearAllFormatting

5.   With the category and command selected in this area, underneath the area labeled **Specify keyboard sequence**, Word will display any assigned keyboard shortcuts. If none are displayed, this means that no keyboard shortcuts are currently assigned to that command.

6.   To assign a new keyboard shortcut, click inside the box labeled **Press new shortcut key**, type a keyboard shortcut, and click **Assign**:

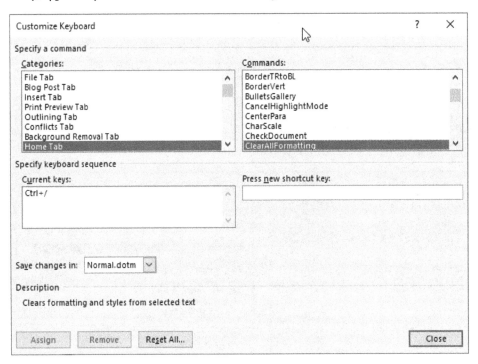

Figure 9.6 – Assigning keyboard shortcuts

Important Note

If that keyboard combination is already assigned, Word will display which command that keyboard combination is assigned to. If it is available, Word will display "unassigned."

After you click the **Assign** button, the window should update and display **Current keys** and the keyboard shortcut you programmed previously. In the preceding screenshot, we used the *Ctrl + /* shortcut after we hit the **Assign** button, so now it is the shortcut for **ClearAllFormatting**.

Now, this won't save a ton of time, but it will add up if this is something that I do a lot. What this is most useful for is for commands not displayed in the ribbon:

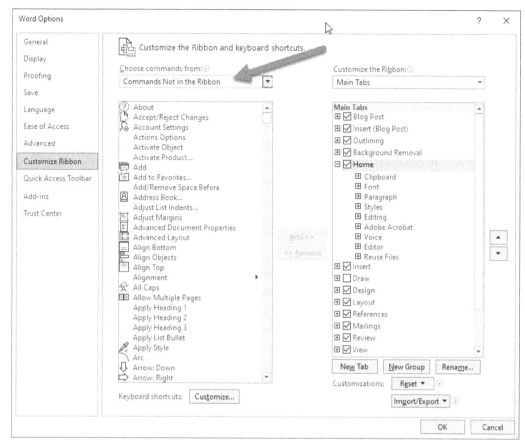

Figure 9.7 – Commands not in the ribbon

If you go back to the **Customize Ribbon** area in the **Word Options** window and select the
Commands Not in the Ribbon option from the **Choose commands from:** dropdown,
you will find a huge list of tough-to-find commands in Word – ones that require a lot of
clicks with the mouse to get to in the interface. All those little clicks do add up to a lot of
time. And replacing those clicks with a keyboard shortcut really can save you a lot of time
if you use any of these commands.

The thing is, many of these commands have been removed from the Ribbon because they
aren't used very often by most people. In the rare event that you are an exception, create
a keyboard shortcut for this command and save yourself some valuable time hunting and
pecking for the command.

In addition to creating keyboard shortcuts, there are other features of Word that you can
leverage to automate common tasks, and these aren't ones that people will typically think
of for customization – AutoCorrect and AutoFormat.

AutoCorrect and AutoFormat

You may already be familiar with some of Word's helpful (or in some cases, more annoying) AutoCorrect features. If you have ever misspelled a word and Word has automatically corrected it for you, that is AutoCorrect helping you. Or, conversely, if you type your last name and Word "corrects" it to a more common word that is not your name, that is Word being not so helpful.

Regardless of what is happening, helpful or harmful, this feature can be used for automating commonly used names and phrases.

AutoFormat as You Type

For this purpose, we will be using a specific feature called **AutoFormat as You Type**, which corrects something that you type into something else that is programmed in. To create a new **AutoFormat as You Type** entry, from any open document, follow these steps:

1. Go to the **File** menu and click on **Options**. This will open the **Word Options** window to the **General** tab.

2. From there, click on the **Proofing** tab in the left-hand corner of the window:

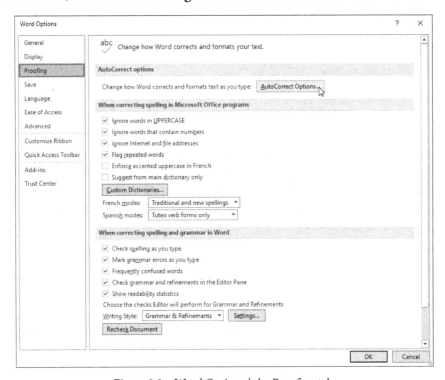

Figure 9.8 – Word Options | the Proofing tab

Toward the top of the **Proofing** screen, you should see an area labeled **AutoCorrect options**, with a button also labeled **AutoCorrect Options…**.

3. Clicking on the **AutoCorrect Options…** button will open the **AutoCorrect** window to the **AutoCorrect** tab:

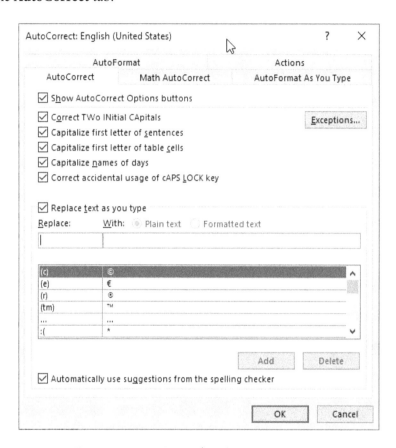

Figure 9.9 – AutoCorrect | Replace text as you type

At the bottom of the **AutoCorrect** tab, you will see a checked option called **Replace text as you type**. Underneath that option is a large table. If you scroll through that list, you will find everything that Word is preprogrammed to replace. On the left is everything that is typed, followed by what will be its replacement. The very first option is an open parenthesis, followed by the letter c, followed by a closing parenthesis. If you type that sequence out, it will be automatically replaced with the copyright symbol.

But upon scrolling down the list a little, you will find a very large list of frequently misspelled words:

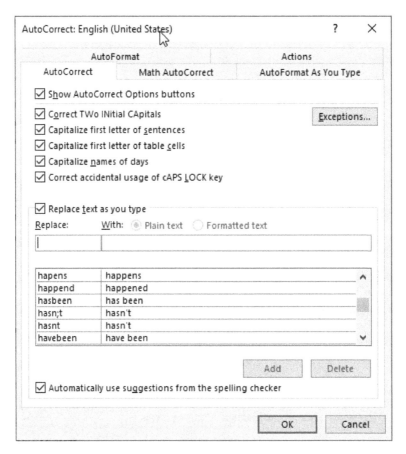

Figure 9.10 – AutoCorrect | frequently misspelled words

Misspellings and typos happen. Microsoft has taken the most common misspellings and typos and placed them into a list to be automatically corrected. This list isn't foolproof. If there is a word that you frequently misspell or mistype, you can add it to this list yourself.

Just type the word that you mistype or misspell into the **Replace** box, and then type its correction in the **With** box. Then, click **Add**.

But I don't just use this for mistyped or misspelled words. I also use this box for shorthand. If there is some name or list or short legal phrase that I need to reference frequently, I have also used this feature to reference longer strings of text.

For example, let's say I need to reference the names of the people in my IT department frequently. I could use this feature to quickly replace a string of letters with a list of those names:

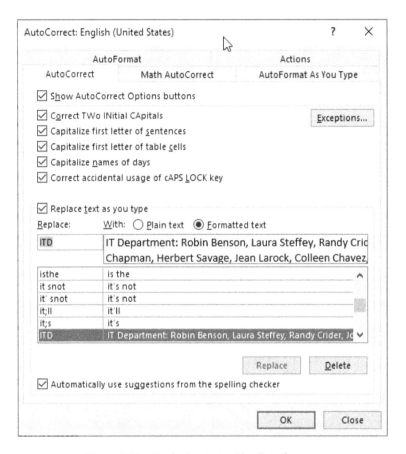

Figure 9.11 – Replacing text with a list of names

In the preceding screenshot, I've written the letters ITD as my replacement text. And then, in the **With** box, I've written out IT Department: Robin Benson, Laura Steffey, Randy Crider, Jordan Hixson, Sandra Knapp, Becky Chapman, Herbert Savage, Jean Larock, Colleen Chavez, Louis Moore, Peter Cates, John Fine. So, now, whenever I want to use this in Word, all I need to do is type out the letter ITD and press *the Spacebar,*, and then Word will automatically convert those three little letters into my full list:

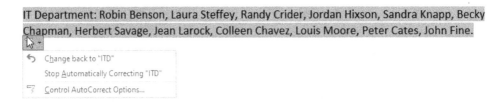

Figure 9.12 – AutoCorrect tag

Typing three letters is a lot faster than typing or even copying and pasting the text. And like with all **AutoCorrect** options, you should see the **AutoCorrect** tag appear immediately appear after the change. Upon clicking on the tag (see the preceding screenshot), you will have the option to **Change back to "ITD"** or whatever you had typed before the change if you choose.

Creating custom Quick Parts

We've discussed how to use Quick Parts in *Chapter 5, Working with Short Documents,* as a great way to save time when working with short documents, where pieces of documents (think letters, memos, resumes, and so on) tend to be reused. In that chapter, we talked about using some of Word's built-in features, such as fields, Building Blocks Organizer, and the AutoText feature to build customizable text blocks that you can add to your document with just a click of a button.

In this chapter, we will continue where we left off there and discuss how to create custom Quick Parts that will appear in various galleries, such as a custom header.

Creating a custom header

To create a custom header that will appear in the header gallery alongside the other sample headers, the easiest way is to first design your header as you would normally. Open the header, add any text or decorative elements you like, such as spacing, page numbers, and document info, and be sure to set things such as **Different First Page** or **Different Odd & Even Pages** right away:

Figure 9.13 – Your company header

Once you have your header styled the way you like, select everything in that header by pressing *Ctrl + A* while in the header area. You can tell that everything is selected if there is a gray shaded box around all the objects in the header:

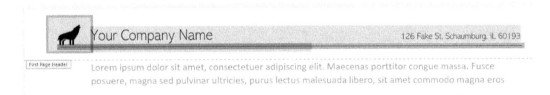

Figure 9.14 – All header objects selected

With all the objects selected, we can now create a custom Quick Part from our selected objects.

Creating a custom Quick Part

To create a custom Quick Part, follow these steps (PC only):

1. With our objects selected, go to the **Insert** tab and click on the **Quick Parts** button. This will open a menu of options.

2. Click on the **Save Selection to Quick Part Gallery...** option:

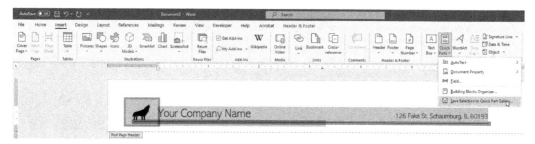

Figure 9.15 – Save Selection to Quick Part Gallery

3. Next, in the **Create New Building Block** window, enter the name of your Quick Part, the gallery you'd like to save it to, a brief description, which template you'd like the Quick Part saved to, and any other options:

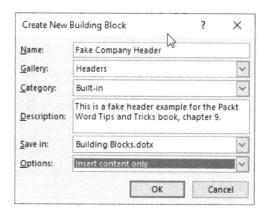

Figure 9.16 – Create New Building Block options

In our example, we are going to save ours to the **Headers** gallery, to the **Built-in** category, and save it to our building blocks template so that the building blocks will appear in our header gallery, alongside all the other options for all new and existing Word documents on this computer.

4. Once you've set all your options, click **OK**.

5. Now, navigate to the **Insert** tab, click on **Header**, and confirm that your custom header appears in the **Header** gallery:

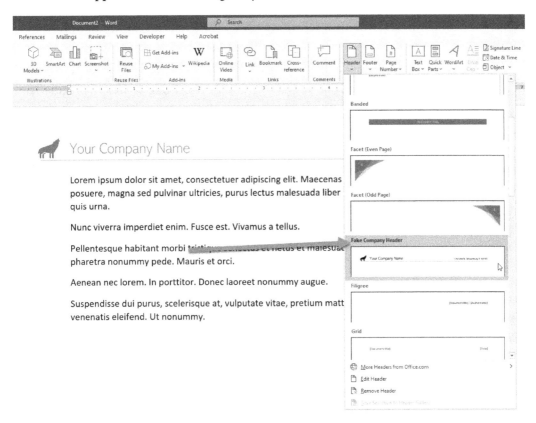

Figure 9.17 – Custom header in the Header gallery

Note – Mac Users

If you are on a Mac and looking for **Quick Parts** on the **Insert** tab, you will not find it. This feature is currently only available on PCs. If this feature is something you would like to use, click on the **Feedback** button in the top right-hand corner of the title bar of any open Word document to send feedback to Microsoft; tell them you want Quick Parts on Mac and what you would use it for.

So, as you can see, by creating a custom Quick Part to appear in one of Word's galleries, you can save time formatting a lot of the parts or pieces of a document that you typically reuse, things such as title pages, headers, footers, text boxes, and even cited entries. By taking a few minutes now and creating a custom Quick Part, you can save yourself hours in the future.

Quick Parts are great, but they are still, by far, not the fastest method. If you have a multi-step procedure or process in Word that you find yourself performing or creating regularly, creating a macro to automate that task is by far the biggest time-saver. In the next section, we will briefly cover how to create and run a simple macro.

Creating and running a macro

As mentioned earlier in this chapter, a macro groups commands, instructions, and keystrokes together and runs them as a single command. For example, you can use macros and record and repeat all the steps required for the following:

- Composing a form letter
- Company letterhead
- Custom page layouts and formats
- Object formatting (such as special designed tables or pictures)
- So much more

You can assign a macro to a button on your **Quick Access Toolbar** or even assign a macro to a keyboard shortcut. You can do whatever you think is easiest to save you time. Remember, macros are about making time-consuming, complicated, and often repeated processes faster.

To begin creating your first macro in Microsoft Word, you will need to turn on or display your **Developer** tab. If you have not done so already, the next section will walk you through how to do just that.

Turning on the Developer tab

To get the most out of creating, recording, and using macros in Word, you will want to display your **Developer** tab. If you do not see the **Developer** tab displayed on your **Word** Ribbon, follow these steps:

1. Click the **File** tab and select **Options** to open the **Word Options** window:

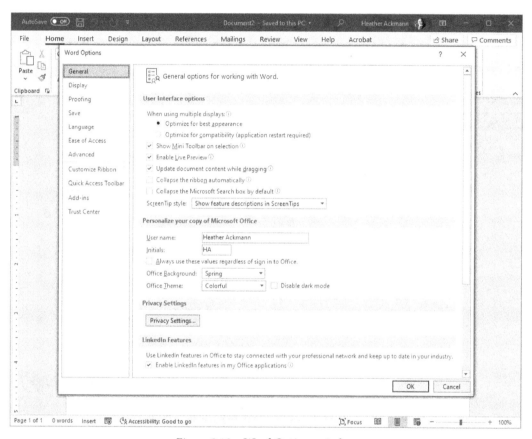

Figure 9.18 – Word Options window

2. Next, on the left-hand side of the screen, click on **Customize Ribbon**.

3. Toward the right of the screen, under the section labeled **Customize the Ribbon**, check the box next to **Developer** to turn on the **Developer** tab:

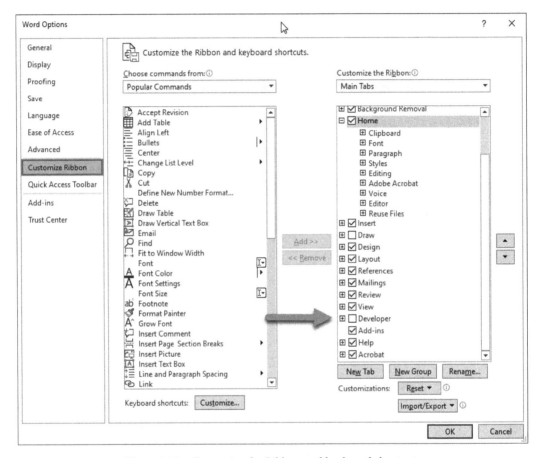

Figure 9.19 – Customize the Ribbon and keyboard shortcuts

4. Click **OK** to save the changes.

The **Developer** tab should now appear in your Ribbon between the **View** and **Help** tabs:

Figure 9.20 – The Developer tab

You will find a lot of advanced features from this tab, most of which are outside the scope of this book. But to the far left of this tab, we will be primarily working with buttons located in the **Code** group, specifically those buttons that relate to **Macros** and **Macro Security**.

Because macros contain a series of commands and code that are executed with a click of a button or a simple keyboard shortcut, in just a matter of seconds, a letter or a document that might have taken you an hour to format could be completely done. That's the positive side. On the other hand, macros can also be used by hackers to install viruses, malware, or to gain access to your organization's network or other sensitive data. For that reason, it is up to us to be aware of what kinds of documents we are opening on our computers, as well as knowing the source of where those documents are coming from. And that starts with knowing about how Word warns you about potential security risks.

Understanding macro security

Let's face it. Cybercriminals use macro-based malware to infect companies because it still works, despite companies' best efforts to prevent and protect themselves. But let's not focus on how it works. Let's focus on why it works. It works because a select number of individuals inside a company trust something they shouldn't. It could be any of the following:

- An email from a potential client with a Word attachment

- A website offering free Word templates

- A link, ad, or Facebook message that links to a file-sharing site

And despite company policies and education programs warning against malicious or suspicious attachments or banning and blocking certain websites, and the fact that companies can now prevent and block macros from running in Office applications that come from the internet from any or all of the preceding scenarios via Group Policy, sometimes, these files still find their way in. As such, each of us must be vigilant and know what each security warning we see in Word means. To begin, let's start with what we see when we open a variety of files.

Opening a file from the internet

Sometimes, when you open a file from the internet, or as an email attachment, or if your company has certain policy settings, you may see a warning that looks a lot like this:

Figure 9.21 – Protected View

You will see a message in yellow underneath the Ribbon that says **PROTECTED VIEW**, and then explains that your file is read-only or that editing has been restricted somehow. Sometimes, there is a button you can press to enable editing.

Protected View is a safeguard in the event of one of the aforementioned malicious scenarios. It gives you time to inspect the document's content safely without too much worry. If your company allows editing for these types of documents, and you trust the person who sent the file and the content on the inside seems okay and isn't causing any issues once opened, then you are probably okay to click the **Enable Editing** button if you must edit the file. But if all you need to do is read the file, there is no reason to click the **Enable Editing** button. You can stay in **Protected View** and just close the file when you're finished.

There are other yellow messages, though, that you will see appearing in this same location below the Ribbon in Word. Not all of them are necessarily warnings or bad.

Recovered Unsaved File

At some point, you may see this yellow banner stretch across underneath the Ribbon. This is when Word has recovered an unsaved file for you. In the event of a computer or software crash or malfunction, Microsoft Word may grab and recover any unsaved file(s) you had open. The next time you open Word, you will see a yellow message bar appear that looks like those same protected view warnings that you see all the time:

Figure 9.22 – Recovered Unsaved File

The only difference is that this isn't anything to be cautious about. Word has temporarily stored the file on your computer and all you need to do is decide whether you want to save it.

Another yellow message box that should not be confused with the other yellow messages is the one that pertains to the topic of this section: macros.

Security Warning

When you see a yellow message bar below your Ribbon that says **SECURITY WARNING**, be sure to read the message that follows and pay attention to who sent you the file and where the file came from. This message is a bit more serious than the previous messages, even though the message bar's appearance looks nearly identical:

Figure 9.23 – SECURITY WARNING Macros have been disabled

In the preceding screenshot, the message bar states **Macros have been disabled..** Then, next to that warning, there is a button stating **Enable Content**.

Do not enable content unless any of the following apply:

- You know the author.
- You trust the source.
- You know that the file has not been compromised.

If anything seems suspicious at all, do not enable the content. When in doubt, contact the author of the file and ask or have your IT department investigate.

Viewing our Trust Center settings

If you aren't seeing any of these warnings, this could be because of your **Trust Center** settings or your company's Group Policy settings. If you are an individual managing your Office subscription and would like to view or manage your **Trust Center** settings, follow these steps:

1. Go to **File | Options | Trust Center** and click on the **Trust Center Settings...** button:

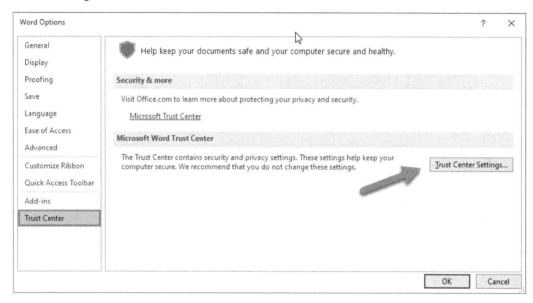

Figure 9.24 – Trust Center Settings

This will open the **Trust Center** window.

2. Navigate to **Macro Settings**:

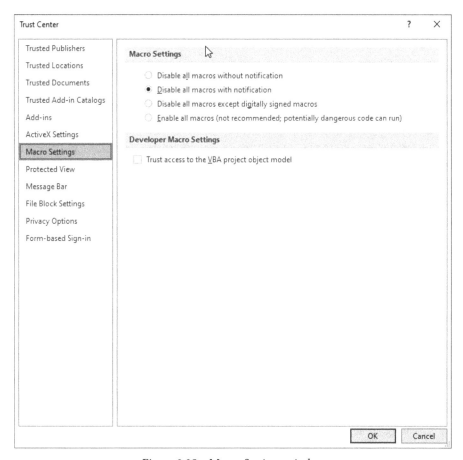

Figure 9.25 – Macro Settings window

Underneath the **Macro Settings** section, you will find four options to choose from:

- **Disable all macros without notification**
- **Disable all macros with notification**
- **Disable all macros except digitally signed macros**
- **Enable all macros (not recommended; potentially dangerous code can run)**

You will not receive any warnings or notifications for the first option, which disables all macros and is the most secure, while the last option enables all macros and is the least secure. I keep mine on **Disable all macros with notification**.

There is more to know about **Trust Center** but that is a bit outside the scope of this book. If you would like to learn more, you can learn more about it on Microsoft Support's Trusted Documents page: `https://support.microsoft.com/en-us/topic/` `trusted-documents-cf872bd8-47ec-4c02-baa5-1fdba1a11b53`.

Now that we understand a bit more about macro security, it's time to dive in and begin creating our very first macro.

Creating a macro

To record a macro, we are going to start small and just record a simple macro that adds our name and Twitter handle to the beginning of any document. For this example, if you want to follow along, just open a blank document and follow these steps:

1. To begin recording, navigate to the **Developer** tab and click on the **Record Macro** button:

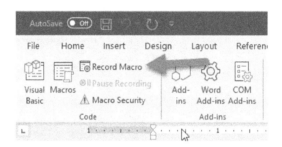

Figure 9.26 – The Record Macro button

This will open a **Record Macro** window.

2. From the **Record Macro** window, enter a unique macro name. For our example, type `NameAndTwitterTop`.

> **Important Note**
> Macro names cannot contain any spaces, periods, or use any non-alphanumeric characters. The name may contain numerals, but the name must begin with a letter. Names must be less than 80 characters and cannot conflict with any reserved commands or keywords.

3. You may choose to assign the macro to a button or a keyboard shortcut if you like, though these are optional. If you do not choose either of these options, you would have to run the macro through the **Macros** window (which adds a few more clicks). For our example, assign it to a button on your **Quick Access Toolbar**. However, we will do this step last because doing so will start the recording process.

4. You may also choose where to store the macro. The default choice is **All Documents (Normal.dotm)**, which makes the macro available across all the documents on your computer. But if there is a particular template or file that you would like this macro to be saved to, you can save this macro to that document.

5. Next, you may add a description to help viewers (and yourself) understand what commands this macro executes or does within the Word document. I strongly recommend writing descriptions. If you are anything like the authors of this book, you will forget what, why, and how you wrote something, even if you wrote it yesterday.

6. And finally, circling back toward the top, click the **Button** button to assign the macro to your **Quick Access Toolbar**.

    That will open your **Word Options** window directly to the **Customize the Quick Access Toolbar Macros** area.

7. Select the **Normal.NewMacros.NameAndTwitterTop** macro and click **Add > >** and then **OK**:

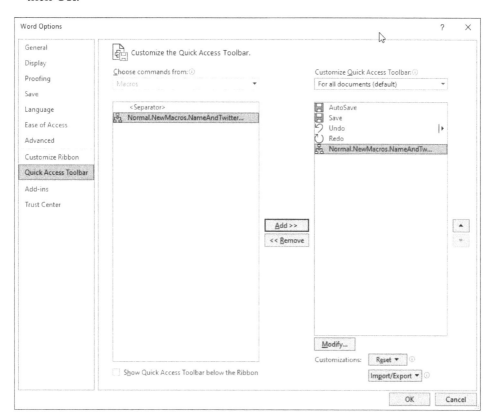

Figure 9.27 – Adding a macro to the Quick Access Toolbar

Once you click **OK**, even if you had not finished with the previous **Macro** window, your macro will begin recording.

> **Important Note**
> This is why I like to save this step for last. Ideally, assigning a button or keyboard shortcut would appear last in the **Macro** window, but in the end, it is not very hard to edit descriptions or macro details after the fact, as you will see.

But do be careful at this point. Everything you do, upon clicking **OK**, everything you type, and everything you click is now being recording as a step in your macro. If you do something unexpected, you can always delete the macro and start over, or edit the code in the VBA editor. There isn't an undo option when recording a macro. Therefore, you must plan through your steps very carefully before you begin. Keep in mind that it may take a couple of tries to get your macro just right if there are a lot of steps involved or if you get interrupted while recording or, simply, if you can't tell whether Word is recording your macro or not.

How to tell whether you are recording a macro

You will know whether you are recording from three locations in Word:

- From the **Developer** tab
- From the appearance of your cursor
- From the status bar

From the **Developer** tab, if you are currently recording a macro, in the **Code** group, the button that normally says **Record Macro** will instead display **Stop Recording**. You will also see another button below that says **Pause Recording**:

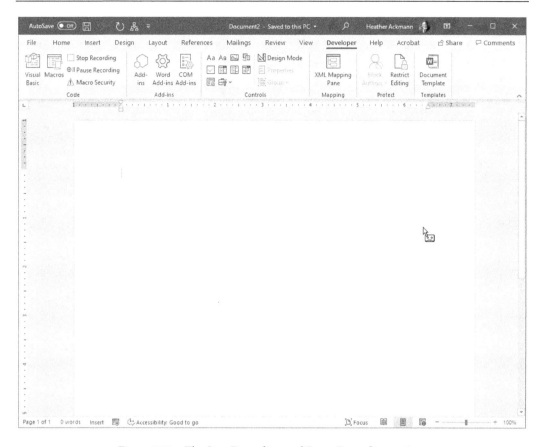

Figure 9.28 – The Stop Recording and Pause Recording options

If your **Developer** tab isn't visible, because you have clicked away from the tab and are no longer sure whether you are recording, you can always look at your cursor. If your cursor has a cassette tape icon behind the arrow, you are recording:

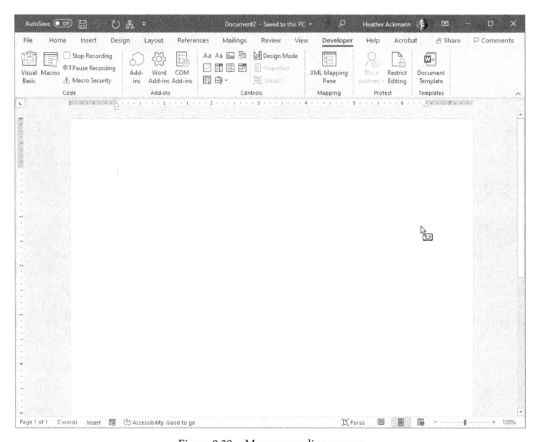

Figure 9.29 – Macro recording cursor

If you see that cursor, you are still recording. And finally, another way not only to tell whether you are recording but to start and stop recording as well is to use the **Macro** button on the status bar:

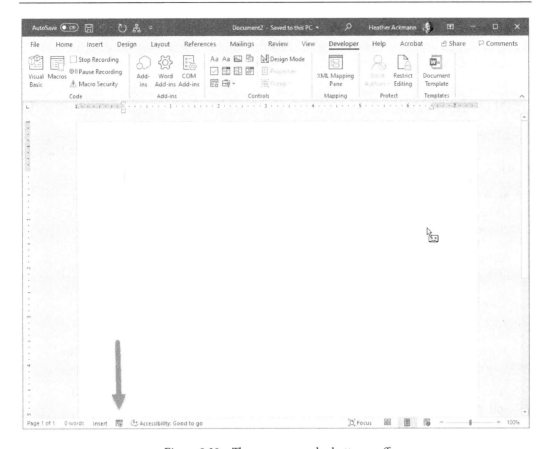

Figure 9.30 – The macro recorder button – off

If you see the macro icon with a recording symbol over it, you are not recording. Clicking that icon will open the **Record Macro** window. If you see a square, however, you are recording:

Figure 9.31 – The macro recorder button – on

You can click the square to stop recording at any time.

Now that we know whether we are recording, let's start recording a simple macro that includes our name at the very top of our document, no matter how long the document may be, and on the second line of the document, our Twitter handle.

Recording a macro

In the previous section, we began recording our macro in Word. That was the easy part. The hard part is figuring out the steps we need to perform to get the output we want our macro to do.

Since we want our name to appear at the top of our document, no matter where our cursor is when we run our macro, we have to figure out a way to tell Word to go to or rather move our cursor to the top of our document:

1. Press *Ctrl* + **Home** to tell Word to move the cursor to the beginning of the document.

    Knowing keyboard shortcuts in Word helps when recording macros.

2. Type your name and press *Enter*.

3. Type your Twitter handle, hold down the *Shift* key, and press *Home* to select the Twitter handle you just typed.

4. Press *Ctrl* + *K* to open the **Create Hyperlink** window. Enter your Twitter URL and press *Enter*.

5. Press *Enter* again.

6. Stop recording the macro.

So, here is what I have so far:

Figure 9.32 – Macro end result

I know it doesn't look like much, but like most things in life, when you are just beginning, it is good to start small and simple.

7. Now, go ahead and delete everything you just typed. Then, type =lorem() and press *Enter*.

Now, you should have a page that looks like this:

Figure 9.33 – Lorem document

With our page all set up, we are ready to run and test our newly created macro.

Running a macro

In the previous section, we recorded a macro that displays our name and our Twitter handle at the very top of the page. And it should display that at the top of the page, no matter where our cursor is within the page and no matter what is on the page.

If, when recording a macro, you created a button on your **Quick Access Toolbar** or created a keyboard shortcut, you may click that button or use that keyboard shortcut to run your macro. In the previous section, we attached the macro to a button on our **Quick Access Toolbar**:

1. First, I am going to move my cursor to the very end of my document.

2. Next, on my **Quick Access Toolbar**, I am going to click on my newly created **Macro** button:

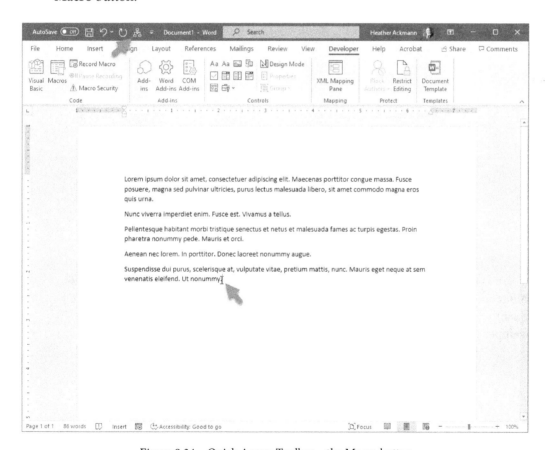

Figure 9.34 – Quick Access Toolbar – the Macro button

Upon clicking the button, my macro will run, and my name and Twitter handle will be added to the top of my document:

Figure 9.35 – Macro running

And that is one way to run a macro. If you run quite a few macros, the **Quick Access Toolbar** could get quite crowded. I usually reserve this area for the commands I use frequently. For macros that I use less often, such as those I prefer to run from the **Developer** tab, I select them from the **Macros** button.

Clicking on the **Macros** button will open a window where you can view, run, manage, organize, edit, and delete previously created macros:

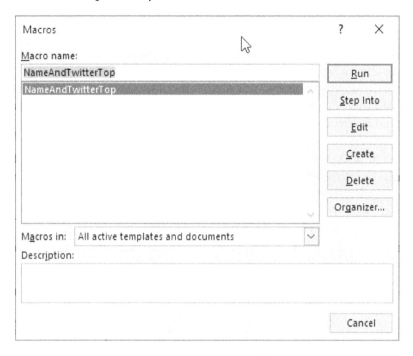

Figure 9.36 – Macros window

To run a macro from this view, simply select the macro from the list and click the **Run** button. Its is the same as using the button from the Quick Access Toolbar or the keyboard shortcut, just not as fast.

Summary

As you can see, Microsoft Word offers many no-code methods for automating tasks, formatting, workflows, keystrokes, and commands on the PC, and each method has advantages and disadvantages. With custom keyboard shortcuts, you can save time and open specialized or hidden Word commands or simply create a keyboard shortcut that is easier for you to remember. Keeping your hands on the keyboard does save time in the long run but having to remember and memorize a lot of keyboard shortcuts takes time and is not for everyone. For others, using Word's AutoCorrect and AutoFormat features in not-so-common ways to create short lists and add hard-to-remember and -spell words or company jargon and acronyms can be a timesaver. Or, for bigger lists and blocks of text, using some of Word's custom Quick Parts or building blocks might be a good option. The downside is that some of these features are not compatible with Mac users yet. And of course, there are always macros, which is what most people think of when they think of automation in Word. The problem is that hackers can often exploit Office files, so companies have locked down on security, making it harder for some users to even open these types of files in the enterprise. However, with a little education and caution, we can record macros and still save time creating safer and more efficient workflows.

In the next chapter, we will be exploring how to work with graphic elements.

10
Working with Illustrations, Charts, and Tables

In Microsoft Word, graphic items such as pictures, icons, shapes, charts, and several other objects are referred to as illustrations. We can also think of them simply as objects that we can place and manipulate to add visual interest to a document. The tools to add these objects to a document can be found in the **Illustrations** section of the **Insert** tab. In this chapter, we will learn how to insert illustrations into a document and explore the different types of illustrations.

We will also learn how to manipulate the way text wraps around an illustration by selecting different text wrapping styles. We will also learn how to manipulate the boundary around an object to customize how text flows around it.

Sometimes, one of the most frustrating things about working with illustrations is keeping them in the same place as you continue to edit the document. In this chapter, we will look at ways to either allow images to move with the text, or how to make them stay in a specific place.

You might not realize it, but charts and tables are also considered illustrations, or objects, in Word, and they can be treated very similarly. Charts and tables can have text flow around them and be positioned wherever you desire. We will end this chapter by exploring how charts and tables can be used as illustrations.

In this chapter, we will cover the following main topics:

- Inserting illustrations
- Wrapping text around illustrations
- Keeping illustrations in place
- Using charts and tables as illustrations

Inserting illustrations

In this section, we are going to learn about inserting illustrations into a Word document and explore the different types of illustrations.

Many types of graphic objects are considered as illustrations in Word. You can see them by going to the **Insert** tab and looking at the **Illustrations** section:

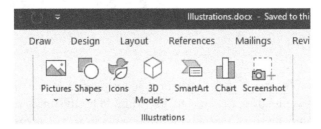

Figure 10.1 – The Illustrations section

Under the **Illustrations** section, we have the following:

- **Pictures**: These are usually photographs or other images saved in one of many digital formats supported by Word. The most common of these are .jpg, .png, and .svg.

- **Shapes**: These are line drawings of various common shapes such as rectangles and ovals. Shapes are scalable and most of their outlines can be manipulated to alter their shape. Shape outlines can be colored or hidden, and shapes can usually be filled with a color or pattern.

- **Icons**: These are similar to shapes but are typically more complex, such as an icon of a computer or a clock. Icons are also scalable, and their outline and fill colors can be changed.

- **3D Models**: These are 3D images that can be tilted and rotated 360 degrees to achieve the desired look of the model in your document. Users of Word can access these models from Microsoft online, right in the Word app. They are then downloaded to your document. You can also add your own 3D models if they are in a supported format.

- **SmartArt**: This is a preformatted and highly stylized type of graphic from Microsoft that you can use to create things such as lists and process diagrams.

- **Chart**: Charts are a visual representation of data that can be added to Word. Charts share many of the same properties as other illustrations.

- **Screenshot**: This allows you to capture an image of an open app and add it to a Word document. You can also use the **Screen Clipping** tool to clip any portion of your screen and add that as well.

> **Important Note**
>
> Support for .svg files is only available in Word for Office 365 at the time of writing.

In the next section, we will explore how to insert pictures and learn about the different types of pictures you can add in Word.

Inserting pictures

To insert a picture into Word, follow these steps:

1. Go to the **Insert** tab and then to the **Illustrations** section, as mentioned previously.

   We are going to begin by selecting a photo saved locally on our computer.

2. Click on the **Pictures** button and a small menu will drop down with three options:

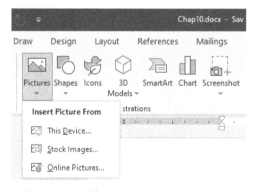

Figure 10.2 – The Insert Picture From menu

Under this drop-down menu, you will get different options for where you want to insert a picture. Let's examine these options:

- **This Device...:** This will open File Explorer and allow you to select a picture stored anywhere on your computer:

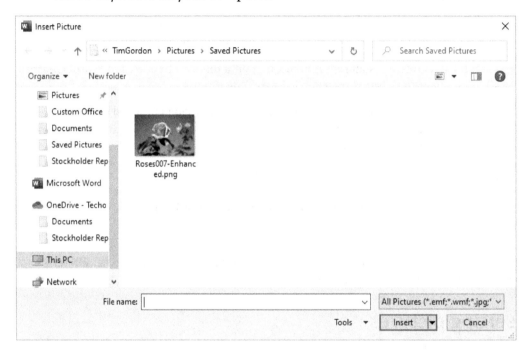

Figure 10.3 – The Insert Picture window in File Explorer

- Stock Images...: This option opens a library of royalty-free images, icons, cutout people, stickers, and illustrations that you can select and use in your documents. These images are copyright-free. This option is only available to Microsoft 365 subscribers:

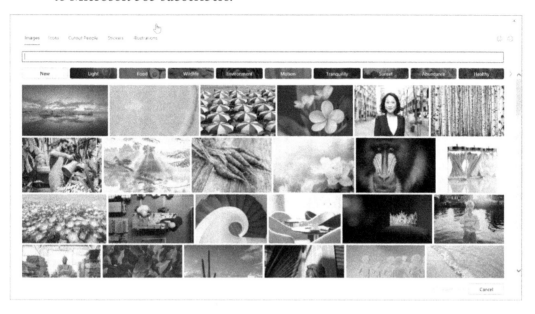

Figure 10.4 – The Stock Images library

- Online Pictures...: This will open a selection of pictures from online sources that you can search through using the Bing search engine. Pictures from online sources may be subject to copyright restrictions. You can also access your OneDrive from here:

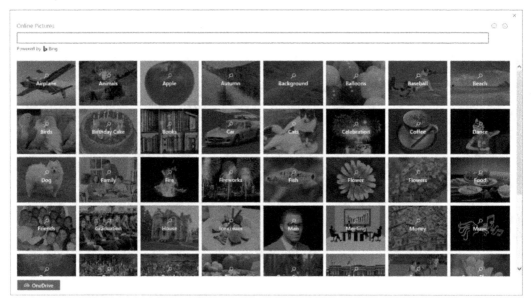

Figure 10.5 – Online pictures

3. Once you have selected the picture you want, click the **Insert** button in the lower-right corner.

    The **Insert** button will be in the lower-right corner for all three options. The picture will then be added to your document at your insertion point.

The next button in the **Illustrations** section is **Shapes**. Shapes are very useful because they can be resized, colored, and manipulated in many ways. So, let's explore how to insert shapes into a document.

Inserting shapes

Shapes are very versatile, and Word provides us with a large selection of shapes to choose from. Shapes in Word are what's known as vector graphics. Vector graphics are made up of points on a plane connected by lines. This differs from raster images, which are most commonly pictures. Vector graphics can be scaled up or down without them losing their quality. The lines will remain sharp and clear, no matter what size or resolution you make them. All of the shapes available in Word are copyright-free.

Follow these steps to insert a shape:

1. Click on the **Shapes** button in the **Illustrations** section. A large panel of shapes will appear, which is further divided into several categories:

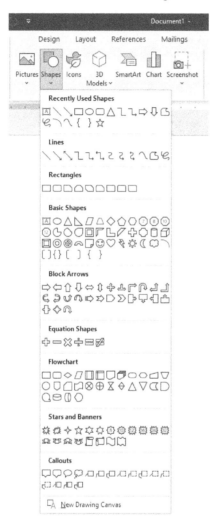

Figure 10.6 – The Shapes panel

2. Once you have decided on a shape, click that shape and the **Shapes** panel will disappear.

3. You will then see a large plus (+) symbol, and you can move it wherever you like with the mouse. Once you have moved the plus near where you want to place the shape, click with the mouse again and the shape will be placed at the spot of the plus (+) symbol.

The following screenshot shows a right-facing arrow that was inserted by clicking once on the plus (+) symbol:

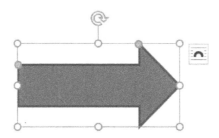

Figure 10.7 – Right-facing arrow

Alternatively, instead of clicking with the plus, if you click and drag, you can make the shape smaller or larger. In some cases, you can even alter the shape. In this example, I have selected a right-facing arrow and changed its size and shape by clicking and dragging:

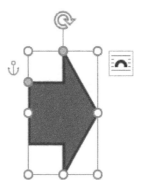

Figure 10.8 – Right-facing arrow resized

Different shapes can be altered in different ways. Some shapes, such as the arrow in the preceding screenshot, have points (shown here as orange dots) that can alter the shape if they're moved in different directions. By moving the dots, I was able to alter the look of this arrow:

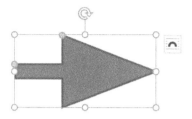

Figure 10.9 – Right-facing arrow altered

Word provides us with many shapes that we can use to enrich our documents and add emphasis.

Another very effective type of illustration is an icon. Icons are drawings of familiar symbols or representative images that can be added to a document. Word provides us with a large library of icons, and in the next section, we will learn how to insert an icon into a Word document.

Inserting icons

Icons are representative images. In Word, they are black and white line drawings, usually with multiple versions of the image. Icons in Word, just like shapes, are vector graphics. They are also copyright-free, which will save you the effort of trying to find free icons on the internet.

Follow these steps to insert an icon into a Word document:

1. Go to **Insert | Illustrations**. Here, you will find the **Icons** option:

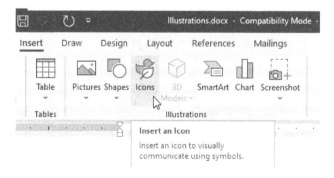

Figure 10.10 – The Icons button

2. Once we click the **Icons** option, the **Icons** window will appear:

Figure 10.11 – The Icons window

Here, you will find thousands of icons to select from. At the top of the window is a search bar that can help you find exactly what you are looking for. Below the search bar, there are category buttons that you can click on to see multiple icons from these different categories. You can scroll through the categories by using the right arrow at the right edge of the window, next to the category buttons:

Figure 10.12 – The icon categories scroll arrow

3. Once you find the icon you want, just click on it and this will place your icon in your document at the place of your insertion point.

You also have a variety of options to change the color and size of the icon. These options, plus more, can be found in the **Graphics Format** tab:

Figure 10.13 – The Graphics Format tab

Now that we know more about the types of illustrations and how to add them to our documents, let's learn how to wrap text around them.

Wrapping text around illustrations

When you add an illustration to a Word document that contains text, you will have to decide how you want your text to flow around that illustration. Depending on the type of illustration, Word will either place it on top of the text or in line with the text by default. In this section, we will learn how to use different layout options to change the way an illustration interacts with the text on the page. This feature is called **Wrap Text**.

Exploring the default layout for illustrations

When a picture is inserted into a document with text, Word will place it in line with the text. The following screenshot shows a picture that has been inserted at the beginning of a paragraph:

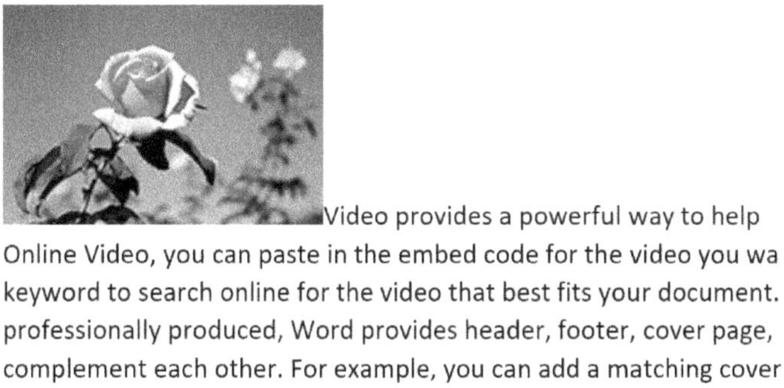

Video provides a powerful way to help
Online Video, you can paste in the embed code for the video you wa
keyword to search online for the video that best fits your document.
professionally produced, Word provides header, footer, cover page,
complement each other. For example, you can add a matching cover

Figure 10.14 – An in-line picture

As you can see, the picture has been placed in line with the rest of the text, as if it were just more text. Word does this by default with pictures, icons, SmartArt, charts, and screenshots. In contrast, Word places shapes and 3D models in front of text by default. In the following screenshot, you can see that a circle shape has been drawn and placed on top of the text:

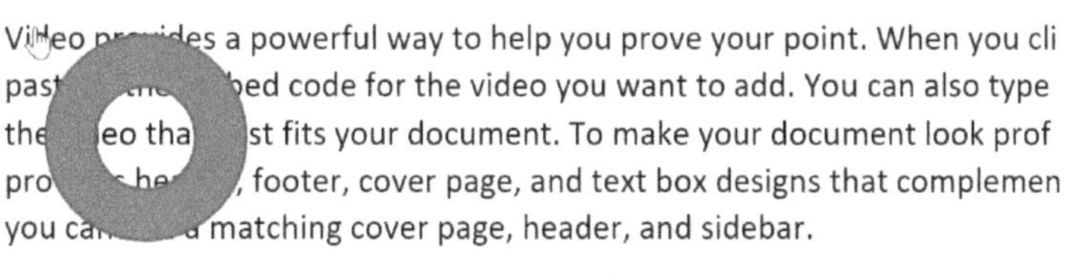

Video provides a powerful way to help you prove your point. When you cli
pas   ed code for the video you want to add. You can also type
the   eo tha   st fits your document. To make your document look prof
pro   he   , footer, cover page, and text box designs that complemen
you ca   matching cover page, header, and sidebar.

Figure 10.15 – Shape in front of text

Because shapes are drawn by the user by using a click-and-drag method, they are not placed at the insertion point. They are placed wherever you first click to begin drawing the shape.

The default wrap text may be exactly what you want but remember, no matter what type of illustration you have, there are several different ways that you can wrap the text around it. Now, let's explore how to wrap text.

Different text wrapping options

To see the list of **Wrap Text** options, you must have the illustration selected. You will know that it has been selected if you see a bounding box with small white dots, or handles, around the illustration:

Figure 10.16 – The bounding box and handles

At this point, a contextual tab will appear on the Ribbon, depending on the type of illustration, either a **picture, graphic, or shape format**. On this Ribbon, in the **Arrange** section, you will see a **Wrap Text** button. This is where you will find various **Wrap Text** options:

Figure 10.17 – The Wrap Text options

There are seven options listed here. Let's go through them, one by one:

- **In Line with Text**: This is the default option. With this option selected, the illustration is placed on the line at the insertion point as if it were simply more text. The image will move along the line as more text is added.

- **Square**: With this option selected, the text will flow around the image in a square. The text will attempt to create a straight line around the square.

- **Tight**: This option will bring the text tight to the image while following the shape of the wrap points around the illustration.

- **Through**: This is very similar to **Tight** and in most cases will be indistinguishable. Text will fill gaps in the image if your image has a transparent background.

- **Top and Bottom**: This will place the image on its own line and the text will appear above and below the image.

- **Behind Text**: This will place the image behind the text on a separate layer. An example would be a watermark or background image.

- **In Front of Textext**: This is the default option for **shapes** and **3D models**. The image will appear on top of the text on a separate layer and may obscure it.

The **Wrap Text** options can also be found by clicking on the **Wrap Text** icon in the top-right corner of a selected image:

Figure 10.18 – The Wrap Text icon and menu

The images in this menu give you a visual indication of how the text wraps around the image. This menu will also show a tooltip when you hover your mouse over one of the **Wrap Text** options:

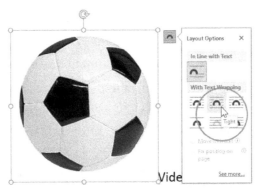

Online Video, you can paste in the embed

Figure 10.19 – The Tight option tooltip

Now, let's take a detailed look at these text wrapping options with some examples. The first option on the list is **In Line with Text**, which we have seen previously.

The second option is **Square**. The square option will make the text flow around the image's bounding box. This creates a square frame around the image and keeps the text on the right edge of the image aligned in a straight vertical line:

Figure 10.20 – An image with square text wrapping

You will notice that the text on the left edge of the image does not adjust to keep the text in a straight vertical line. By default, the text on the left of the image does not hyphenate either.

The next **Wrap Text** option is **Tight**. The **Tight** option will bring the text as close as it can around the image. If the image has a transparent background, the effect can be much more dramatic, as we can see in the following example:

Figure 10.21 – The Tight Wrap Text option

You can still see the bounding box, but the picture in this example has a much more extreme edge to illustrate how the text follows the edge of the branches and not the bounding box.

The next option is **Through**. **Through** is very similar to **Tight** and in most instances, you will not notice any difference. **Through** will fill in any gaps in the white space of the image, assuming your image has a transparent background. We will look at the same image I used for the **Tight** example, and see that the text fills in more of the space around the image:

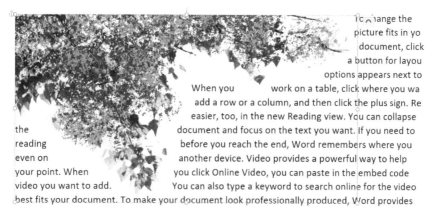

Figure 10.22 – The Through Wrap Text option

In some instances, you may need to adjust the wrap points around the image to get the full effect of the **Through** option. We will discuss how to edit wrap points in the *Edit wrap points* section, later in this chapter.

With these first four options, if you move the illustration, the text will continue to flow around it in the manner of the option you have selected. This offers great flexibility for the placement of an illustration, and you can achieve some amazing visual effects in your documents. If you add more text to the page, by default, the illustration will move with the text. If you open the **Wrap Text** menu, you will see that the **Move with Text** option is checked by default:

Figure 10.23 – The Move with Text option

The **Fix Position on Page** option, when checked, will keep the image in the same place, even when you add more text.

The **Top and Bottom** option is next on the list. With this option, the text does not flow around the image, but rather the image is placed on its own line and the text appears above and below, as shown in the following screenshot:

To change the way a picture fits in your document, click it and a butto
to it. When you work on a table, click where you want to add a row or

sign. Reading is easier, too, in the new Reading view. You can collapse
on the text you want. If you need to stop reading before you reach th

Figure 10.24 – Top and Bottom Wrap Text

With the **Top and Bottom** option, you can move the picture anywhere, and the text will remain alone on the line and will stay in the top and bottom positions.

The next **Wrap Text** option is **Behind Text**. Like we saw with the **Top and Bottom** option, the text does not flow around the illustration but behind it, on its own layer, as the name suggests. Depending on the image, this may make it difficult to read the text. In the following screenshot, I turned down the transparency of the picture to make the text easier to see:

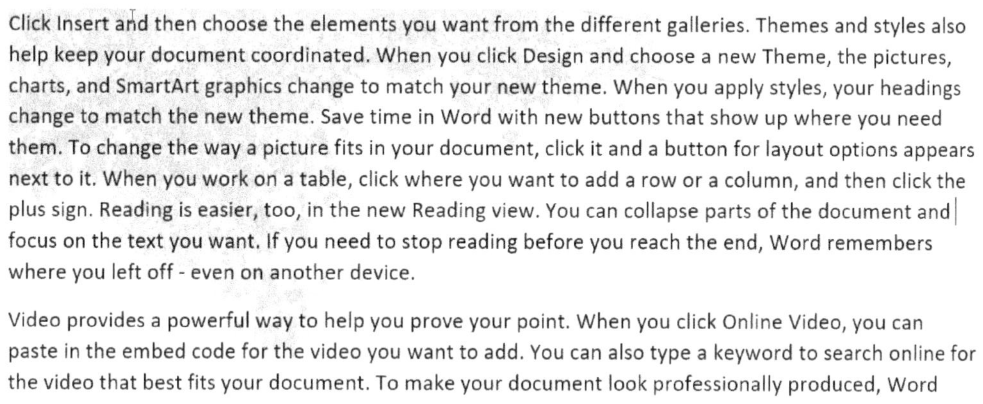

Click Insert and then choose the elements you want from the different galleries. Themes and styles also help keep your document coordinated. When you click Design and choose a new Theme, the pictures, charts, and SmartArt graphics change to match your new theme. When you apply styles, your headings change to match the new theme. Save time in Word with new buttons that show up where you need them. To change the way a picture fits in your document, click it and a button for layout options appears next to it. When you work on a table, click where you want to add a row or a column, and then click the plus sign. Reading is easier, too, in the new Reading view. You can collapse parts of the document and focus on the text you want. If you need to stop reading before you reach the end, Word remembers where you left off - even on another device.

Video provides a powerful way to help you prove your point. When you click Online Video, you can paste in the embed code for the video you want to add. You can also type a keyword to search online for the video that best fits your document. To make your document look professionally produced, Word

Figure 10.25 – The Behind Text Wrap Text option

A good scenario for using the **Behind Text** option would be for a watermark image or text in a document.

The final **Wrap Text** option is **In Front of Text**. This places the illustration on top of the text and depending on the image, it may obscure the text. This is the default setting when inserting shapes and 3D models, as we discussed earlier in this chapter. Here is an example of the **In Front of Text** option:

To change the way a picture fits in your document,
to it. When you work on a table, click where you wan
sign. Reading is easier, too, in the new Re   ew.
on the text you want. If you need to   ing bef
you left off - even on another   deo provides
When you click Online Video,   an paste in the em
also type a keyword to search online for the video tha

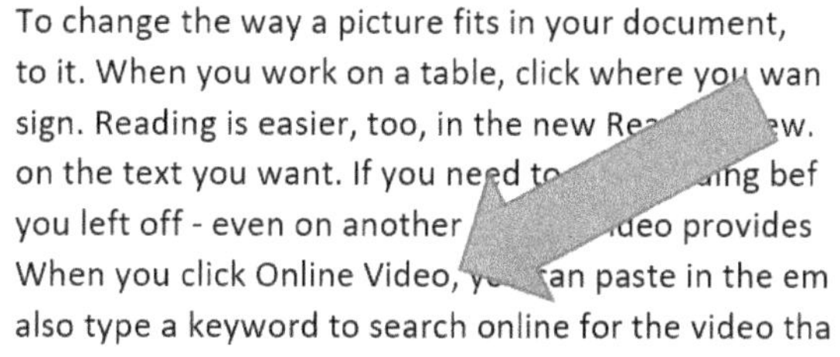

Figure 10.26 – The In Front of Text option

As you can see, the image obscures the text, but the arrow has also been used to point out text in the document. This can be a very effective use of the **In Front of Text** option.

For both the **Behind Text** and **In Front of Text** options, moving the image will not affect the text at all because the illustration is placed on a separate layer from the text. If you add more text to the page, by default, the illustration will move with the text.

Editing wrap points

Earlier, we spoke about editing wrap points. Wrap points create a path around an image, called a wrap boundary. Word will follow that boundary when wrapping text around an illustration. These wrap points are placed around the illustration automatically, based on the type of image. In this first example, we have a `.jpg` image with a white background. The wrap points appear as small black squares and are connected by red lines to create the wrap boundary, which appears square around this image:

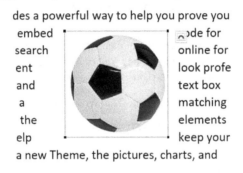

Figure 10.27 – Wrap points around a .jpg image

In the following example, we have a `.png` image with a transparent background around the image of the ball. In the following screenshot, we can see that the wrap boundary has wrapped closely around the shape of the ball:

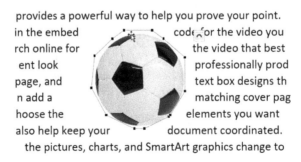

Figure 10.28 – Wrap points around a .png image with a transparent background

The great thing about wrap points is that you can move them around to create whatever boundary you want around an illustration, even if it does not have a transparent background. For example, I could take the .jpg image of the ball with the square wrap boundary, add more points, and manipulate them to create a circular shape or any other shape. This allows you to have your text flow around an image however you wish.

To edit these wrap points, follow these steps:

1. Select the image.

2. Then, from the **Format** tab, in the **Arrange** section, click on the **Wrap Text** button to expose the menu.

3. Near the bottom of the list, you will see the **Edit Wrap Points** option; click on that to expose the wrap points around the image. Remember that they will be connected by red lines:

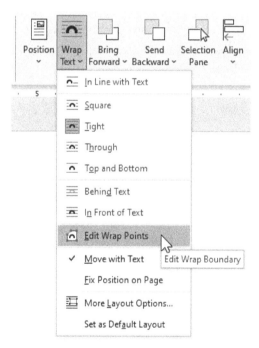

Figure 10.29 – Edit Wrap Points

4. To change the position of a wrap point, you must select it, hold down the mouse button, and drag it to where you want it.

    While moving the wrap point, the red boundary line will be replaced by a black dashed line until you let go of the mouse button:

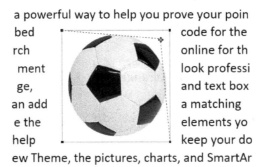

a powerful way to help you prove your poin
bed   code for the
rch   online for th
ment   look professi
ge,   and text box
an add   a matching
e the   elements yo
help   keep your do
ew Theme, the pictures, charts, and SmartAr

Figure 10.30 – Editing the wrap points

It is also helpful to be able to add additional wrap points so that we can manipulate the shape however we like.

5. To add a wrap point, bring your mouse to the place on the connecting red line where you want the point.

6. Hold down your mouse button and drag. The point will be added when you release the mouse button:

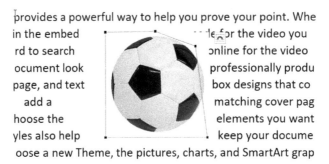

provides a powerful way to help you prove your point. Whe
in the embed   le for the video you
rd to search   online for the video
ocument look   professionally produ
page, and text   box designs that co
add a   matching cover pag
hoose the   elements you want
yles also help   keep your docume
oose a new Theme, the pictures, charts, and SmartArt grap

Figure 10.31 – Adding a wrap point

You can continue to add and move points until you achieve the desired shape. If you want to delete a wrap point, you will need to move your mouse over it and hold down the *Ctrl* key. Then, a small **x** will appear over the wrap point. Now, click the left mouse button and the point will be deleted:

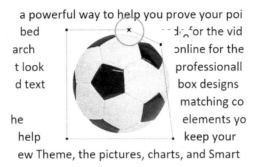

Figure 10.32 – Deleting a wrap point

Being able to edit wrap points allows you to have full control over how the text flows around your illustrations. Let's take another look at the image of the tree branches, this time with the wrap points and boundary lines revealed:

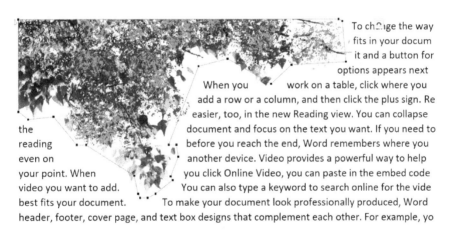

Figure 10.33 – Wrap points and their connecting lines revealed

To achieve the desired effect, I had to add and manipulate several wrap points, but it was worth it to get the desired look.

In this section, we learned about the many ways Word can wrap text around an image and what the defaults are for different types of illustrations. We saw how to make text flow around an image, as well as how to place it behind or on top of an illustration. We also explored how to edit wrap points and the wrap boundary so that we can customize how text wraps around an image. In the next section, we will look at how to fix the position of an illustration on a page and how to use anchors to lock an image to a paragraph.

Keeping illustrations in place

When working with illustrations, it may be important for you to be able to keep your illustrations from moving if more text is added, or if other changes would cause them to change their position. Fortunately, Word has tools to help us keep our illustrations in place. In this section, we will learn how to keep illustrations in place.

When you choose a **Wrap Text** option other than **In Line with Text** for an illustration, by default, Word will apply the **Move with text** attribute to the image. So, what does this mean? Imagine that you have placed an image in a paragraph and applied the **Tight** style, and you then add another paragraph of text before the one with the image. Here, the image will keep its position in the current paragraph and move down the page with the rest of that text.

In the following screenshot, we can see an image of a ball with the **Square** style applied. It is in the paragraph that begins with *When you apply...*:

In this section we learned the many ways Word can wrap text aroun are for different types of illustrations. We saw how you could make to place it behind, or on top of an illustration. We also explored how Boundary so that we can customize how text wraps around an imag how to fix the position of an illustration on a page and how to use paragraph.

When you apply styles, your headings change to
Word with new buttons that show up where you
picture fits in your document, click it and a bu
to it. When you work on a table, click where you
then click the plus sign. Reading is easier, too, in th
collapse parts of the document and focus on the text you want. If yo
reach the end, Word remembers where you left off - even on anoth
way to help you prove your point.

Figure 10.34 – Move with text before adding additional text

Now, we will add another paragraph before the paragraph with the image:

Boundary so that we can customize how text wraps around an image. In the next secti
how to fix the position of an illustration on a page and how to use anchors to lock an
paragraph.

Save time in Word with new buttons that show up where you need them. To change
fits in your document, click it and a button for layout options appears next to it. When
table, click where you want to add a row or a column, and then click the plus sign. Rea
in the new Reading view. You can collapse parts of the document and focus on the te
need to stop reading before you reach the end, Word remembers where you left off -
device. Video provides a powerful way to help you prove your point. When you click
can paste in the embed code for the video you want to add.

When you apply styles, your headings change to match the new th
Word with new buttons that show up where you need them. To
picture fits in your document, click it and a button for layout
to it. When you work on a table, click where you want to add a
then click the plus sign. Reading is easier, too, in the new Reading
collapse parts of the document and focus on the text you want. If you need to stop
reach the end, Word remembers where you left off - even on another device. Video
way to help you prove your point.

Figure 10.35 – After adding additional text

You will notice that the image kept its position in the paragraph and simply moved down.
This is because of the **Move with text** option, which was automatically applied when we
selected the **Square** style. To determine whether **Move with text** has been applied, select
the image and click the **Wrap Text** icon in the top-right corner. This will open the **Wrap
Text** menu. Near the bottom, you will see the **Move with text** option. If the radio button is
selected, then **Move with text** is on:

Figure 10.36 – The Move with text option applied

This is applied automatically when you choose any **Wrap Text** option other than **In Line
with Text**.

The next thing we want to look at is the **Fix position on page** option. If selected, this will keep the illustration in its place on the page, even if more text is added. In the following screenshot, the **Fix position on page** option has been applied. Notice that the image is in the paragraph that begins with *When you apply styles…*:

In this section we learned the many ways Word can wrap text around an image and what the
are for different types of illustrations. We saw how you could make text flow around an image,
to place it behind, or on top of an illustration. We also explored how to edit Wrap Points and
Boundary so that we can customize how text wraps around an image. In the next section we
how to fix the position of an illustration on a page and how to use anchors to lock an image to
paragraph.

When you apply ... styles ... e to match the new theme.
in Word with new ... e you need them. To change
picture fits in your ... docu ... tton for layout options appe
it. When you work ... on a t ... want to add a row or a colur
then click the plus ... sign. ... in the new Reading view. Yo
collapse parts of the document and focus on ... you need to stop reading bef
reach the end, Word remembers where you ... her device. Video provides a
way to help you prove your point.

Layout Options ✕

In Line with Text

With Text Wrapping

○ Move with text ⓘ
◉ Fix position on page

See more...

When you click Online Video, you can paste ... the video you want to add.
also type a keyword to search online for the ... ur document. To make your
look professionally produced, Word provides ... page, and text box designs
complement each other. For example, you c ... er page, header, and sideba
Insert and then choose the elements you wa

Fix Position on Page
Keep your object in the same place
on the page as text is added or
deleted.

Remember, if its anchor moves to
the next page, your object moves as
well.

keep your document coordinated. When you
and SmartArt graphics change to match your new theme. When
to match the new theme.

Save time in Word with new buttons that show up where you
fits in your document, click it and a button for layout options ap

Figure 10.37 – Fix position on page

Now, we will add another paragraph. You will see that the image has not changed its position on the page:

In this section we learned the many ways Word can wrap text around an image and
are for different types of illustrations. We saw how you could make text flow around
to place it behind, or on top of an illustration. We also explored how to edit Wrap Po
Boundary so that we can customize how text wraps around an image. In the next sec
how to fix the position of an illustration on a page and how to use anchors to lock an
paragraph.

You can also type a ... keyword to search online for the video that
document. To make ... your document look professionally produced,
header, footer, cover ... page, and text box designs that complement
example, you can ... add a matching cover page, header, and sideb
then choose the ... elements you want from the different gallerie

styles also help keep your document coordinated. When you click Design and choose
pictures, charts, and SmartArt graphics change to match your new theme. When you
headings change to match the new theme. Save time in Word with new buttons that
need them.

When you apply styles, your headings change to match the new theme. Save time in
buttons that show up where you need them. To change the way a picture fits in your
and a button for layout options appears next to it. When you work on a table, click
add a row or a column, and then click the plus sign. Reading is easier, too, in the new

Figure 10.38 – Fix position on page after adding text

We can see that the image stayed in place and is now in a different paragraph because we have added another paragraph before the image. This is what happens when the **Fix position on page** attribute is applied to an illustration in Word. Next, we will learn how to work with anchors.

Working with anchors

In this section, we will look at using object anchors to lock an illustration to a specific paragraph or page.

When you apply any wrap text style to an illustration (that is, object), other than inline, Word applies the **Move with Text** attribute to the object. We have seen and discussed this previously. This also applies to **Object Anchor**. To see **Object Anchor**, we must select the illustration. Once the image has been selected, you will see a small blue anchor icon in the left margin:

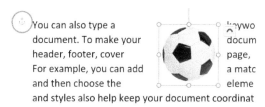

Figure 10.39 – The anchor icon

This indicates that the object is anchored to that paragraph, even if more text is added. If you add enough extra text, the illustration will move to another page, but it will still stay with that specific paragraph itself.

If you change to the **Fix position on page** option, the object will stay in place, as we discussed previously, but will still be anchored to the same paragraph:

Figure 10.40 – The object is still anchored to the same paragraph

You can see that the object did keep its position, but it is still anchored to the paragraph that begins with *You can also....*

We can use the **Lock anchor** option to keep an object anchored to the same page as the paragraph it's anchored to. To enable the **Lock anchor** option, follow these steps:

1.   Select the object.

2.   Right-click the image and select the **Size and Position...** option:

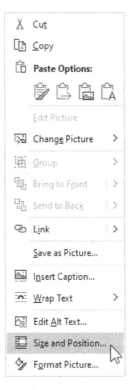

Figure 10.41 – The Size and Position... option

3. This will open the **Layout** window. Go to the **Size** tab of the **Layout** window:

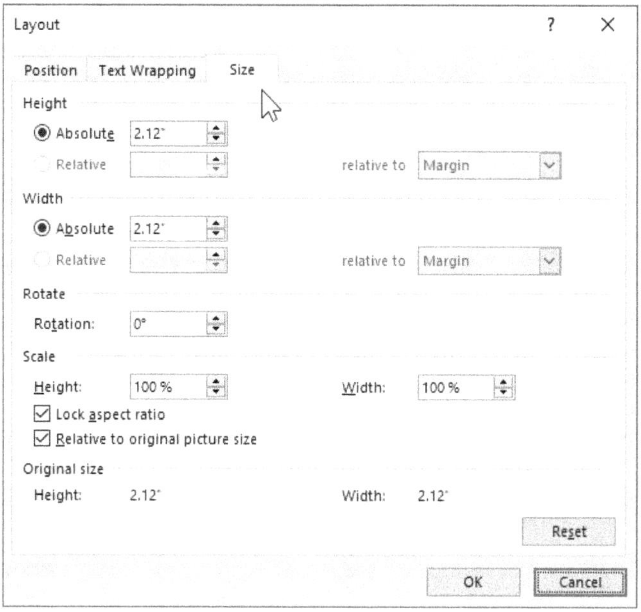

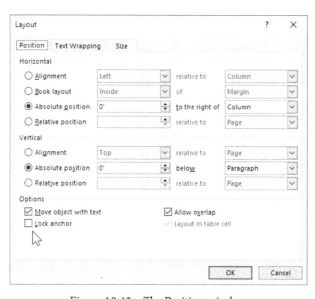

Figure 10.42 – The Size window

4. In the **Size** tab, you will see three tabs at the top of the window; that is, **Position**, **Text Wrapping**, and **Size**. Click on the **Position** tab. At the bottom left, you will see the **Lock anchor** checkbox:

Figure 10.43 – The Position window

5. Check this box and click **OK**.

Now, if we select our image again, we will see that the anchor icon now has a small lock symbol on it:

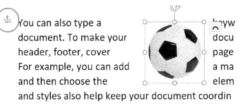

You can also type a
document. To make your
header, footer, cover
For example, you can add
and then choose the
and styles also help keep your document coordin

Figure 10.44 – The locked anchor icon

Now, the image is anchored to the paragraph and locked to the same page as that paragraph:

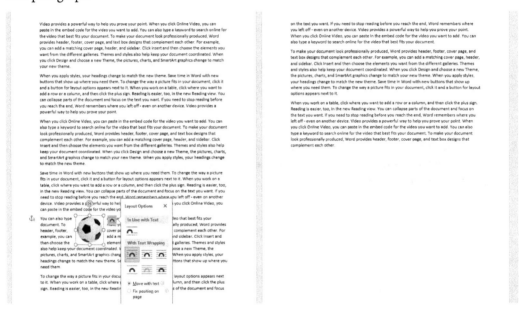

Figure 10.45 – Before adding text

At this point, if the **Move with text** option is applied and enough text is added to move the paragraph to another page, the object will stay with that paragraph and in its same position:

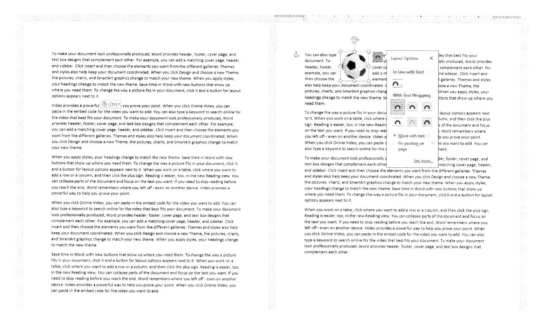

Figure 10.46 – Move with text and Lock anchor

If we apply the **Fix position on page** option to the object while **Lock anchor** is on, the object will still be anchored to the paragraph:

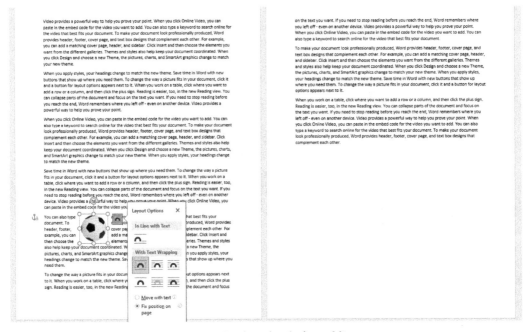

Figure 10.47 – Lock anchor before adding text

However, if enough text is added to move the paragraph to another page, the locked image will move to the same position on the new page but remain anchored to the original paragraph:

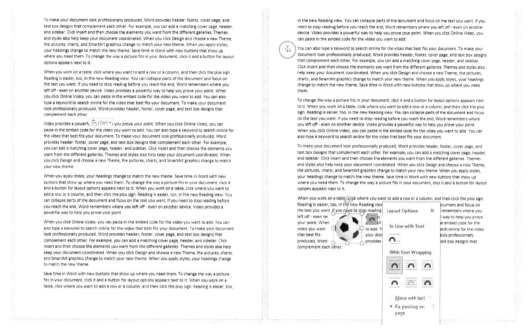

Figure 10.48 – Lock anchor after adding more text

The **Lock anchor** option is very useful when working with long documents to keep images anchored to a particular paragraph.

In this section, we've seen how to use the **Move with text** and Fix **position on page** options to keep objects within a specific paragraph or in a specific position. We also saw how to work with anchors to help keep objects where you want them. In the next section, we are going to look at working with charts and tables as illustrations.

Using charts and tables as illustrations

You may not think of charts and tables as illustrations, but Word certainly thinks of them in those terms. More specifically, Word treats charts and tables as objects just as it does any picture, shape, icon, or 3D model. In this section, you will see that tables do not have as many options for text wrapping, but you can still make text flow around a table, just as you would in any other illustration.

To insert a chart into a Word document, you simply need to go to the **Insert** tab and look in the **Illustrations** section, just as you would any other illustration. When you click the **Chart** button, the **Insert Chart** window will open:

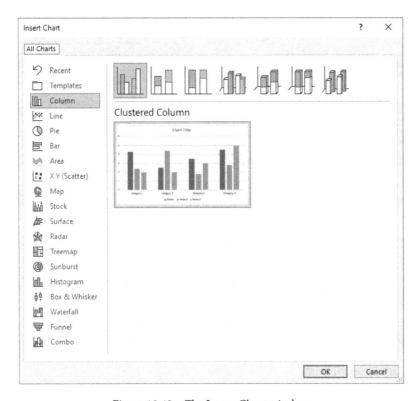

Figure 10.49 – The Insert Chart window

Now, you can select the type of chart you wish to use and add your data.

When you insert a chart into a document, Word will place it at your insertion point, in line with the text, the same as it does with most other illustrations:

To make your document produced, Word provides header, footer, cover page, and text box designs that For example, you can add a matching cover page, header, and sidebar. Click Inser elements you want from the different galleries. Themes and styles also help keep

Figure 10.50 – A chart in line with text

Once the chart has been added to your document, you can treat it like any other illustration. If you select the chart, you will notice a familiar icon – the **Layout Options** button in the top-right corner. Click this and you will see the **Layout Options** menu with all the same **Text Wrapping** options that we saw earlier in this chapter:

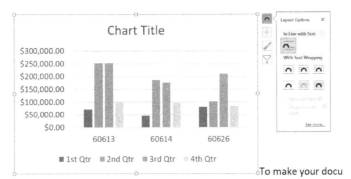

To make your docu produced, Word provides header, footer, cover page, and text box designs For example, you can add a matching cover page, header, and sidebar. Click elements you want from the different galleries. Themes and styles also help

Figure 10.51 – The Layout Options menu

Now, you can treat a chart the same as you would any other illustration. In the following screenshot, you will notice that I have applied the **Tight** style. You can also see the **Lock anchor** icon in the top-left corner:

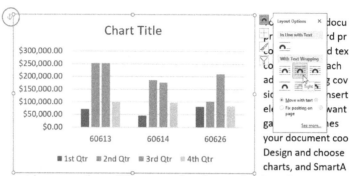

Figure 10.52 – A chart with the Tight text wrap style

The same **Lock anchor** options are also available for charts.

As I mentioned earlier, tables are a bit different than other illustrations, but you can still make text flow around a table.

To insert a table into a document, you will need to go to the **Insert** tab but instead of the **Illustrations** section, you must look for the **Tables** section:

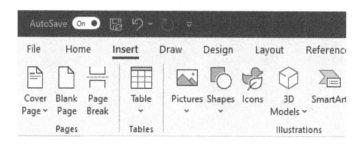

Figure 10.53 – The Tables section

The **Tables** section has only one option, **Table**, and this is used to create a table in your document. When you click on the **Table** option, the **Insert Table** menu will appear, at which point you can choose the method you want to use to create a table:

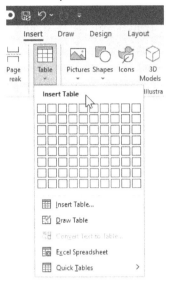

Figure 10.54 – The Insert Table menu

Whichever method you use to create a table, Word will add it to the document at the placement of the insertion point. It will also be placed on a separate line, not in line, as we have seen with other types of illustrations:

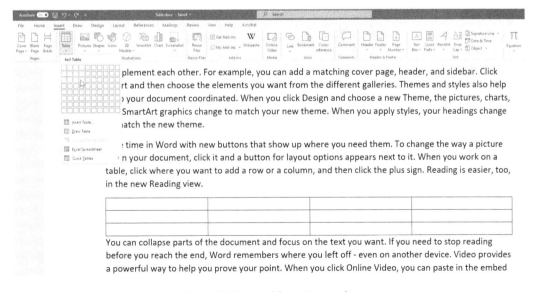

Figure 10.55 – A table on its own line

In the preceding example, I drew a 4x3 table using the grid method. You can see the cells highlighted in orange. With this method and the **Insert Table** method, Word will make the table fill the entire space between the margins, and the rows are a standard height. If you use the **Draw Table** method, you have more control over the width and height of the table. Once the table has been created, you can add data, resize the table, apply styles, and work with many other options that can be found on the contextual **Table Design** and **Layout** tabs.

When you want the text to wrap around the table, you will find that the process is a bit different than what we have talked about with other illustrations, but you can still achieve the desired effect. You need to begin by selecting the table. Simply click somewhere on the table to select it. You will know that the table is selected if you see the contextual **Table Design** and **Layout** tabs on the Ribbon. You will also see the **Table Selection** icon in the top-left corner of the table:

First	Last	Address	City	State
Amanda	Long	4959 Wenninger Street	Houston	TX
Donna	McMullin	4783 Southside Lane	Gardena	CA
Danny	Sampson	4770 Giraffe Hill Drive	Mesquite	TX
Jason	Turner	637 Gambler Lane	Houston	TX
Lucy	Davis	3752 Tennessee Avenue	Southfield	MI

When you work on a table, click where you want to add a row or a column,
Reading is easier, too, in the new Reading view. You can collapse parts of the

Figure 10.56 – The Table Selection icon

Next, you will need to go to the **Layout** tab and then to the **Table** section, which is located on the left-hand side of the Ribbon:

Figure 10.57 – The Table section of the Layout tab

Now, click the **Properties** button and the **Table Properties** window will appear:

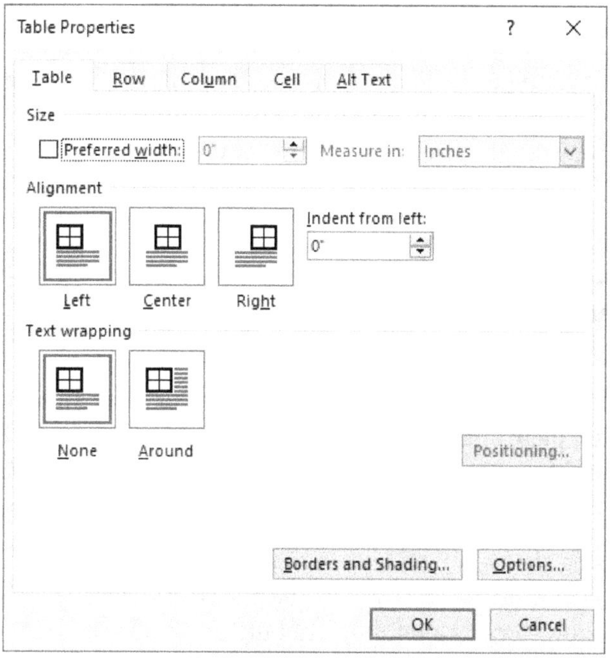

Figure 10.58 – The Table Properties window

The bottom portion of the **Table Properties** window is the **Text wrapping** section. By default, the **None** option is selected, so the table is placed on its own line. By clicking the **Around** option, the text will now wrap around the table, and you will be able to position the table however you want within the text:

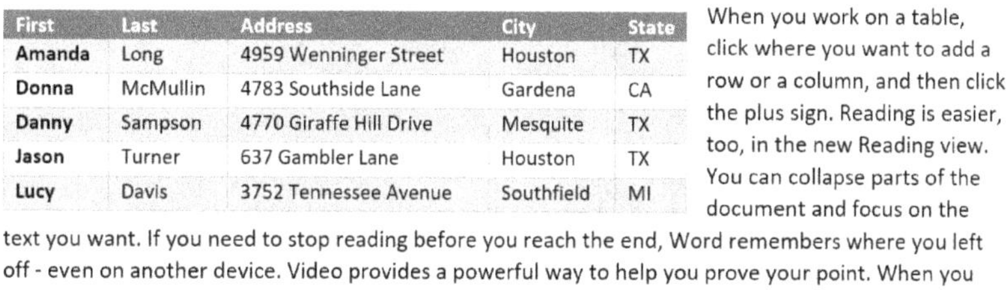

First	Last	Address	City	State
Amanda	Long	4959 Wenninger Street	Houston	TX
Donna	McMullin	4783 Southside Lane	Gardena	CA
Danny	Sampson	4770 Giraffe Hill Drive	Mesquite	TX
Jason	Turner	637 Gambler Lane	Houston	TX
Lucy	Davis	3752 Tennessee Avenue	Southfield	MI

When you work on a table, click where you want to add a row or a column, and then click the plus sign. Reading is easier, too, in the new Reading view. You can collapse parts of the document and focus on the text you want. If you need to stop reading before you reach the end, Word remembers where you left off - even on another device. Video provides a powerful way to help you prove your point. When you

Figure 10.59 – A table with the Around option applied

As you can see, the **Around** option is quite similar to the **Square** option, which we looked at previously. To move the table, you can click the **Table Selection** icon in the top-left corner and drag the table to the desired position with your mouse.

Summary

In this chapter, we explored using illustrations in Word documents. Illustration is the term that Microsoft uses to refer to any graphic object that can be added to a document. We learned about the different types of illustrations and how to insert them into a document. We also learned that different types of objects are treated differently when they are placed in a document. Some objects are placed in line with text, while others are placed on their own layer.

Next, we learned how to make text flow around objects and about the many styles of **text wrapping** we have, as well as how to apply them. This included learning about **wrap points and wrap boundaries** and how we can manipulate them to better control how text flows around an illustration.

We also looked at how to keep an illustration in place by using the **Move with text** option and the **Fix position on page** option. We also learned about anchors and how we could use the **Lock anchor** option to keep an object on the same page as the paragraph it's anchored to.

Lastly, we explored using charts and tables as illustrations. We saw that charts are treated just the same as any other illustration. They can be placed and have text wrapping in the same manner. Tables, however, are a bit different but very similar to other objects. We can still wrap text around a table, but the **Text Wrapping** options are limited to just two. We can also still move a table wherever we desire, by clicking and dragging it.

In the next chapter, we will learn about the document accessibility features in Word and what things to consider when creating documents that will be accessible to all audiences.

11
Writing for Everyone – Understanding Document Accessibility

If you're going to the lengths of writing something down in **Microsoft Word**, the chances are your goal is to communicate your ideas with others. Part of communicating effectively is tailoring your message to a target audience.

Unfortunately, in business, we can't always predict everything about the person on the other end of a document. At a minimum, we want them to be able to read what we have written. But what happens when we send a document to a client who is blind or low-vision, who relies on a screen reader to navigate and interpret the document, and we haven't designed our document in a way that makes it easy for a screen reader to do that?

I'll tell you what happens: we fail in our mission to communicate effectively.

In this chapter, we will cover some basics for making your Microsoft Word documents accessible for everyone using some simple, free tools available within Microsoft Word and **Word for the Web**.

We will cover the following topics in this chapter:

- Designing for document accessibility
- Writing concise and contextual alt text
- Using the new and improved Accessibility Checker
- Typing with your voice
- Transcribing audio

Microsoft is dedicated to ensuring that its products and services are **accessible**. I expect that in the coming years, accessibility features will expand beyond what you see in this chapter—but these topics are a good start. So, let's begin by talking about a few accessibility basics.

Designing for document accessibility

Despite even the best intentions, document accessibility in some businesses is sometimes an afterthought—a step or series of checks performed at the end of writing or document design to meet the minimum legal obligations. This is the wrong way to approach document accessibility.

At its core, document accessibility is about ensuring that your message reaches the largest, most diverse audience possible. As with most core aspects of design, designing for accessibility should happen in the earliest design and writing stages, alongside discussions of your document's target audience and rhetorical purpose, rather than a simple "check" when you are finished.

Therefore, the requirements for document accessibility need to be built in at these early stages, when designers are thinking about images and layouts and building Word's templates, themes, and tables, and when writers are planning the scope, target audience, examples, graphs, and other imagery. Then, the designers and writers need to keep accessibility in mind as they work in Word, making sure they are following best practices with regard to formatting to make the Word document accessible. And finally, after working to ensure the most accessible document possible throughout the creation of the document, using Word's accessibility tools to check and recheck the level of accessibility can help creators stay on target.

In the next few sections, you will learn about some simple ways to format and compose your Word document to make it more accessible. You will also learn how to use Word's newest **Accessibility Checker** to ensure you are meeting your accessibility goals.

Applying headings

One of the fastest ways to improve accessibility is to organize your document using **headings**.

Now, by headings, I don't mean selecting text and simply making the text appear larger, or bold, or a different color. I mean formatting the text with a built-in **heading style**. If you are unfamiliar with what a heading style is, refer to *Chapter 8*, *Saving Time and Ensuring Consistency with Styles*.

Headings allow users to explore a document faster with their screen readers. With **Windows Narrator**, for example, users can enable a feature called **scan mode** by pressing *Narrator* + the space bar. To navigate heading levels in Word with scan mode on, readers simply press *1* to jump to the next heading 1 level. To jump back to the previous heading 1 level, readers can press *Shift + 1*. Likewise, to jump to the next heading level 2, readers can press *2*, and for heading level 3, readers can press *3*, and so on.

Ideally, you will also want to ensure that the headings are placed in a logical order. Heading 1 should come first, as it is the most important and represents the main idea within the document. That is then followed by smaller chunks of information, formatted as heading 2. If you can further subdivide information inside heading 2, then you would apply a heading 3 to chunk up that information.

Navigating with headings using popular screen readers

Headings are very important for other screen readers too. For people who use **NonVisual Desktop Access (NVDA)** and **Job Access With Speech (JAWS)**, you can use the *H* key and *Shift + H* key combination to move forward and backward through headings, respectively. Just keep in mind that for these keyboard shortcuts to work, you must be in the correct mode. For example, using NVDA, there are two ways to explore Word: using the **focus mode**, where you can interact with and edit the document, and using the **review mode**, where you can read and navigate the document.

To switch into review mode, users will need to press whatever their NVDA modifier key is set to plus the space bar. On most machines, by default, the *Insert* key will be set as the NVDA modifier key. But you also have the option to set the *CapsLock* key as well.

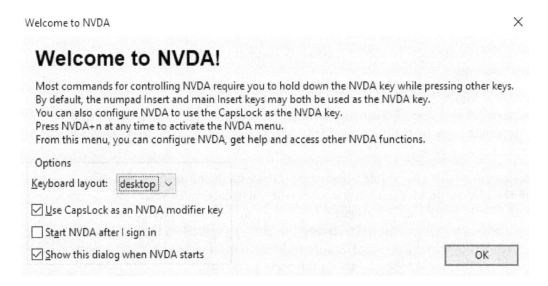

Figure 11.1 – NVDA Welcome screen

Personally, I prefer using *CapsLock* + the space bar to toggle between modes in NVDA, as I rarely use *CapsLock* when typing. When toggling between modes, you will hear two different tones to indicate which mode you are in. When you are in review mode, you can simply press *H* to jump to the next heading. If you are in regular mode, you will simply end up typing the h letter into your document.

To use shortcut keys such as the *H* key to navigate, documents must be properly formatted or styled with Word headings. All headings inside the document must be styled correctly as Word headings and named as such. Unfortunately, the reader using the screen reader often has little control over this. It is therefore up to authors, editors, and designers of documents and document templates to be aware of how to create properly styled headings for screen reader accessibility.

Common accessibility problems with headings

For many writers and designers using Word, customizing heading styles away from the default can be confusing. To review, Microsoft Word comes preloaded with many styles, including nine heading styles. When you open the **Styles** pane for the first time, you may only see two of those heading styles. That's because, by default, Word doesn't show all the styles available—only the recommended styles. However, if you open the **Styles** pane (*Alt + Ctrl + Shift + S*) and click on the **Options...** button in the lower right-hand corner of the pane, that will open a window where you can view all available styles.

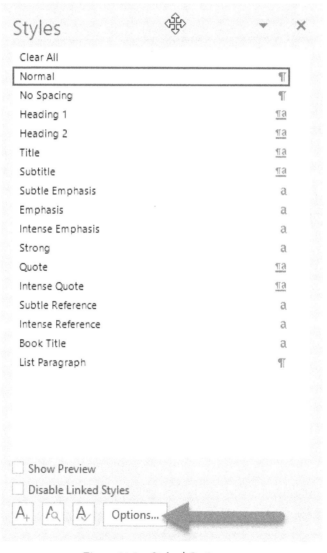

Figure 11.2 – Styles | Options...

When you display **All styles,** you will see the full list of available styles in Word.

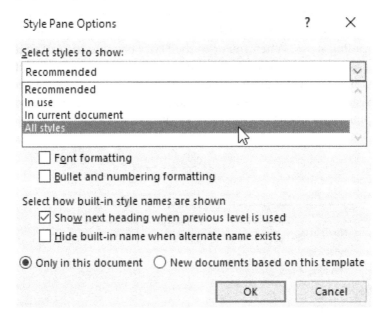

Figure 11.3 – Showing All styles

Accessibility problems arise when an author attempts to create new or additional heading styles to live alongside these default Word styles. Screen readers are programmed to look for Word's default styles, such as **Heading 1**, **Heading 2**, and **Heading 3**. If you create another style named **H1 – Section** and base it off the Heading 1 Word style, screen readers such as NVDA will not recognize that style as a Heading 1 style.

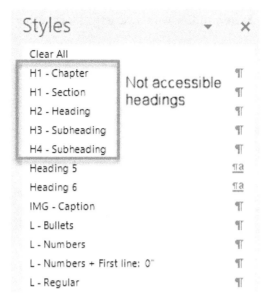

Figure 11.4 – Not accessible headings

Therefore, if you want to create accessible headings that look the way you want, be sure to modify the heading style from the **Styles** pane. To do this, you can right-click on any style and click **Modify…**.

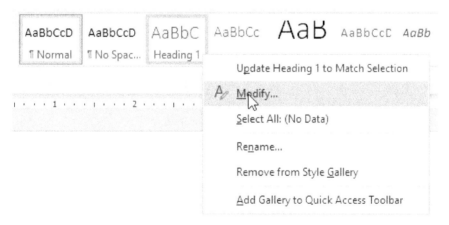

Figure 11.5 – Modifying the Heading 1 style by right-clicking

This will open the **Modify Style** window with a variety of formatting options:

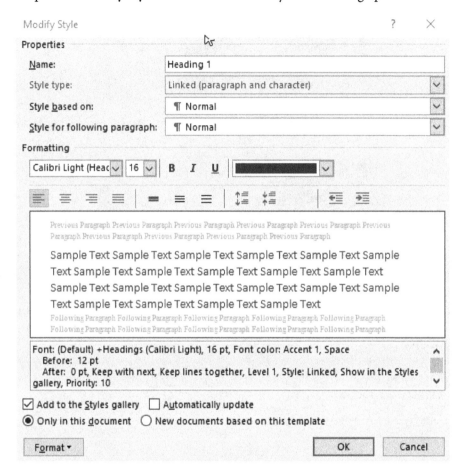

Figure 11.6 – Modify Style options

Simply select any options you like. A preview of how your text will appear will display in the sample text window. Then, click **OK** to save the style changes.

For additional information regarding how to properly format styles, refer to *Chapter 8, Saving Time and Ensuring Consistency with Styles*.

Other ways to navigate headings

Within Word, all readers can take advantage of headings for quick and easy document navigation, with or without a screen reader. When opening the **Navigation** pane from the **View** tab on the ribbon, headings will appear in the first tab of the **Navigation** pane:

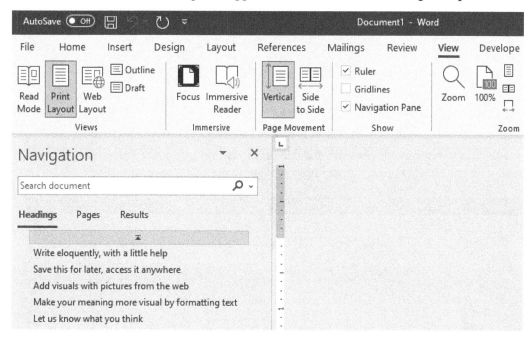

Figure 11.7 – Navigation pane headings

As shown in the preceding figure, all headings will appear as a neatly organized list for viewers to use to jump to sections of their document. Inside the **Navigation** pane, readers can use their mouse or press the *Tab* key to cycle through elements and the *Enter* key to select a heading item to jump to a section. Screen readers will read items as they are selected with the keyboard.

Creating Word lists

Who doesn't love a good **list**? Lists provide concise, easy-to-read, and scannable information. Even better, for accessibility purposes, screen reader users can easily jump to and navigate properly formatted lists and list items, just as they do with headings in Word. The problem is that writers using Word sometimes have some strange ways of creating bulleted and numbered lists. Sometimes, they will add hyphens or use an asterisk before a line to visually indicate a new bullet. In these circumstances, screen readers have no way of knowing that these symbols indicate a bulleted list item.

If you want your lists to be accessible to screen readers, be sure to use Word's bullets, numbering, and multi-level list buttons to create them.

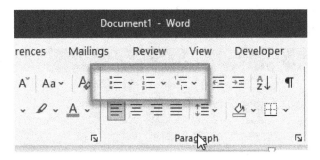

Figure 11.8 – List buttons

You'll find these buttons conveniently located on the **Home** tab, in the **Paragraph** group. Clicking on the bullets button, for example, will apply the **List Paragraph** style.

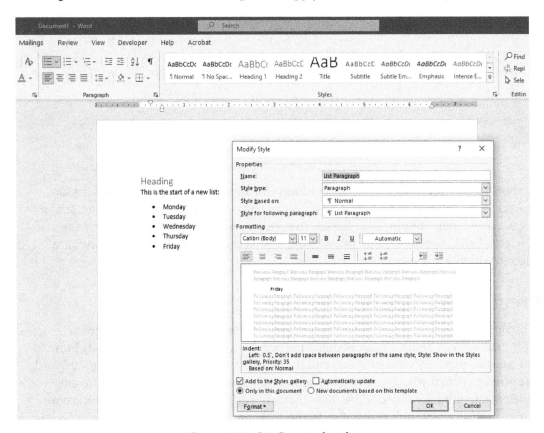

Figure 11.9 – List Paragraph style

Like any other style in Word, you can easily make changes to this style by right-clicking on the style in the **Styles** pane and selecting **Modify…** to open the **Modify Style** window. Any changes to the formatting you make here will be reflected anywhere you have this style applied. But, more importantly, regardless of how the style looks, screen readers will be able to read it and recognize it as a bulleted list.

Inserting meaningful hyperlinks and ScreenTips

You may have noticed that when copying and pasting URLs or hyperlinks from a web browser, Word will automatically convert them to hyperlinks or an active link that points to another place. This could be somewhere on the web, within the same document, or another document on the computer.

This autoformatting is both a blessing and a curse. On the one hand, copying and pasting a URL into Word will save you time and ensure that you haven't made any errors. On the other hand, you've just copied an ugly and unreadable link for everyone, not just screen reader users.

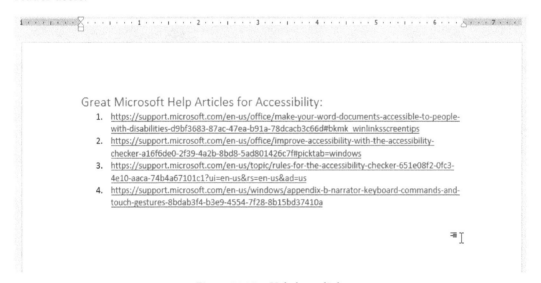

Figure 11.10 – Ugly hyperlinks

If this happens to you, there is an easy way to fix the appearance of hyperlinks, which we will look at in the next section.

Fixing hyperlinks

Follow these steps to fix ugly hyperlinks:

1. Right-click on the URL you've just pasted in and select **Edit Hyperlink...** (or, press *Ctrl + K*).

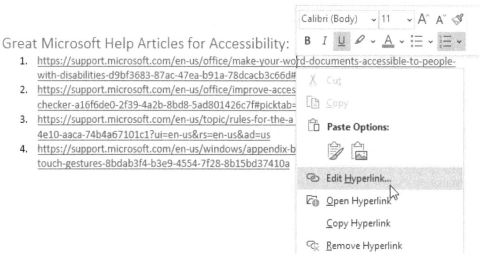

Figure 11.11 – Edit Hyperlink...

This will open the **Edit Hyperlink** window.

2. In the **Edit Hyperlink** window, change the display text by replacing the text that appears inside the box labeled **Text to display**.

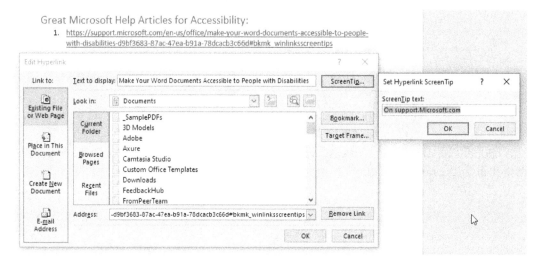

Figure 11.12 – Changing the Text to display field in the Edit Hyperlink window

3. To add a ScreenTip, click on the **ScreenTip…** button. A separate window will open where you can type in text that will appear when users hover over or select the link.

4. When finished typing in the display text and ScreenTip, click **OK** to save.

Your hyperlinks will still be formatted and function as hyperlinks. They will just be a lot easier to read for all people.

Great Microsoft Help Articles for Accessibility:
1. Make Your Word Documents Accessible to People with Disabilities
2. Improve Accessibility with the Accessibility Checker
3. Rules for the Accessibility Checker
4. Narrator Keyboard Commands and Touch Gestures

Figure 11.13 – Accessible hyperlinks

The only issue you may encounter is if you attempt to print a file that contains accessible hyperlinks. In this situation, you can temporarily display field codes to print the full hyperlink and any display text contained within the field.

In the next section, we will have a detailed look at this.

How to print accessible hyperlinks

Follow these steps if you want to print accessible hyperlinks:

1. Go to **File** and click on **Options** to open the **Word Options** window.

2. From the **Word Options** window, click on the **Advanced** tab and scroll down until you see the **Print** section.

3.   Check the checkbox labeled **Print field codes instead of their values**.

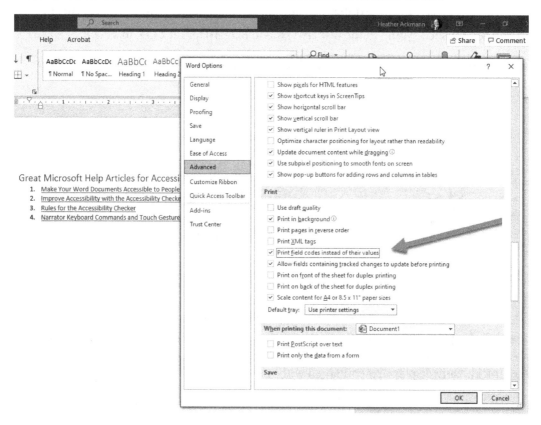

Figure 11.14 – Displaying full URLs when printing with the Print field codes instead of their values option selected

4.   Click **OK.**

With this option enabled, when you view the **Print** preview, you should be able to see all your hyperlinks and any other information contained within them displayed inside a curly brace.

Figure 11.15 – Print preview with field codes

This way, you have the best of both worlds: accessible and clickable hyperlinks to use on the computer, but the full URL available in print for when electronic devices will not be used.

So, as you can see, there are built-in tools in Word to make almost everyone happy. It just may take a while to learn about all the features and remember where to go to find them.

One such feature that is easy to forget about when in a hurry is the addition or editing of your images' alt text.

Writing concise and contextual alt text

Within the context of a Word document, *Alt text* (or *alternative text*) refers to text that is attached to graphical objects to assist people with visual impairments in interpreting the object's meaning within the document. Alt text is important for any reader who is blind or low-vision and relies on a screen reader to describe what an onscreen object not only looks like but what its purpose is within the document.

I am going to confess that writing effective alt text still stresses me out. I always seem to question what I have written. Is it too much? Too little? Repetitive? Too vague? Too annoying? I just can't tell sometimes.

I will give you the advice I give myself when I freak out—relax, and just write something. Something is better than nothing. But here are some tips:

- Be concise.

- Describe the subject (that is, the most important element) of the image.

- Optional: Describe the setting (if it is relevant to the visual's context or meaning).

- Optional: Describe the actions and interactions (if it is relevant to what you want to focus on).

- Optional: Any other relevant details contained in the visual.

Remember that when it comes to alt text, you are not writing a novel (or even a paragraph). That is what the body of your document is for.

Ideally, your alt text should be no more than one or two descriptive sentences, and they don't have to be complete sentences in a grammatical sense. But most importantly, they shouldn't reference the type of object that is being described. For example, if you are describing a picture, you would not say "*A picture of a lamppost.*" Screen reader users will know that the screen reader has come to a picture because the screen reader will announce the type of object that's been selected.

Writing alt text for pictures

In **Microsoft Word 365**, if you insert a picture from the **Stock Images** option, alt text will more than likely be automatically generated for the image:

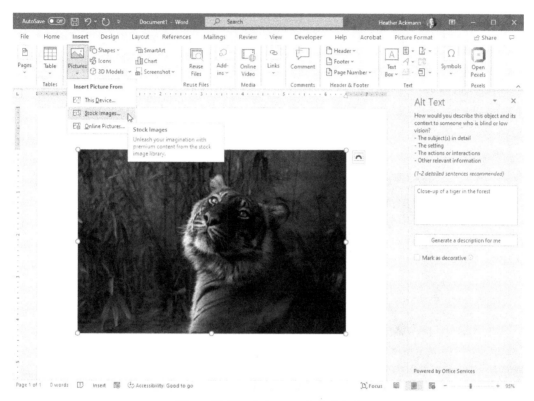

Figure 11.16 – Autogenerated alt text

However, this doesn't mean that you shouldn't check, edit, and write your own alt text for these images. In fact, I strongly encourage you to double-check the autogenerated alt text. Checking alt text is just a good habit to form and to keep up.

Writing or editing image alt text

To check, write, or edit image alt text, follow these steps:

1. Select the image. That will make the **Picture Format** contextual tab appear on your Word ribbon.

2. Click on the **Alt Text** button located in the **Accessibility** group.

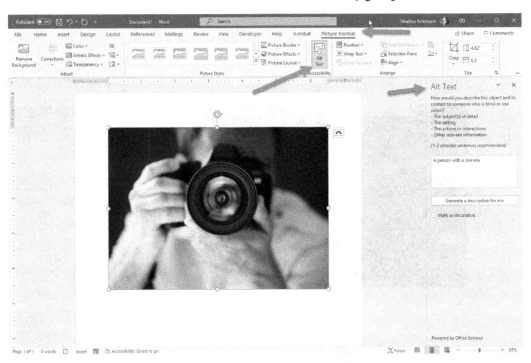

Figure 11.17 – Adding alt text to images

This will open the **Alt Text** pane to the right of your screen.

> **Important Note**
>
> The location of the **Alt Text** button may vary depending on your version of Word. The preceding instructions apply to the Word subscription, Microsoft 365 product, PC version 2015. If you cannot find the button in your version, try right-clicking (control-click on a **Mac**) on the image. Alt text is often an option in the shortcut menu.

Even if some text is autogenerated, there will be times where you may want to write more context-specific alt text for your audience. An example of this is shown in the following figure:

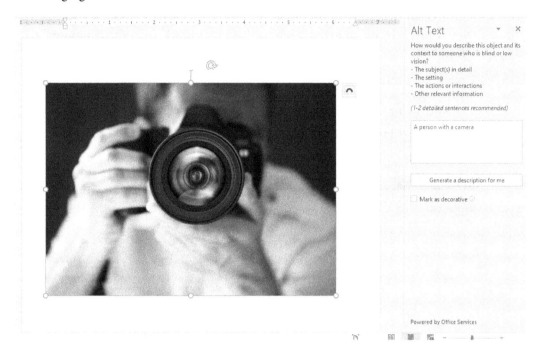

Figure 11.18 – Ways to describe a camera

In most circumstances, the alt text, A person with a camera is a perfectly fine description. The image does contain a person and a camera. But if you are writing an article that is comparing photography lenses, you may want the alt text to highlight something specific about the camera, for example, the lens, and make that the focus of the alt text, much like the lens is the most dominant element in the picture.

So, instead, we would edit the alt text to read, A close-up of the Canon EF-S 17-55mm f/2.8 IS USM lens. Alternatively, if you would like to keep a mention of the man in the alt text, we could write, A close-up of a man holding the Canon EF-S 17-55mm f/2.8 IS USM lens.

How specific and detailed you make alt text will depend on how many details you include in your article. Again, your alt text shouldn't repeat information contained elsewhere unless it is to help clarify what this image goes with in the body text.

Inserting alt text for charts

Charts are a complicated subject, mainly because they are meant to summarize a representation of data quickly and at a glance. At their heart, good charts are meant to tell a story with data. So, strong alt text for a chart should reflect the data story—that is, the point your chart is trying to make. Keeping that in mind will help you compose meaningful alt text.

The steps to follow are similar to adding alt text to pictures:

1. Select the entire chart (rather than an element within the chart).
2. Click on the **Chart Format** contextual tab on your ribbon.
3. Click the **Alt Text** button in the **Accessibility** group.

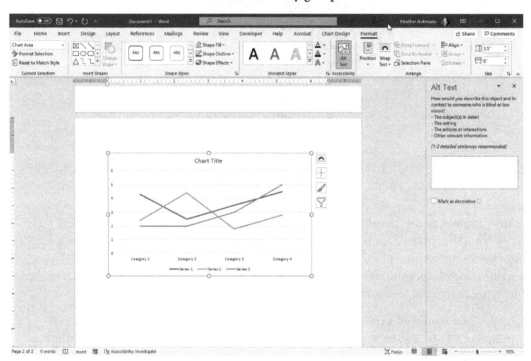

Figure 11.19 – Chart Alt Text pane

In addition to adding accessible alt text for charts, make sure that all colors used are visible and all text contained within the charts contrasts enough with the background color. Running the Accessibility Checker will check for these items, as well as a few other accessibility items as well. The next section will help you with some additional suggestions.

The new and improved Accessibility Checker

The name of this tool, the Accessibility Checker, would seem to imply that it should be run at the end of the document design or writing process as a series of final proofing checks. However, please do not think of this tool as something to be run only at the end. In fact, I strongly urge you to open a blank Word document and run this tool now. When you do, although it is highly unlikely you will find any issues in a blank document, you will find some additional helpful accessibility information and settings.

Running the Accessibility Checker

The steps for running the Accessibility Checker will vary depending on your version of Word. In Office 365, however, you can start the Accessibility Checker from your **Review** tab:

1. Go to your **Review** tab.

2. Click on the top part of the **Check Accessibility** button.

Figure 11.20 – Check Accessibility button

The Accessibility Checker will open in a pane to the right side of your screen.

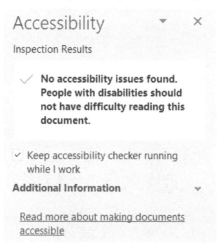

Figure 11.21 – Accessibility Checker with no issues found

Once opened, the Accessibility Checker will quickly scan your document for issues and make any suggestions. In *Figure 11.21*, the Accessibility Checker states that **No accessibility issues were found. People with disabilities should not have difficulty reading this document.**

But scanning for issues isn't the only thing that the Accessibility Checker does. From here, you can also learn about accessibility guidelines and check accessibility from the Status Bar.

Learning about accessibility guidelines

In *Figure 11.21*, toward the bottom of the **Accessibility Checker** pane, you should see a link that states, **Read more about making documents accessible**. Clicking that link will open your **Help** pane on the topic, *Improve accessibility with the Accessibility Checker*. Within this help article, you will find a lot of tips and additional help for using the Accessibility Checker, as well as quick links to related articles, and even links to technical support for customers with disabilities.

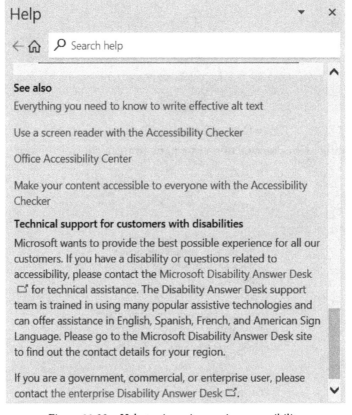

Figure 11.22 – Help topic on improving accessibility

So, in case you ever need guidance on accessibility in Word and you don't have this book handy, just remember that you can easily find additional help through the Accessibility Checker.

Checking accessibility from the status bar

In *Figure 11.21*, the checkbox next to the **Keep accessibility checker running while I work** option will allow you to check accessibility as you design and write documents. But best of all, Word will notify you, discretely, from the status bar should any issues arise.

Figure 11.23 – Accessibility: Investigate warning

The trick is remembering to look at the status bar. If you have the option to investigate accessibility as you work enabled, Word will quietly alert you to investigate accessibility issues as they arise by displaying a warning on the status bar in the lower left-hand corner of your Word window, right next to your macro recorder button.

All you need to do is click this button on the status bar to launch the Accessibility Checker, and Word will display the inspection results.

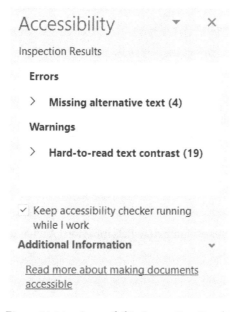

Figure 11.24 – Accessibility Inspection Results

Word will also categorize its inspection results. In *Figure 11.24*, there are four listed errors and 19 warnings. There are other categories you may see in this pane, including suggestions and even intelligent services. Typically, the ones you will need to be most concerned about are the errors and warnings, as they apply to almost all audiences. But I recommend reading and paying close attention to the other advice and considering its relevance to your readers or target audience.

Once you've decided which suggestions apply to your situation, fixing any errors directly from the Accessibility Checker is quite simple.

Fixing accessibility issues from the Accessibility Checker

When you locate an issue you'd like to correct, there is no need to close the checker or hunt around in your document or the Word interface to try and figure out how to correct the issue. The new and improved Accessibility Checker has made the process very simple.

Simply click on the error or suggestion and you will see a drop-down arrow to the right of the suggestion. Clicking on that arrow will reveal a **Recommended Actions** menu:

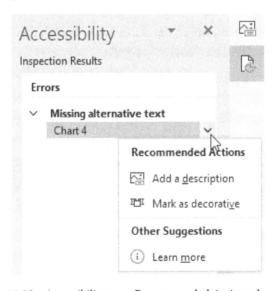

Figure 11.25 – Accessibility pane Recommended Actions dropdown

In *Figure 11.26*, there is a chart with missing alt text. I have a choice of adding a description or marking the chart as decorative. If I click **Add a description**, Word will open the **Alt Text** pane for that chart where I can immediately begin writing alt text for that chart.

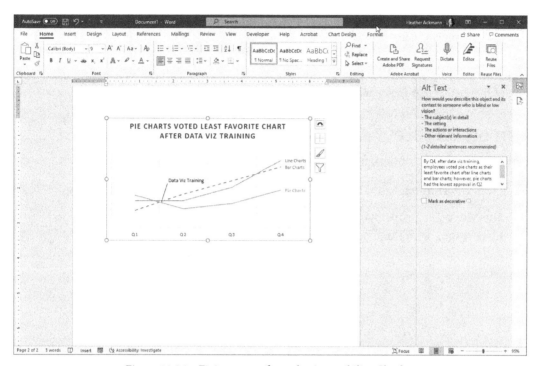

Figure 11.26 – Fixing errors from the Accessibility Checker

After I've written my description, I can close the **Alt Text** pane to return to the **Accessibility** pane and continue checking and fixing issues.

Typing with your voice

So far in this chapter, we have focused on features to help people read a document—that is, to help people with visual impairments: people who are blind, low-vision, or color blind. But other people may require tools to help with other needs.

For those who have trouble typing, there is a newer feature called **Dictate**. When the feature first came out a few years ago, it wasn't very responsive or impressive. However, the tool does seem to have improved quite a bit. So, if you haven't used it lately, be sure to give it another try.

> **Tips for Typing with Dictate**
>
> If you plan on typing successfully with Dictate, make sure you use a headset microphone. Even though the feature will work with the built-in microphone on your laptop or webcam, those microphones will pick up a lot of room and ambient noise. To ensure that the mic only types what you are saying (and not anybody else in the room), a headset microphone is preferred. A quiet environment is also helpful.

In the next section, we will see how to turn on Dictate to type with our voices, and use some of the newer features, such as punctuation and the profanity filter.

Turn on Dictate

To turn on the dictate option, follow these steps:

1. From the **Home** tab, on the far right of the ribbon, click on the **Dictate** button.

    This will open a small window toward the bottom of your Word screen that says **Listening...**, with three buttons underneath.

Figure 11.27 – Dictate launch window

2. To configure dictation settings, click on the gear icon in the left-hand corner.

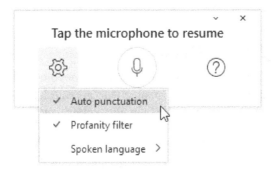

Figure 11.28 – Dictation settings

3. From the **Dictation Settings** menu, you can toggle **Auto punctuation** and **Profanity filter** on or off and change **Spoken language**.

4. To view what commands you can use, click on the question mark icon to view Word's help article. Under the **What can I say?** section, you will find a list of commands you can use, including **new line**, **delete**, **bold that**, **start list**, **pause dictation**, and **exit dictation**.

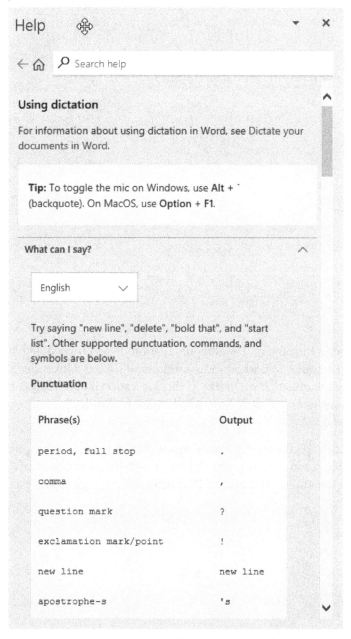

Figure 11.29 – Using dictation Help article

5.   To begin typing with your voice, click the microphone icon and begin speaking.

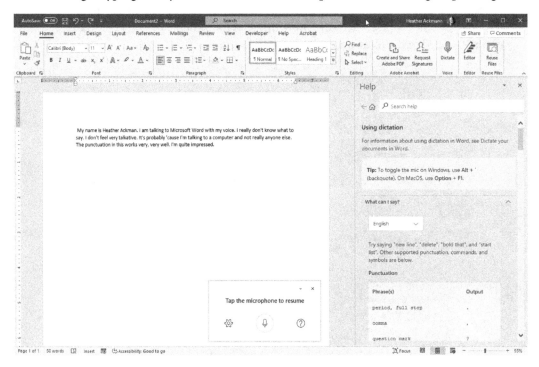

Figure 11.30 – Dictation practice

I strongly recommend turning on the auto punctuation. It isn't turned on by default, but I found that it worked quite well when I was speaking. Plus, it is a lot easier and more natural than saying the punctuation marks. If there is a special punctuation mark that you want to add, such as an em dash, you can always say it while speaking even with auto punctuation turned on.

The best part about the dictation feature is that you do not need a subscription to use it. If you have a free Microsoft account, you can log in with that account at office.com, create a new Word document, and use the **Dictation** feature, right from the web.

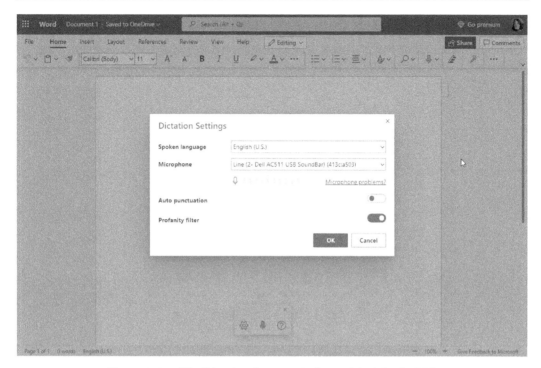

Figure 11.31 – The Dictation Settings window in Word for the Web

For the most part, although the buttons and windows may look a little different, the feature works the same way it does on the desktop version of Word.

So, now that you've seen the Dictation feature, there is a brand-new feature that, at the time of this writing, is only available in Word for the Web: transcription of pre-recorded audio.

Transcribing audio

If this feature is something that sounds exciting, but you don't have a Microsoft 365 subscription, I am sorry to tell you that **Transcribe** is a premium subscription feature.

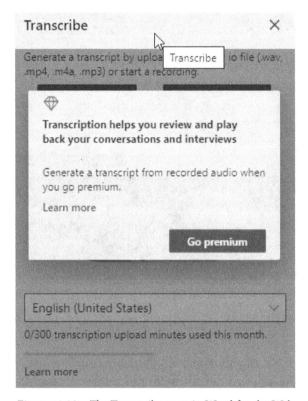

Figure 11.32 – The Transcribe pane in Word for the Web

Even though there is a button for Transcribe in Word for the Web, that does not necessarily mean you have access to the feature. You do need to have a Microsoft 365 subscription, whether it's a personal, school, or work subscription.

But if you do, you can sign in with that premium subscription account, open a Word document, and click on the **Transcribe** button to upload and transcribe audio files.

Transcribing audio

Follow these steps to transcribe audio:

1. Open a Word for the Web Word file with a subscription Microsoft 365 account.
2. Click the arrow next to the microphone icon to open a menu.

3. Click on the **Transcribe** button.

Figure 11.33 – The Transcribe button in Word for the Web

This will open the **Transcribe** pane to the right of your screen. From this pane, you can either upload an audio file (`.wav`, `.mp4`, `.m4a`, or `.mp3`) or record your own audio.

4. To upload an audio file to transcribe, click the **Upload audio** button.

Figure 11.34 – Transcribe pane

5. Select the audio file from your computer and upload it.

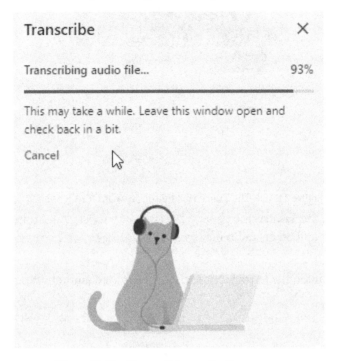

Figure 11.35 – Transcribing audio file message

Depending on the size of your file, the transcription can take quite a while. Don't close Word—leave the window open. You can continue working in other windows on your computer while Word transcribes the audio.

When your transcription finishes, the complete transcript will appear within the **Transcription** pane for you to review.

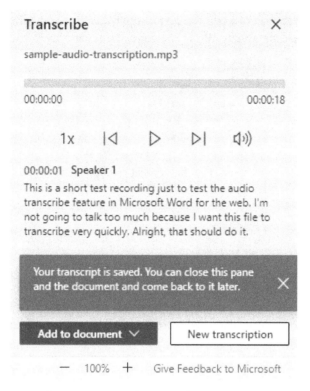

Figure 11.36 – A short sample transcription

You can edit the transcription by hovering your mouse over the selected dialog and clicking on the pencil icon.

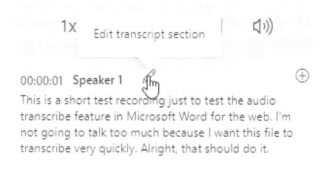

Figure 11.37 – Edit transcript section button

From inside the edit area, you can edit the text of the transcript and edit the speaker's name. You can even cascade update all the speakers' names at once if you like.

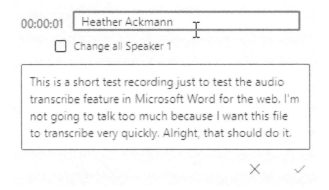

Figure 11.38 – Editing the speaker's name

When you are finished editing the transcript, click on the checkmark to save the changes. If you would like to add portions of the transcript to your Word document, you can hover your mouse over dialog selections and click on the plus sign to add that section to your document.

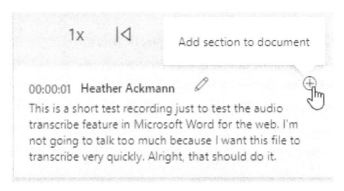

Figure 11.39 – Add section to document button

Alternatively, you can add the entire transcript to your document using the **Add to document** button at the bottom of the pane.

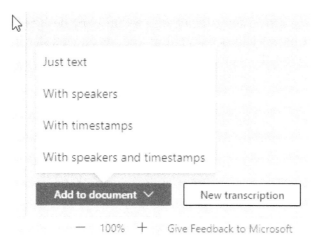

Figure 11.40 – Add to document button

There, in the menu that appears upon clicking the button, you will find options to add just the text of the transcript, the text plus the speaker's names, the text with timestamps, or the text with both names and timestamps.

To stay up to date on the latest US government standards and practices for creating accessible electronic documents, visit the following websites:

- `section508.gov`
- `https://www.section508.gov/create/documents/`
- `webAim.org`
- `https://webaim.org/techniques/word/`

These websites are great to keep bookmarked in your browser and to check for additional resources and document types other than Word.

Summary

In this chapter, we first learned how to design for document accessibility. We discussed the importance of using Word headings and how screen readers need these headings to navigate and "see" the structure of a document. We also briefly discussed how to write concise and contextual alt text. We talked about what alt text is, what it is used for, and how to write and edit effective alt text within the rhetorical context of images and other graphical content.

Next, we dove into some special accessibility tools within Word designed to help you locate and improve the overall accessibility within your document, starting with the Accessibility Checker. We walked through how to use the checker to fix problems, seek advice, and learn more about accessibility.

Finally, we covered two newer tools available with a subscription: Dictate and Transcribe. There, we learned how to type and add punctuation with our voice from both the full version of Word and Word for the Web. Then, we took a very short audio file and had Word convert the file to text.

In the next chapter, we will look at some common problems that people face when working with spacing.

Section 3: Help! Word Is Being Strange! Troubleshooting Common Problems

For all the speed and ease that word processing programs deliver, they sure can offer their fair share of frustrations at times too. In this section, you will learn how to troubleshoot some common problems that may arise when working with documents in Microsoft Word. You will learn the initial steps to take to diagnose what is causing the specific issue, things to try to remedy the issue, and some creative or fast workarounds to alleviate the core problems even if you don't know the cause.

This section comprises the following chapters:

- *Chapter 12, Formatting Problems – Too Much Space*
- *Chapter 13, Transforming Annoying Automation*
- *Chapter 14, Fixing Frustrating Numbers and Bullet Lists*
- *Chapter 15, Stuck Like Glue – Word's Deceptively Simple Paste Options*

12
Formatting Problems – Too Much Space

It will happen; you are collaborating on a group project, maybe at work or at school, and you open the Word document that your group has been collaborating on, and it looks, well, strange. The words are fine, but there is all of this extra space, perhaps between the letters or paragraphs, or there are margins appearing that weren't there before.

You don't want to play the blame game. That would be a waste of time. All you know is that this is extra space that you didn't put there, you don't know how it got there, and you aren't sure how to remove it. This document has to go out soon, so it has to be fixed quickly. However, it contains blank spaces and is invisible. So, how do you remove it if you can't actually see it?

That is what this chapter is all about; situations that occasionally arise where someone has sent you a document with all of this random extra space in it, and you have to figure out how to fix it. In this chapter, we'll cover the following topics:

- Removing different types of spacing

- Hidden formatting marks

- Troubleshooting paragraph spacing, line spacing, indents, and tab stops

- The magical **Clear All Formatting** button

Each of the preceding topics will help determine the underlying issue and cause of the extra space in your document. Although this chapter isn't exhaustive in terms of explaining what might be causing the issues, it does provide the most common reasons as to why people get frustrated and how they can solve the issue quickly, no matter what document they are working on.

Removing different types of spacing

If you open a document and find that there is an unnecessary or unintended amount of space somewhere, there are a variety of reasons as to why this can occur. It could be caused by people typing or formatting the document in an unexpected way, copying a style over from an old document, or simply by typing in, clicking on, or accepting a change they didn't intend to. Whatever the reason, there is now space in the document, and we are not sure how it got there. The reason doesn't matter as much as the type of space you are seeing and where you are seeing it inside the document. In Word, you can view extra spacing between the following:

- Letters or characters

- Words

- Lines or sentences

- Paragraphs

- Pages

Depending on where you see the extra space will determine how you can troubleshoot, fix, and remove that extra space in your document. To begin, let's start by examining how Word handles spacing between characters.

Removing extra space between letters

On occasion, you might find extra space between characters or letters in your Word document that cannot be removed by simply moving your cursor between the characters and hitting the Backspace key. In other words, the person didn't create that extra space by hitting the spacebar. The space was created using another method:

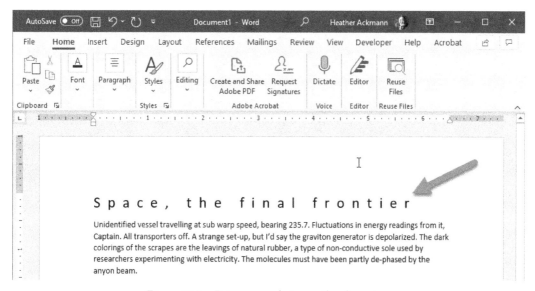

Figure 12.1 – Extra spaces between the characters

The most common method in which to adjust the spacing between characters in most programs is to adjust the kerning and tracking for a typeface or font.

Strangely enough, this is not a very common method used to adjust spacing in Microsoft Word because the feature that adjusts the spacing between letters is not easy to find or even called by these names, kerning and tracking.

Kerning refers to the space between two letters, whereas tracking refers to the overall spacing between groups of letters. In other words, kerning is for minor, individual adjustments, and tracking is for larger, wholescale adjustments. The problem in Word is that you will not find a command on the Ribbon for "kerning and tracking." However, that does not mean you can't adjust the spacing between letters in Word—it just means that we'll have to go digging for those options a bit.

In Word, to adjust anything related to how your typeface or font appears, there are a few steps you should take to troubleshoot. The first thing you can do is to check whether the character style is not the cause. You can easily check this by opening your **Styles** pane. If it is a character style, you can simply remove or clear that particular style. In our example, when we open it, the **Normal** style is the only style that is selected:

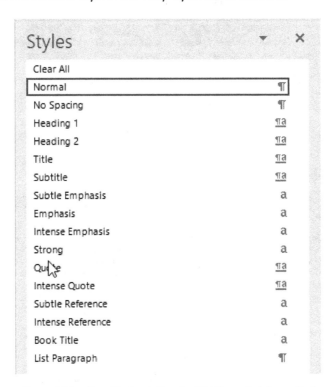

Figure 12.2 – Troubleshoot Step 1 with Normal style applied

So, evidently, a style is not the cause of the spacing. Something has been applied in addition to the **Normal** style. The next step is to check your font's advanced settings.

To check your font's advanced settings, follow these steps:

1.   Go to the **Home** tab and click on the **More settings** button in the lower-right corner of the **Font** group, or just press *Ctrl + D*:

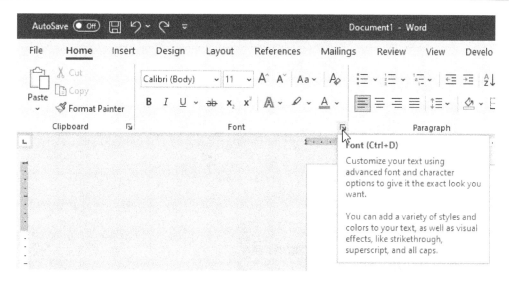

Figure 12.3 – The Font More settings button

This will open the **Font** settings window on the **Font** tab:

Figure 12.4 – The Font settings window

2. At the top of the window, click on the **Advanced** tab:

Figure 12.5 – The Font settings window Advanced tab

From the **Advanced** tab, toward the very top, you will find a section labeled **Character Spacing**. This is where you will go to adjust the spacing between the letters or the kerning and tracking. In *Figure 12.5*, next to the **Spacing** option, the combobox says that the selected text is set to **Expanded** by **9.3** pt. This is what is causing our text to appear extra wide with spaces between all of the letters or characters.

3. Next, click on the **Spacing** combobox, and change it to **Normal**:

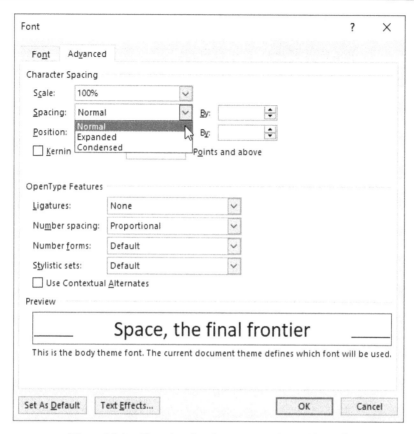

Figure 12.6 – Changing the character spacing to Normal

4. And, finally, click on **OK**.

Now, the selected text should appear with spacing that is similar to the rest of your text:

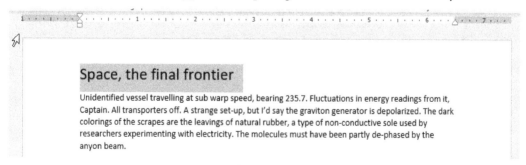

Figure 12.7 – Character spacing is Normal

If this technique doesn't work, there are still other things that we can do to continue troubleshooting our text, lines, and paragraphs. The first is to show our hidden formatting marks. Let's take a look at how to do that in the next section.

Hidden formatting marks

If you ever see something strange happen in your document and aren't sure what is going on, turning on your formatting symbols is a good first step in troubleshooting. Doing this can help you view everything that has been physically entered into the document, whether it is a space, a tab, a paragraph return, an object anchor, or simply a page break.

Turning on the hidden formatting marks and symbols

To turn on or display your document's hidden formatting marks and symbols, there are a couple of approaches you can use. You can toggle them on and off, as needed, from the **Home** tab, or you can turn select symbols on permanently from your **File** menu.

Method 1 – toggling on and off

To temporarily see what formatting is hiding in your document, perform the following steps:

1. From the **Home** tab, in the **Paragraph** group, click on the **Show/Hide paragraph** symbol, or use the keyboard shortcut, *Ctrl + *:

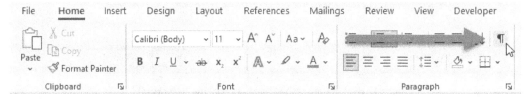

Figure 12.8 – Showing/hiding the formatting symbols

This will toggle on the formatting symbols inside your document:

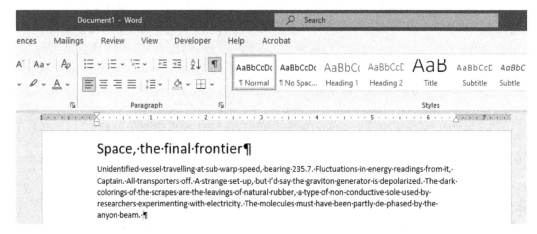

Figure 12.9 – The formatting symbols are displayed

In *Figure 12.9*, you will see an example of what a document looks like with the formatting symbols displayed. Spaces will appear as tiny dots between each word. Paragraph marks will appear at the end of each paragraph. If you have used a tab to indent the start of a paragraph, you might not see the tab symbol depending on your AutoCorrect settings. We will discuss that behavior in more detail in *Chapter 13, Transforming Annoying Automation*.

2. To turn off the symbols, click on the **Show/Hide paragraph** button on your **Home** tab, or press *Ctrl + ** on your keyboard.

This method is useful when you have something quick that you need to check or troubleshoot inside your document. This view is also great for finding most types of page and section breaks:

Figure 12.10 – Page and section breaks

With the formatting symbols displayed, you can easily determine what kind of break is on display and where it is within the document with only a glance.

There are some formatting marks that you might want to permanently display. Personally, I like to have my object anchors displayed all of the time. By default, object anchors are usually turned on, as anchors are known to cause trouble. However, there are other formatting marks that you can consider turning on permanently too, such as tab characters. If you are someone who works with tab stops, then turning on the tab characters but leaving other formatting symbols hidden might be an option to consider. For that option, you will need to permanently turn on or display your tab stop characters from your **Word Options** window.

Method 2 – permanently turning on select formatting symbols

Perform the following steps to permanently turn on the selected formatting symbols:

1. Go to the **File** menu, and click on **Options** to open the **Word Options** window.

2. Click on the **Display** tab:

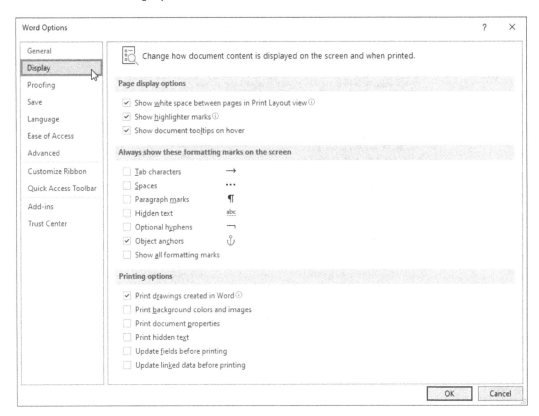

Figure 12.11 – The Word Options Display tab

3. In the area labeled **Always show these formatting marks on the screen**, you can select from a list of several marks to always display:

    - **Tab characters**

    - **Spaces**

    - **Paragraph marks**

    - **Hidden text**

    - **Optional hyphens**

    - **Object anchors**

    - **Show all formatting marks**

4. To display the tab characters, check the box next to **Tab characters**.

5. Click on **OK**.

With the tab character option turned on or displayed, any time you press the *Tab* key, you will see a tiny arrow displayed on the screen every 0.5 inches (that's the default) or wherever you have a tab stop on your ruler:

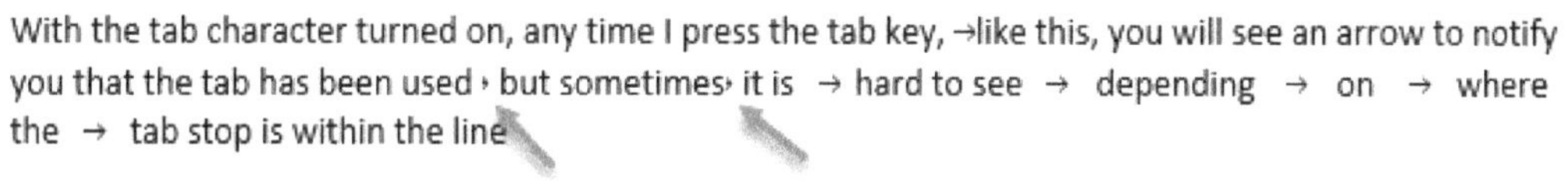

With the tab character turned on, any time I press the tab key, →like this, you will see an arrow to notify you that the tab has been used ‧ but sometimes‧ it is → hard to see → depending → on → where the → tab stop is within the line

Figure 12.12 – Difficult-to-see tab stops

Sometimes, these tab stop arrows might be difficult to see depending on where they are in relation to your text. So, I wouldn't rely on a visual check for tabs if this is something important. Instead, I would use the **Advanced Find** feature to hunt for hidden marks and symbols.

Method 3 – using the Advanced Find box for hidden symbols

You might already be familiar with the **Find** box in the **Navigation** pane. You can use this feature to quickly search your document for a name or location to jump to within your document. However, you can also use the **Advanced Find** box to search for hidden formatting marks and symbols. Let's learn how to use this box by following these steps:

1. To use the **Advanced Find** box, navigate to your **Home** tab and click on the arrow next to the **Find** button in the **Editing** group:

Figure 12.13 – The Advanced Find menu

Clicking on this will open a drop-down menu.

2. From this drop-down menu, click on the **Advanced Find…** option, which will open the **Find and Replace** window:

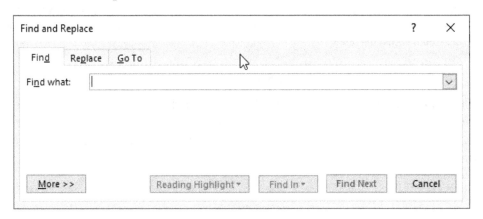

Figure 12.14 – The Find and Replace window

3. Toward the bottom-left corner, click on the **More >>** button to display additional find options:

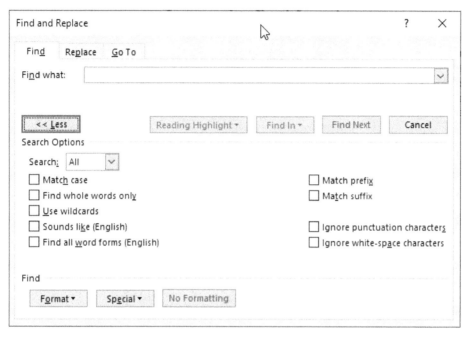

Figure 12.15 – The advanced Find options

4. Click on the button labeled **Special** to open a menu of special characters. Here, you can select the special character that you would like to search for in your Word document:

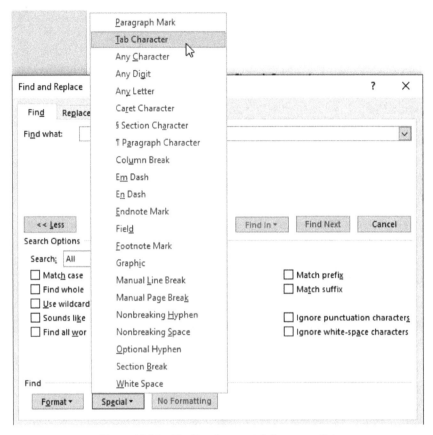

Figure 12.16 – Finding the special characters list

5. Select the **Tab Character** option.

As soon as you click on **Tab Character**, you should see ^t inserted into the **Find what** box of your **Find and Replace** window.

6. To search for tabs within your document, click on the **Find Next** button.

Word will then jump to and select the next tab character within your document:

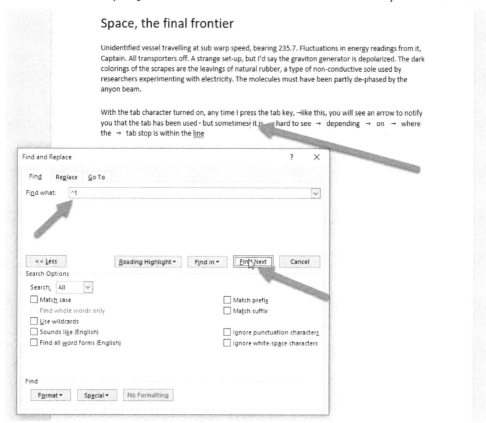

Figure 12.17 – Selecting the tab character

So, if your goal is to locate special formatting that might be causing you trouble, often, the first step is to locate where that formatting is within your document. Sometimes, the problem is finding or seeing where it is inside your document. It is nice to have several methods at your fingertips to find those hard-to-see formatting marks, no matter what they might be.

Now that we've examined how to locate tiny hard-to-see formatting issues that might be lurking between letters and characters but are easy to fix, let's expand our search to issues that are easy to spot but sometimes hard to troubleshoot.

Troubleshooting paragraph spacing, line spacing, indents, and tab stops

Now that we've looked at how to troubleshoot space between characters and letters and how to view hidden formatting symbols, we can move on to troubleshoot slightly harder spacing issues. These spacing issues won't necessarily be caused by anything that has been typed or inserted into the document itself. Instead, it is likely to be created by a setting within Microsoft Word that is difficult to see at a glance unless you know where to go look. In the following screenshot, you will find an example document with a variety of sample line and paragraph spacing problems where it is difficult to determine what might be the exact cause:

Figure 12.18 – Example line and paragraph spacing problems

When we turn on our hidden formatting marks and our ruler, we can observe a few clues as to what might be the problem. To tackle these various spacing issues, we are going to divide and conquer by addressing the space issues by type. First, we are going to tackle horizontal space issues (that is, the tab stops and indents) and then move on to investigate the vertical space issues (that is, spacing between lines, paragraphs, and breaks).

Horizontal space issues – the ruler, tab stops, and indents

To begin investing our horizontal space, we will need to turn on our most important tool—our Word ruler.

Turning on the ruler

In newer versions of Word, the ruler is hidden by default. I have no idea why Microsoft made this decision. I speculate it was because they thought it would make the interface "cleaner" and provide more room for the document, but really, I don't know. The ruler is so useful for formatting and referencing that I leave it on all the time (and strongly suggest that you do, too). Follow these steps to turn on the **Ruler** box:

1. Navigate to the **View** tab in your Ribbon.

2. In the **Show** group, check the box marked **Ruler**:

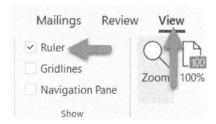

Figure 12.19 – Navigating to View and checking the Ruler box

With the **Ruler** box now enabled, you should see two rulers along the top and left-hand side of your document. In the upper-left corner, you will also see a box where you can click through a variety of different tab and indent options that you can place onto the ruler to set various tab and indent marks:

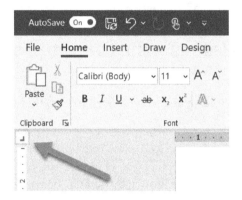

Figure 12.20 – The tab stop button

Users who do not know that these options, or even this button, exist, can sometimes accidentally place tab stops onto the ruler by clicking on the ruler:

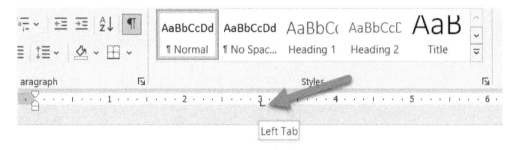

Figure 12.21 – Clicking on the bottom area of the ruler to apply the tab stop

That is how you add a tab stop. First, you select a tab stop, and then quickly click on the bottom area of the ruler to apply the tab stop. It is not very intuitive, discoverable, or easy to do. Even a pro like me has a very difficult time applying tabs stops this way. However, it seems that newbies will often accidentally apply stops all the time without knowing it. That is one way we can end up with strange spacing in our document! What's more, as soon as you navigate away from the line or paragraph with the applied tab stop, the symbol for the tab stop disappears from the ruler. This is great to help you see what is causing the spacing issues, tab stops or not. It's one of the reasons why I like to keep my ruler on. However, when using my ruler to apply or modify my tab stops or other paragraph and line settings, I prefer to do that through my paragraph settings menu.

The easiest way to work with tab stops

My preferred method of working with tab stops (and other spacing issues) is to go through the **Paragraph** settings menu rather than the ruler. The ruler provides a quick at-a-glance way to check whether there are tab stops or indents inside your document. However, as for adjusting those settings, I just don't like using my mouse to drag things around on the ruler. It's just too difficult and cumbersome. To adjust tab stops, follow these steps:

1. Go to your **Home** tab and click on the **Paragraph** settings button:

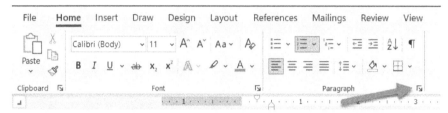

Figure 12.22 – The Paragraph settings button

This will open the **Paragraph** window at the **Indents and Spacing** tab.

2. Toward the bottom of the **Indents and Spacing** tab, you will find a button labeled **Tab…**. Click on that:

Figure 12.23 – The Indents and Spacing tab

In the Tabs window, you can view the tab stops for your selected paragraph, the default tabs setting, and the tab alignment and leader options. You will also find buttons for you to use to set and clear the current tabs, and an option to clear all tabs from the entire document:

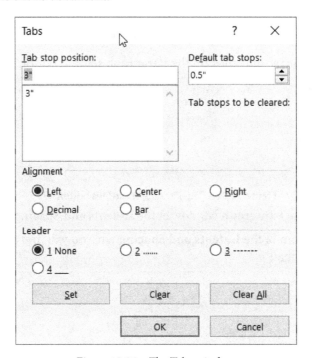

Figure 12.24 – The Tabs window

3. Click on the **Clear All** button to clear all of the tab stops in the document.

4. Click on **OK**.

Your tabs should now be removed from your document.

Now, the extra space at the beginning of our fourth paragraph has gone:

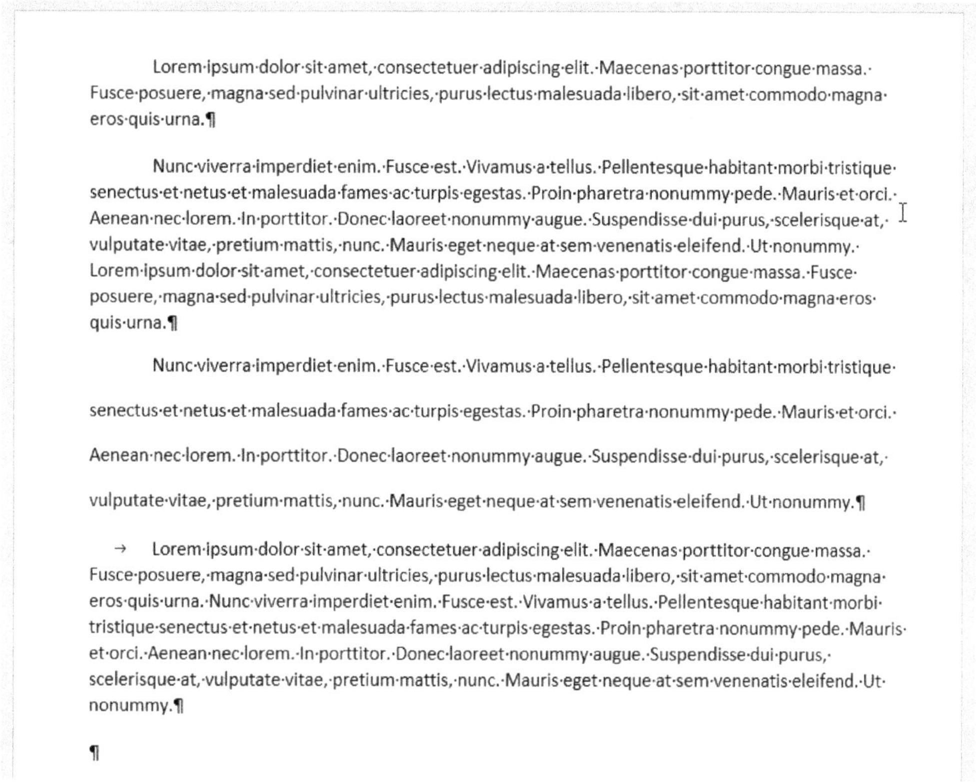

Lorem·ipsum·dolor·sit·amet,·consectetuer·adipiscing·elit.·Maecenas·porttitor·congue·massa.·
Fusce·posuere,·magna·sed·pulvinar·ultricies,·purus·lectus·malesuada·libero,·sit·amet·commodo·magna·
eros·quis·urna.¶

Nunc·viverra·imperdiet·enim.·Fusce·est.·Vivamus·a·tellus.·Pellentesque·habitant·morbi·tristique·
senectus·et·netus·et·malesuada·fames·ac·turpis·egestas.·Proin·pharetra·nonummy·pede.·Mauris·et·orci.·
Aenean·nec·lorem.·In·porttitor.·Donec·laoreet·nonummy·augue.·Suspendisse·dui·purus,·scelerisque·at,·
vulputate·vitae,·pretium·mattis,·nunc.·Mauris·eget·neque·at·sem·venenatis·eleifend.·Ut·nonummy.·
Lorem·ipsum·dolor·sit·amet,·consectetuer·adipiscing·elit.·Maecenas·porttitor·congue·massa.·Fusce·
posuere,·magna·sed·pulvinar·ultricies,·purus·lectus·malesuada·libero,·sit·amet·commodo·magna·eros·
quis·urna.¶

Nunc·viverra·imperdiet·enim.·Fusce·est.·Vivamus·a·tellus.·Pellentesque·habitant·morbi·tristique·

senectus·et·netus·et·malesuada·fames·ac·turpis·egestas.·Proin·pharetra·nonummy·pede.·Mauris·et·orci.·

Aenean·nec·lorem.·In·porttitor.·Donec·laoreet·nonummy·augue.·Suspendisse·dui·purus,·scelerisque·at,·

vulputate·vitae,·pretium·mattis,·nunc.·Mauris·eget·neque·at·sem·venenatis·eleifend.·Ut·nonummy.¶

→   Lorem·ipsum·dolor·sit·amet,·consectetuer·adipiscing·elit.·Maecenas·porttitor·congue·massa.·
Fusce·posuere,·magna·sed·pulvinar·ultricies,·purus·lectus·malesuada·libero,·sit·amet·commodo·magna·
eros·quis·urna.·Nunc·viverra·imperdiet·enim.·Fusce·est.·Vivamus·a·tellus.·Pellentesque·habitant·morbi·
tristique·senectus·et·netus·et·malesuada·fames·ac·turpis·egestas.·Proin·pharetra·nonummy·pede.·Mauris·
et·orci.·Aenean·nec·lorem.·In·porttitor.·Donec·laoreet·nonummy·augue.·Suspendisse·dui·purus,·
scelerisque·at,·vulputate·vitae,·pretium·mattis,·nunc.·Mauris·eget·neque·at·sem·venenatis·eleifend.·Ut·
nonummy.¶

¶

Figure 12.25 – A document with removed tab stops

In *Figure 12.24*, even though the tab stop has been removed, we still have a tab opening the paragraph. In the other paragraphs, Word has automatically converted those tabs into an indent. We will discuss this strange behavior in Word in more detail in *Chapter 13, Transforming Annoying Automation.*

Important Note

Clearing all of the tab stops from the **Tabs** window does not remove the default tab stops that appear in the header and footer. If you open the header and footer, you will still find the center-align tab and the right-align tab. To remove the tab stops from that area, you will have to open your header and footer and repeat the same steps for that section.

Now that we've covered how to remove one type of extra space that appears at the beginning of a line, we can explore how to remove or adjust another type of space that appears at the beginning of a line—indents.

Working with indentation

From the same window where we found our tabs button to fix and clear our tab stops, you will also find options for working with indentation. You can refer to the preceding section for step-by-step instructions on how to open your **Paragraph** settings window and navigate to the **Indents and Spacing** tab:

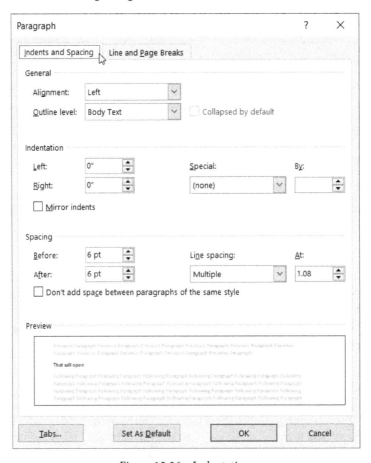

Figure 12.26 – Indentation

In *Figure 12.25*, halfway down the **Paragraph** window, there is an area for indentation. From there, you can adjust everything from the left and right indents or create special indents such as a first-line indent or a hanging indent. There is even a checkbox for creating mirror indents, which is useful if you want book-like margins for binding.

However, most of the time, if you want to increase your paragraph indent, you will want to do so quickly. There are three methods that are quick and easy, depending on your needs:

- Pressing the *Tab* key
- Using the increase/decrease indent buttons
- Using the **Set As Default** button to save indent and spacing settings

To begin, we are going to discuss the most popular method to create a left or first-line indent, which is simply by using your keyboard and allowing Word to automatically format or correct your tab and turn it into an indentation.

Setting the left and first-line indent with tabs

One way to quickly set a left or first-line indent is to simply use your *Tab* key. One of Word's AutoCorrect features is to automatically set a left or first-line indent for you when you press your *Tab* key at the start of a paragraph or first line. To add a first-line indent using the *Tab* key, perform the following steps:

1. First, make sure your ruler is on (navigate to **View** | **Ruler**). This will help you determine whether or not the method worked.
2. Next, move your insertion point to the start of a new line in your document.
3. Press the *Tab* key on your keyboard.
4. Please refer to the top ruler to make sure a left indent has been inserted:

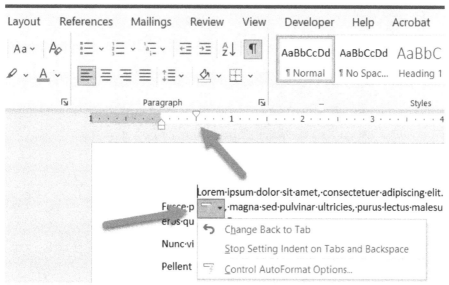

Figure 12.27 – The first-line indent tab

If it worked, on the ruler, you will see the first-line indent mark set to its default position or the position you have it set to in your document. You might also see an **AutoFormat** flag appear beneath your insertion point. By clicking on the flag, you will find a menu with options appearing to change the indent back to a tab or to turn off the **AutoFormat** setting entirely. That is one quick method for adding a first-line or left indent. However, if you want to add these types of indents to all of your paragraphs, this isn't the most efficient or reliable method (as you will discover in *Chapter 13, Transforming Annoying Automation,* sometimes, it can be a nuisance). Another method is to use your increase and decrease indent buttons to indent all of your paragraphs at once.

The increase and decrease indent buttons

When you have a lot of paragraphs and you need to adjust the indentation all at once, the quickest method is probably to use your increase or decrease indent buttons. To indent all your lines at once, follow these steps:

1.   Select all of your paragraphs. Take your mouse and triple-click inside the left margin of your document or use the keyboard shortcut *Ctrl + A* to select all of your document text:

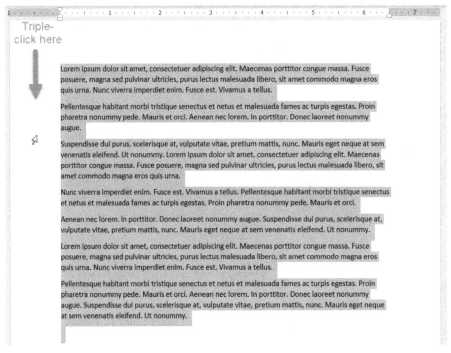

Figure 12.28 – Triple-clicking inside the left margin

2. Next, from your **Home** tab, in the **Paragraph** group, click on the **Increase Indent** button to move your paragraph farther away from the margin:

Figure 12.29 – The increase indent button

This will increase the indent by whatever your default tab stop is set to. In our example, our tab stop is set to **1** inch:

Figure 12.30 – Default tab stops example

When we click on the increase indent button once, our lines will increase by **1** inch, and will continue increasing every time we click on the button:

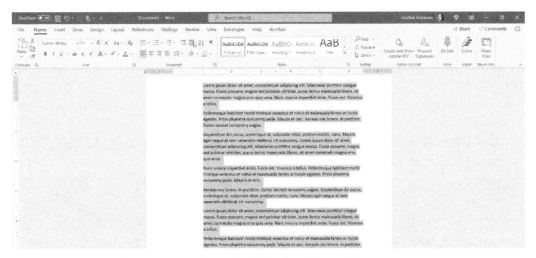

Figure 12.31 – Increasing the indent after one button press

So, if you need to increase indentation for a lot of lines, this method is the fastest. However, if you find yourself having to create these same settings over and over again, you might consider making these settings your default document settings.

Using the Set As Default button in the Paragraph settings window

You might have noticed this option when we were in the **Paragraph** settings window before adjusting our tab stops or our indentation. If not, don't worry—it's easy to miss! There is a lot going on in this window:

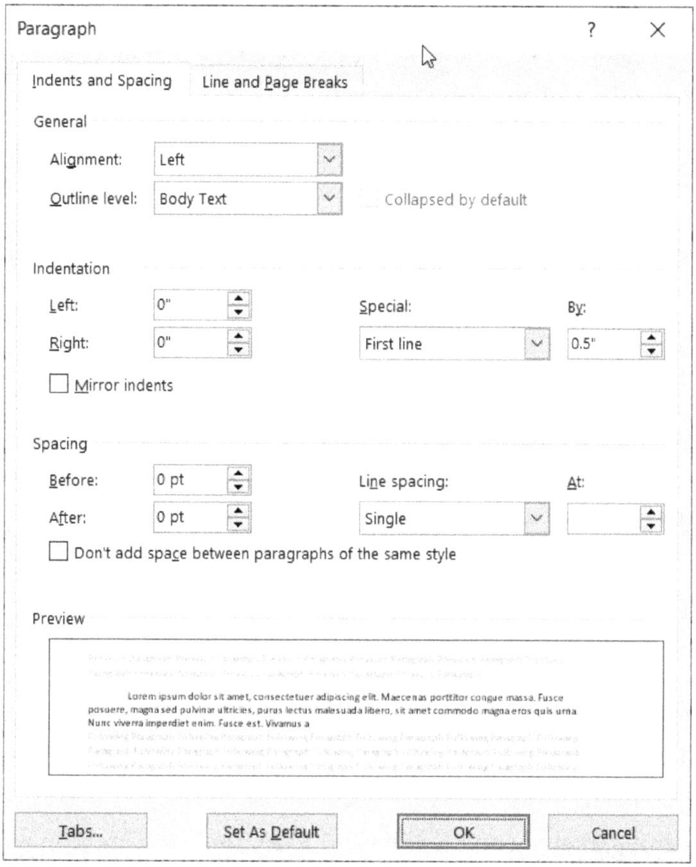

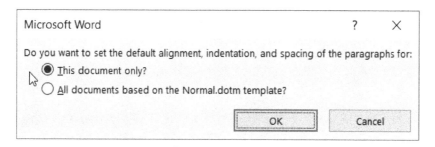

Figure 12.32 – The Paragraph settings window Set As Default button

Toward the bottom of the window, sandwiched between the **Tabs…** button and the **OK** button, you will find a **Set As Default** button. Whatever you have set in the preceding window, when you click on this button, they will become your default settings.

Upon clicking on the **Set As Default** button, you will find two more options that appear in a new window:

Figure 12.33 – The Set As Default options

Here, you can choose whether you want to apply these settings to this document only or whether you want to apply these settings to your **Normal.dotm** template. Applying these settings to your **Normal.dotm** template means that for every new blank document you create on this computer, these settings will be applied.

This is a great way in which to apply settings to custom templates or work or academic documents that follow a vastly different style guide than what Microsoft Word's default settings follow. You can just set it up now, early on, and set it as the default rather than making all those little changes one at a time. It will save you so much time, in the long run, when you are formatting your documents.

That covers troubleshooting horizontal line spacing issues. For vertical spacing issues, including line, paragraph, and page, there are a few more options to discuss. And even though these options can, sometimes, be a bit trickier to work with, fortunately, you will also find these options in the same locations that we've already discussed: the **Paragraph** group on the **Home** tab, and the **Paragraph** Settings window.

Vertical space – line, paragraph, and page

The first type of vertical space that we are going to troubleshoot in our document is line spacing. In Microsoft Word, there are a couple of places you can go to adjust your line spacing options. From your Ribbon, on your **Home** tab, you have a button where you can quickly adjust your line spacing along with some simple(and popular) paragraph spacing options.

In the **Paragraph** group, clicking on the **Line and Paragraph** spacing icon will open a menu of quick options:

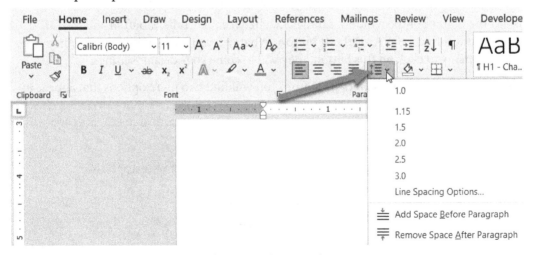

Figure 12.34 – The Line and Paragraph spacing menu

The numbers inside the menu represent options for single and multiple line spacing. Selecting **1.0** is equivalent to single-line spacing. Selecting **2.0** is equivalent to double, and so on. Additionally, you will find shortcuts to add and remove space before and after paragraphs. By default, Word automatically adds spacing after paragraphs as part of the **Normal** style. If you would like to temporarily override the style for one paragraph, you can remove the spaces for one paragraph here, by selecting the **Remove Space After Paragraph** option.

Clicking on **Line Spacing Options…** in the menu will take you right back to the **Paragraph** settings window where we were working before and all the way to the **Line spacing** section:

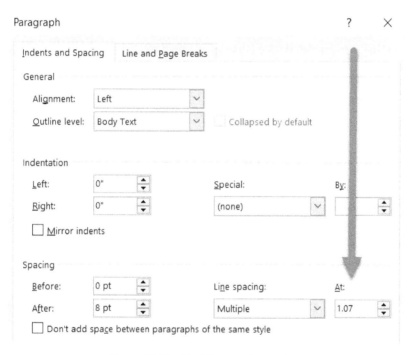

Figure 12.35 – The Line spacing options

Here, you can set **Line spacing** to whatever custom settings you like or remove whatever goofy settings you find. The **Don't add space between paragraphs of the same style** checkbox is a handy little option to check in situations where you want to keep the space after the paragraph but only if the style applied changes. And, just as with your tab stop and indentation options, if you want to set any of these options as your default options, remember that you can click on the **Set As Default** button toward the bottom of the screen to save the settings inside this document or to the **Normal.dotm** template.

Pagination

While we are in the **Paragraph** settings windows, there are other more advanced line and page break options available on another tab. Toward the top of the window, click on the tab labeled **Line and Page Breaks**. Here, you will find a variety of options that you can check on or off. The first option, **Widow/Orphan control**, is the most confusing for folks in terms of what it means, so I am going to make it easy for you to remember. Picture sentences that are afraid to be alone. That's what this control does. It makes sure your sentences are never alone.

Widow/Orphan control

By default, the **Widow/Orphan** control is turned on. For the purposes of Microsoft Word, it doesn't distinguish between widows and orphans—they are the same—they are single paragraph lines that are separated from the rest of the paragraph, usually by a page break or a column break or some kind of break:

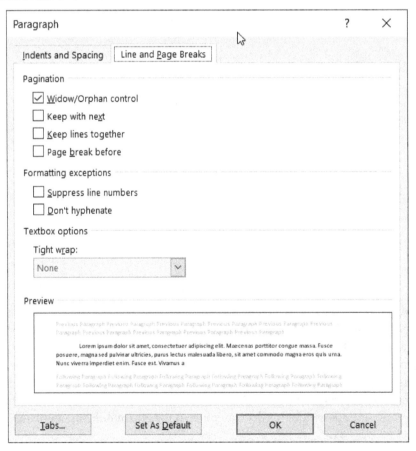

Figure 12.36 – The Widow/Orphan control turned on

With the box checked, when you are typing or writing and continue onto another page or column, Word will make sure your lines always have a buddy. A single line all by itself just doesn't look as appealing on the page. Two is better. Trust us. Leave the **Widow/Orphan** control checked.

Keep with next

The next option, **Keep with next**, is the one I, personally, use the most. Whenever I have a single-line paragraph, such as a heading, that I want to keep with the following body text, I select the paragraph and choose the **Keep with next** option to force Word to keep the paragraphs together. Even if the heading appears on one page and the body text flows to another, this will force the text to stay together, as you can observe in the following screenshot:

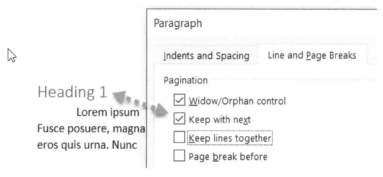

Figure 12.37 – Keep with next checked

With this option unchecked, the **Heading 1** text will then appear on the previous page, as displayed in the following screenshot:

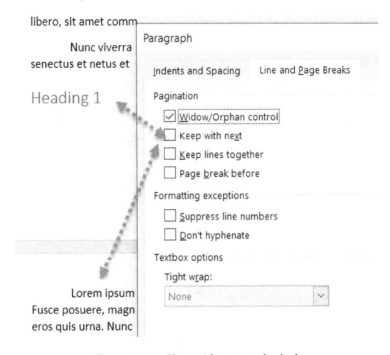

Figure 12.38 – Keep with next unchecked

As you can see, having a heading all by itself on a page is a bit unsightly and potentially confusing for readers.

Keep lines together

The next option might appear to be similar or even the same as the previous option, but there is a big difference in its behavior. Specifically, Keep lines together changes how Word will flow the text and lines within paragraphs on the page, whereas the Keep with next option changes how lines flow with the next or subsequent paragraph.

Going back to our previous example of the **Heading 1** text and the body text, if we select both paragraphs and select the **Keep lines together** option but not the **Keep with next** option, notice what happens:

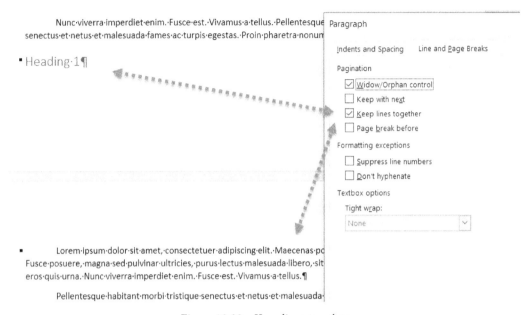

Figure 12.39 – Keep lines together

In *Figure 12.39*, even though we have the **Keep lines together** option checked, our **Heading 1** text appears on the previous page, and the body text appears on the next page. For a lot of people, this seems counter-intuitive. They think, "Hey, I selected these lines and clicked keep together. So, why aren't they staying together?" Technically, they are together. They are together by their paragraphs. In *Figure 12.38*, I've turned on the hidden formatted marks, so you can see where all the paragraphs end. At the end of **Heading 1**, there is a paragraph mark. And at the end of the body paragraph on the next page, there is a paragraph. Those are the lines that will be kept together, within those individual paragraph boundaries. So, Heading 1 is a two-word paragraph that will be kept together according to wherever the paragraph symbol marks the paragraph's end. And Word is doing its job by keeping the words and lines together between paragraphs marks.

So, think of this option not as "keep all the lines I've selected together" but really as "keep the lines within each paragraph together." That is really the more accurate phrasing of what is happening.

Page break before

The last option that we'll discuss is one that I've very rarely seen used in the wild, but I am including it here since we are discussing how to troubleshoot unusual spacing issues that you might encounter:

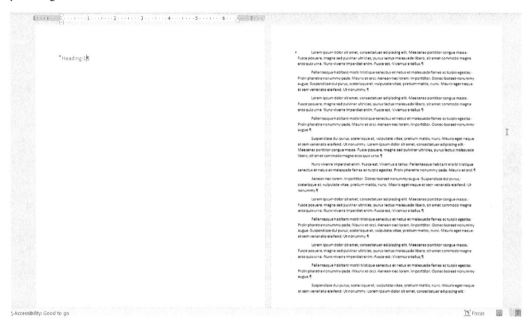

Figure 12.40 – Space after the heading with no break

Figure 12.39 shows a ton of space after a heading. In fact, there's an entire page's worth of blank space. The strange thing is that there's no page break, section break, return characters, or anything else that we can see when we turn on hidden characters. That leaves one other possibility—the page break before setting.

This is a tricky little setting to use in a document where, if you want a certain paragraph to always appear at the top of a page, you could select that specific paragraph and check this option. However, the problem is that if you edit or remove paragraphs before that paragraph, your document can begin to look really odd, just like this one. So, I would advise you to use this setting with extreme caution or to only use it when you are finished writing and toward the end of the editorial and formatting process.

So far, we've looked at a variety of options in which to troubleshoot spacing problems, both horizontal and vertical spacing issues. However, sometimes, you might not have the time (or the patience) to go through all of these steps, or these steps might not even be the solution to the problem. If that's the case, then just skip on over to the magical Clear All Formatting button.

The magical Clear All Formatting button

Perhaps the simplest way of all to fix nearly any formatting issue in Word is to use the magical **Clear All Formatting** button. It's not really magical; it just seems that way because of how fast it works and how many problems it can solve.

You can find the **Clear All Formatting** button within the **Home** tab on the Ribbon:

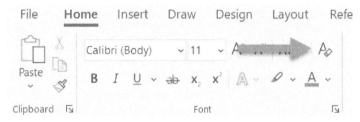

Figure 12.41 – The Clear All Formatting button

The **Clear All Formatting** button is the **A** letter with a little purple eraser next to it. Just select the text that is giving you trouble and click on the button. It really is that easy.

In *Figure 12.42*, you will see an example of some very unusual-looking text. Rather than try to figure out what is going on, let's just reset this text back to the **Normal** style and clear any additional formatting that has been applied on top—all with the click of a button

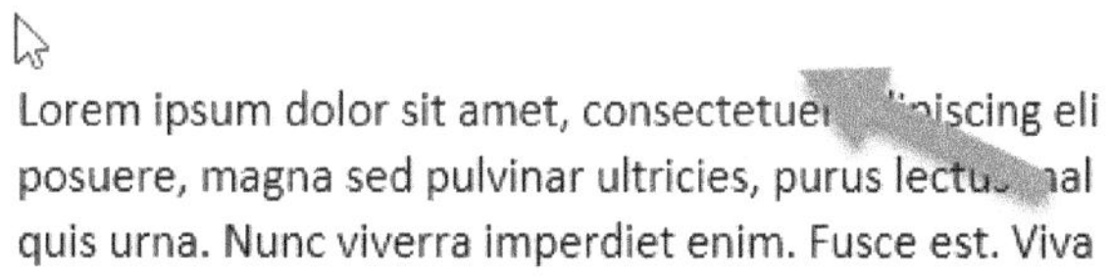

Lorem ipsum dolor sit amet, consectetuer adipiscing eli
posuere, magna sed pulvinar ultricies, purus lectus mal
quis urna. Nunc viverra imperdiet enim. Fusce est. Viva

Figure 12.42 – Problem text beforehand

Let's take a look at how to use this option:

1. Select the problem text.

2. Click on the **Clear All Formatting** button on the **Home** tab:

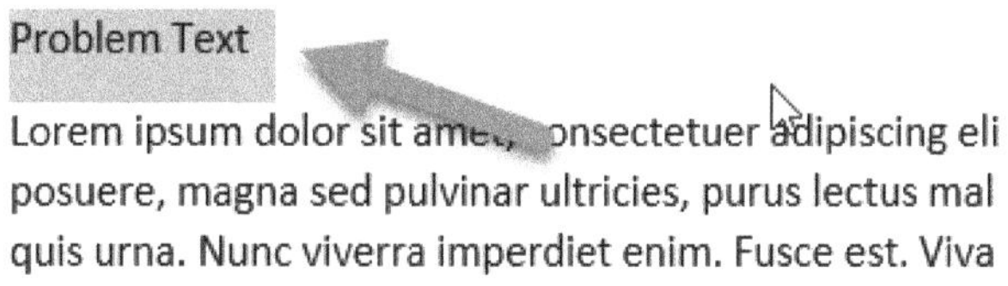

Problem Text

Lorem ipsum dolor sit amet, consectetuer adipiscing eli
posuere, magna sed pulvinar ultricies, purus lectus mal
quis urna. Nunc viverra imperdiet enim. Fusce est. Viva

Figure 12.43 – Problem text afterward

Now, our text has been returned to the **Normal** style and any additional formatting has been removed, giving us a clean slate to work with.

Summary

In this chapter, we discussed how to troubleshoot, find, and fix a variety of problems related to extra or unusual spacing found within a Word document. These spaces could be anything related to the horizontal space such as the space between letters or characters and the space between words or lines. Additionally, we discussed vertical spacing issues related to lines or sentences, paragraphs, and pagination.

When troubleshooting spacing problems, don't forget to check and be sure that a particular style is not at the root of your problems. Removing, clearing, or updating a style will save you more time in the long run, if a style is the root cause of any spacing issues. If the spacing issue is something that someone accidentally typed into your document, then turning on hidden formatting characters or using the advanced find tool will help you to locate and view hidden formatting marks in particularly dense documents. Also, remember that most of the options related to spacing will appear either on the **Home** tab within the **Paragraph** group or in the **Paragraph** settings window.

However, most importantly, remember the **Clear All Formatting** button. That button has solved the toughest of formatting issues for me in the shortest amount of time. If you take away anything from this chapter, make it be to use that button.

In the next chapter, we will be shifting things around a bit to focus on some less-than-perfect situations where Word automation, though a time saver in most situations, is not very helpful. We will discuss how to turn those settings off or make them work better for us in our specific situations.

13
Transforming Annoying Automation

There are many things to love about Word. Throughout this book, we have covered several tools and features of Word to help make you more efficient and productive in your workflows: from using and modifying Word's Styles, Quick Parts, and building blocks to utilizing Word's proofing and accessibility tools more effectively.

However, there will be times when Word will automatically add or change text when you don't want it to. Word will think it is being helpful, but for you, it will be so annoying trying to figure out what is happening and where you need to go to stop and correct the problem. That is what this chapter is all about. In this chapter, we will discuss the following topics:

- Stopping Word from automatically adding or changing text
- Understanding and working with AutoFormat
- Creating custom keyboard shortcuts
- Customizing custom dictionaries

The preceding topics will all work together to help you turn on, turn off, or work around Word's built-in AutoCorrect and AutoFormat features. However, first, we are going to discuss a few common real-world scenarios where Word automatically adds or changes a piece of text for you, starting with your very own name.

Stopping Word from automatically adding or changing text

A very common scenario (or issue) in Word happens when Word automatically inserts your name (or a company name) unexpectedly. How you prevent or update this automatic behavior depends on what information is being automatically populated or corrected in Word.

Sometimes, in Microsoft Word, when using features such as **Track Changes** or **Comments**, Word will automatically insert your name for you. However, you might find that Word thinks your correctly spelled name is misspelled and automatically correct it for you. And at other times, Word will just automatically insert your name or initials into your documents, or even some generic placeholder name instead, such as "author." The following screenshot presents some examples:

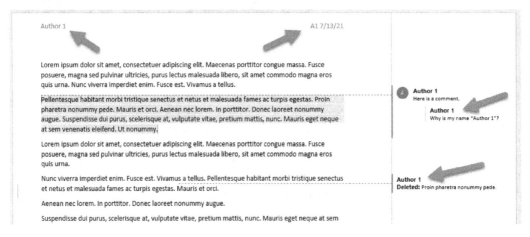

Figure 13.1 – Incorrect name examples

Many Word templates use field codes that insert the author of the document automatically. However, when you are not the one who created the document, it can sometimes be hard to know where to go to update the document or the field.

In a lot of these examples, Word pulls your name information from your copy of Microsoft Office, from the **User name** area of your general **Word Options** properties. In other instances, the issue is not a property field but an **AutoCorrect** property or setting. In this chapter, we will explore how to troubleshoot and correct both of these problems.

Updating your name and initials in Microsoft Word

If the problem you are encountering is that Word is automatically inserting your name incorrectly somewhere, the first and easiest place to go on your computer is to your **Word Options** window. To update your name and initials, follow these steps:

1. Navigate to your **File** menu and click on **Options**:

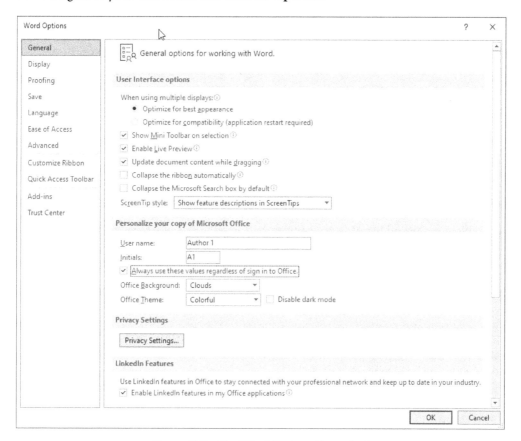

Figure 13.2 – The Word Options General tab

This will open the **Word Options** window at the **General** tab.

2. From there, halfway down the **General** tab, underneath the section labeled **Personalize your copy of Microsoft Office**, you will find an option to update your username and your initials.

3. If you would like to use this entered username regardless of how you have signed into Office, you can check the box labeled **Always use these values regardless of sign in to Office**. Otherwise, ensure that the checkbox has been cleared so that your Office sign-in username will be applied when you sign in.

4. Click on **OK** to apply the changes.

Your new name should now be applied when using **Track Changes**, adding or replying to a comment, or when using a name field code such as within a template.

Problems with names

If the directions in the previous section do not work for you, there could be some administration setting preventing you from changing or updating usernames in Office. If someone else manages your Office account (for example, if your copy of Office was purchased by your company) check with your administrator or IT department first. They are the ones most able to help in your specific situation.

If you are the one who manages the user options and would like to know where to go to troubleshoot strange or unusual user options, you can reset certain options from the registry. Just be very careful when doing so, and be sure to back up anything and everything beforehand.

For a complete guide and list of Word options and where they are stored within the registry, please refer to the full guide on Microsoft Docs.

You can locate the link to *How to reset user options and registry settings in Word* at `https://docs.microsoft.com/en-US/office/troubleshoot/word/reset-options-and-settings-in-word`.

This guide will take you through a few different methods regarding how to reset user options and registry settings in Word. In the next section, we will understand what AutoFormat is and how to work with it.

Understanding and working with AutoFormat

In *Chapter 9, Working Faster with Automation,*, we discussed how to use the **Replace Text as You Type** feature, which automatically corrects commonly misspelled words. We also discussed how to add our own entries to create our own shorthand and lists to type frequently used words, phrases, and hard-to-remember lists easier and faster. That's one example of how Word's built-in automation features can be helpful. However, sometimes, they aren't always so helpful. Let's say you are writing a date range, and since you paid attention in school, you know that the punctuation mark, the en dash, should be used to separate dates or a span of time, for example, "*The 2019–2020 school year was a difficult year for teachers in the US.*"

Also, notice that in the preceding example, there are no spaces before or after the en dash. Now, in Word, there are **AutoFormat** options for hyphens and dashes. When you type a hyphen followed by a space and something else, you might notice that Word will automatically convert your hyphen into another kind of dash. The problem is that how Word converts and formats these dashes doesn't always follow many traditional style guides, or at least the style guide that you might be using for your school, your company, or the conventions for your region. As such, you might need to adjust how Word automatically formats symbols as you type.

AutoFormat as you type

There is a specific feature in Microsoft Word called **AutoFormat as You Type**. You might have activated this feature accidentally by typing any of the following character combinations into Word:

- `--`
- `1/2`
- `" "`
- `http://www.packtpub.com`

Typing any of these combinations into Microsoft Word followed by a space or a paragraph will usually result in Word automatically formatting them as follows:

- The two hyphens into a dash
- The fraction into a fraction character
- The straight quotes into smart quotes
- The internet path into a hyperlink

In many word processing situations, this behavior is both desirable and helpful, but not always. For example, when writing code, you will not want smart quotes. When handing in a bibliography or works cited page for school, typically, you will not want hyperlinks.

To adjust any of these settings, you can find this feature within Word's **AutoCorrect** settings area in the **Word Options** window. Perform the following steps:

1. Navigate to your **File** menu and click on **Options**.

    This will open your **Word Options** window at the **General** tab.

2. Click on the tab labeled **Proofing**:

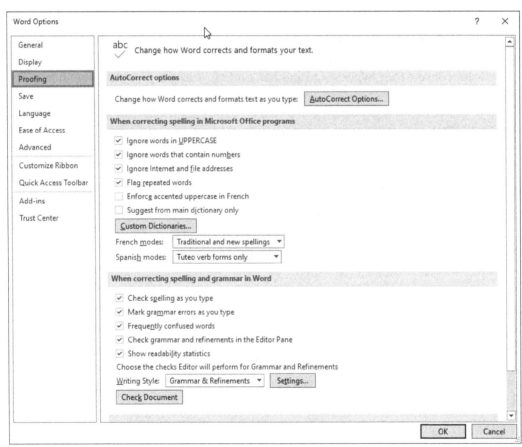

Figure 13.3 – The Word Options Proofing tab

3. In the area labeled **AutoCorrect options**, click on the **AutoCorrect Options…** button.

This will open the **AutoCorrect** options window at the **AutoCorrect** tab:

Figure 13.4 – The AutoCorrect window's AutoCorrect tab

4. Click on the tab labeled **AutoFormat As You Type** to view some of your **AutoFormat** options:

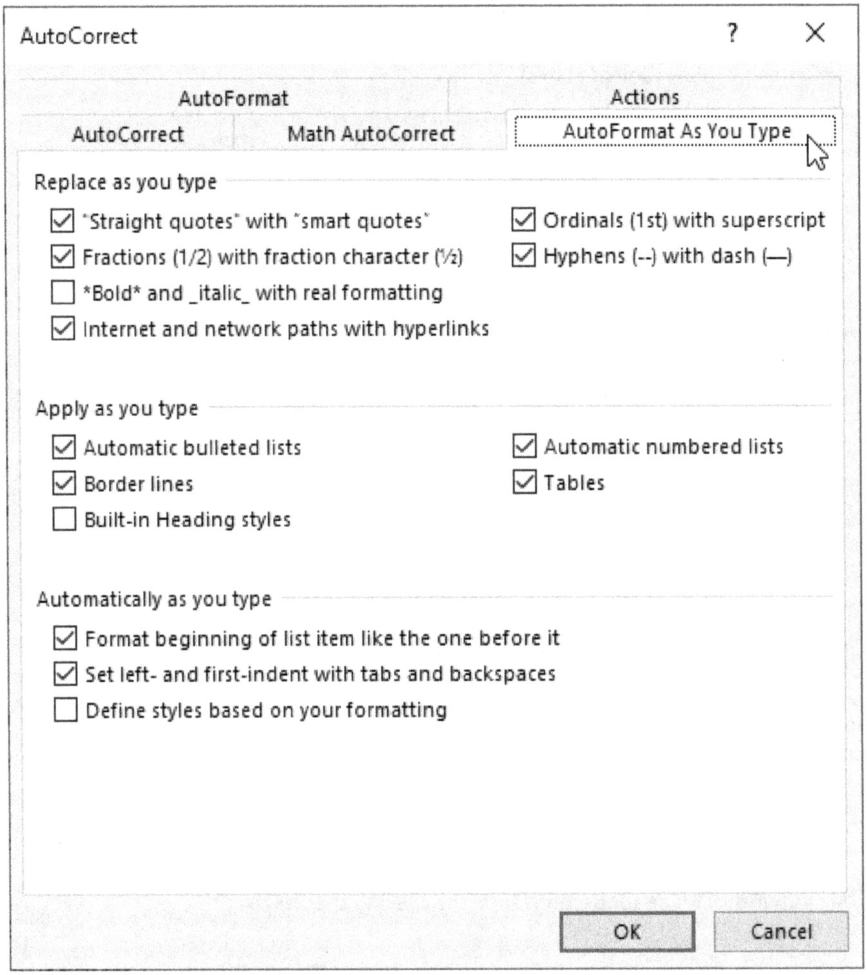

Figure 13.5 – The AutoFormat As You Type tab

From this tab, you will find all the options for what happens when Word automatically formats text *while you are typing*.

> **Important note**
>
> There is another tab inside the **AutoCorrect** window labeled **AutoFormat**; however, the options inside that tab (though, they are virtually the same options) will not control what happens while you are typing text. Those options only control the AutoFormat commands run from the **AutoFormat** button—a button that is hidden from the Ribbon and must be added to the **Quick Access** toolbar manually. As such, no one ever really uses this feature or even knows that it is there. Therefore, they get extremely confused when they see two **AutoFormat** tabs inside the **AutoCorrect** window.
>
> So, why is it there, you ask? Well, it is there in those rare instances when you receive a document from someone where they haven't formatted their document with options that you would typically find on the **AutoFormat As You Type** tab. Maybe they have these options turned off. Maybe they originally composed the document in a different word processing program. Whatever the reason, if you decide you want things formatted with smart quotes, as fraction characters, or anything else, you can choose the settings you like, add the **AutoFormat** button to your **Quick Access** toolbar, click on the button, and those changes will be applied to already typed text (as opposed to text that is currently being typed, which is what the other tab options are for). Yes, it is confusing to have two tabs with the same **AutoFormat** options. And yes, the options do different things. And yes, it can be frustrating.

From this tab, you can check and uncheck any setting you like.

5. Check the **Bold* and _italic_ with real formatting* option.
6. Click on **OK**.

Let's return to our blank document. Now, if we begin typing, all we need to do is surround anything we type with those characters. So, let's type the following sentence:

`*The quick brown fox jumped over the lazy dog*`. Take a look at the following screenshot:

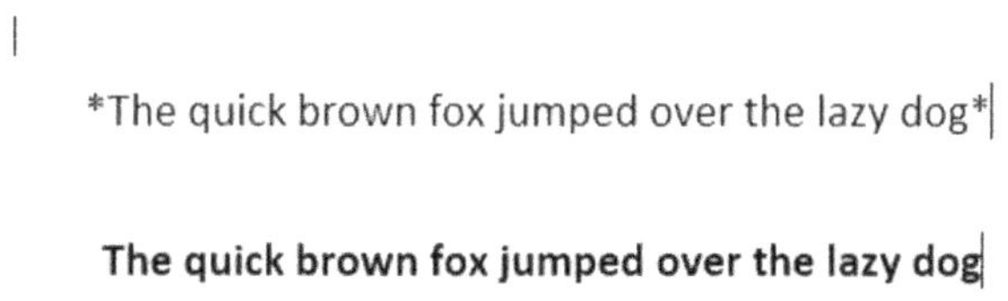

The quick brown fox jumped over the lazy dog|

The quick brown fox jumped over the lazy dog|

Figure 13.6 – AutoFormat to bold before and after

As you can see in *Figure 13.6*, the text inside the asterisks will be automatically converted into bold text. Similarly, if we surround the text with underscore characters, that text will be formatted with italics.

Changing how Word corrects and formats text automatically

In addition to being able to check on and off certain AutoFormat features from within the **AutoFormat As You Type** tab, you can also customize how Word fixes basic **AutoCorrect** options. You can turn AutoCorrect off summarily, or you can be more granular and create more specific exceptions to the AutoCorrect rules that are already in place.

Adding exceptions

To create an exception for any AutoCorrect rule, follow these steps:

1. Go to your **File** menu and click on **Options**.

   This will open your **Word Options** window at the **General** tab.

2. Click on the **Proofing** tab, and then click on **AutoCorrect Options**.

3. In the **AutoCorrect** window, click on the **AutoCorrect** tab.

4. Click on the **Exceptions…** button toward the right-hand side of the window:

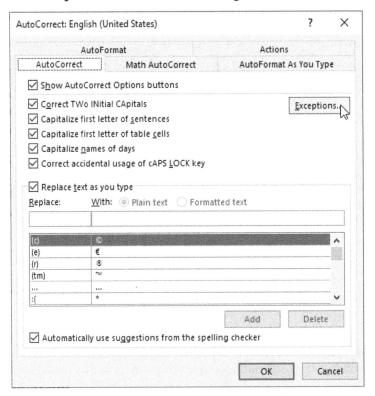

Figure 13.7 – The AutoCorrect Exceptions… button

5. In the **AutoCorrect Exceptions** window, you will see three tabs:

- **First Letter**

- **INitial CAps**

- **Other Corrections**

Each of these tabs corresponds to one or more rules (checkboxes) in the previous window:

- **Capitalize first letter of sentences**

- **Correct TWo INitial CApitals**

From each tab, you can create exceptions for each specific scenario. For example, for the **First letter** capitalization rule, there are certain instances where you wouldn't want Word to capitalize after typing in a certain combination of letters. Words in this list have been added to prevent Word from automatically capitalizing after these letter combinations:

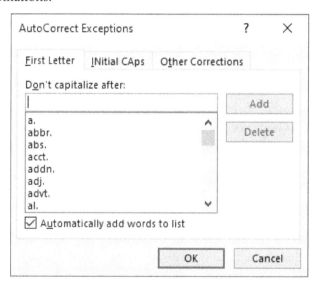

Figure 13.8 – First Letter exceptions

In the preceding screenshot, notice that the **Automatically add words to list** checkbox has been enabled. There are times when users might accidentally add words to this list unknowingly and then don't know where to go to remove that exception. This is where you would go.

6. To remove an exception that is giving you trouble, select the exception and click **Delete**.

7. To add an exception to a rule, type it into the box, and click on **Add**.

8. To apply the changes, click on **OK**.

The preceding steps and options will be very similar to your **INitial CAps** tab and the **Other Corrections** tab, too. By far, the most difficult aspect of this is attempting to troubleshoot the logic of what you need for your specific scenario in Word. Next, let's examine how to create custom keyboard shortcuts.

Creating custom keyboard shortcuts

If you don't have time to mess around creating a bunch of exceptions for **AutoCorrect** and **AutoFormat** (or you simply don't currently have the patience to deal with the logic required to create and master the puzzle that is Word's AutoCorrect rules and exceptions), you can simply turn off all your **AutoFormat** options and use simple keyboard shortcuts for your most-used punctuation and symbols that you need in Word. You can even create your own custom keyboard shortcuts if they do not exist already or if the ones that do exist are difficult to use or remember.

I'm not sure whether this is quicker, as it does require more memorization, but if you have a good memory and like keyboard shortcuts, this might be a good option. It does keep your fingers on the keyboard. However, in this method, we will be inserting symbols using keyboard shortcuts and learning how to customize those keyboard shortcuts from within Word.

Creating a custom keyboard shortcut by inserting symbols

This might seem like a very unusual place to go to create a keyboard shortcut. That's because it is. In fact, it hardly makes any sense at all; that is, unless you use a couple of symbols regularly and want to find a quicker way to insert them without having to constantly go to the buried **Symbols** menu to add them.

Let's say that you frequently use dashes in your writing. The keyboard only offers a hyphen, and you want to insert an en dash. To insert a symbol such as an en dash, perform the following steps:

1. Navigate to your **Insert** tab and click on the **Symbol** button:

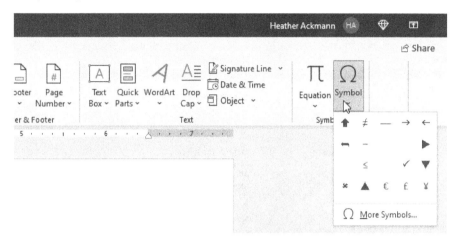

Figure 13.9 – Inserting symbols

This will open a symbol menu and display the most common or recently used symbols.

2. At the very bottom of the menu, click on the option labeled **More Symbols...** to open the **Symbol** window:

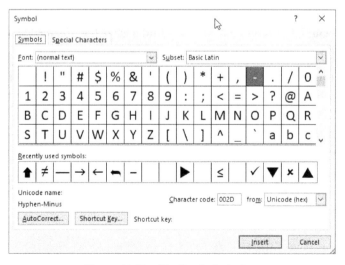

Figure 13.10 – The Symbol window

This will open the **Symbol** window at the **Symbols** tab and display all of the symbols for your normal text.

3.   Click on the tab at the top of the window named **Special Characters**:

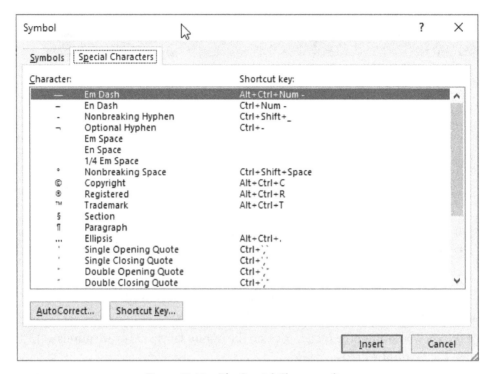

Figure 13.11 – The Special Characters list

4.   From the **Special Characters** list, you will find a large list of special characters and their assigned keyboard shortcuts.

Underneath the **Shortcut key** list, you will see that the em dash and en dash keyboard shortcuts have key combinations that use keys from the keyboard's number pad. That is what *Num* plus a symbol references—the number pad on your keyboard. For the en dash, pressing the *Ctrl* key plus the number pad hyphen key will create the en dash symbol.

However, if I was working from a keyboard that didn't have a number pad, that keyboard combination would be very difficult to use. So, in that case, I might want to change the shortcut key to something easier.

5. Select the **En Dash** keyboard shortcut and click on the **Shortcut Key...** option.

    This will open the **Customize Keyboard** window:

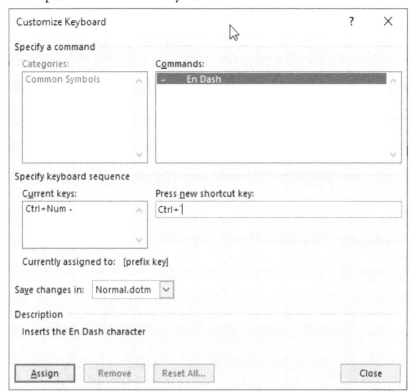

Figure 13.12 – Customize Keyboard

6. Here, you can assign a new keyboard combination inside the area labeled **Press new shortcut key:**. Just click inside that area and type out your key combination.

7. Click on **Assign** and then on **Close** when finished.

Now, you should be able to return to your document and try out your keyboard shortcut. Just select where you have typed in a hyphen, use the keyboard shortcut and watch Word replace your hyphen with an en dash:

The 2021–2022 school year must be better than the 2020-2021 school year.

Figure 13.13 – Keyboard shortcut for an en dash

Likewise, as you are typing, you can simply use the keyboard shortcut to insert an en dash whenever you like. In addition to creating a keyboard shortcut from the Insert Symbol window, you can also create keyboard shortcuts for any action in Word from your **Word Options** window.

Creating a keyboard shortcut from Word Options

If there is another command or action in Word, not just frequently used characters or symbols, that you'd like to assign a keyboard shortcut to, you can create keyboard shortcuts from your **Word Options** window as well. Follow these steps to learn how to do this:

1. Navigate to your **File** menu, select **Options**, and click on **Customize Ribbon**.

    That will open your **Word Options** window.

2. On the left-hand side of the screen, toward the bottom, next to the **Keyboard shortcuts** text, click on the **Customize…** option:

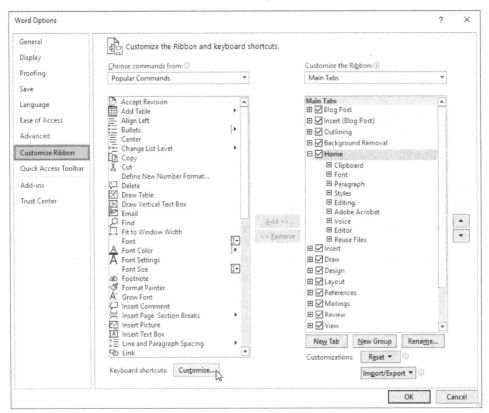

Figure 13.14 – Customizing keyboard shortcuts

This will open the **Customize Keyboard** window:

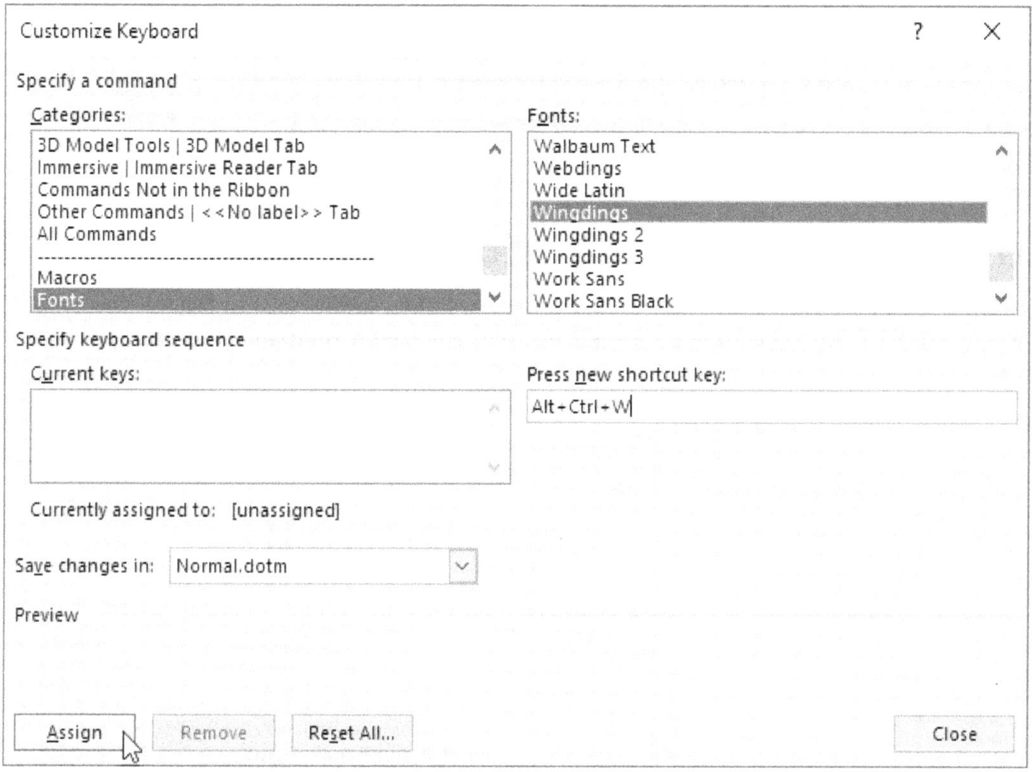

Figure 13.15 – The Customize Keyboard window

Word commands are located in the **Categories** section and are organized by the **Ribbon** tab. Toward the bottom, you will find options for **Commands Not in the Ribbon**, **Other Commands**, **All Commands**, and two additional categories for **Macros** and **Fonts**, too.

3. Scroll to the bottom and select the **Fonts** category.

4. In the **Fonts** section, scroll to the bottom and select the **Wingdings** font.

5. To assign this font a custom keyboard shortcut, click inside the box labeled **Press new shortcut key:** and type in ALT+Ctrl+W.

6. Click on **Assign**.

7. Close any open windows to return to your Word document.

Now, you should be able to try out your new keyboard short in any document. Just open a new document, type in ALT+CTRL+W, and watch your **Home** tab change from Calibri to Wingdings.

In addition to customizing keyboard shortcuts, other things that you can customize are your Office dictionaries. In the next section, we will discuss how you can find and customize these custom dictionaries.

Customizing custom dictionaries

Perhaps this has happened to you (because it has happened to me once or twice); you type in a word and see the red squiggly line and mean to right-click on it and hit the **Ignore All** button for this one document:

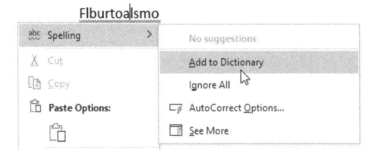

Figure 13.16 – Add to Dictionary from the right-click menu

Or perhaps you are in the **Editor** tool, checking a document's spelling, and instead of clicking through the suggestions or making a change, you accidentally hit the **Add to Dictionary** button instead:

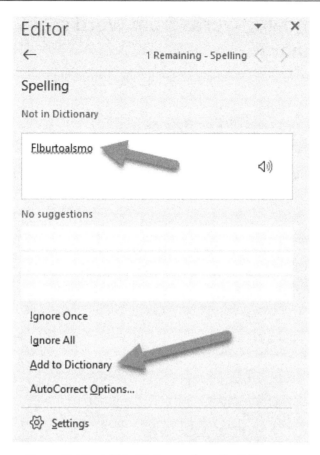

Figure 13.17 – Add to Dictionary from the Editor pane

Wherever you might be, when you accidentally hit that **Add to Dictionary** button, the problem is there isn't an undo option from either of these panes or windows. At least, it is not very apparent or obvious what to do. And although this isn't really automation per se, it is really an annoying issue that does sometimes happen. So, we thought we'd walk through this little tip here.

Adding or removing words from Word's custom dictionary

To remove a word that we've accidentally added to our custom dictionary, follow these steps:

1. Go to your **File** menu and click on **Options**.

    This will open your **Word Options** window at the **General** tab.

2. Click on the **Proofing** tab, and then click on the **Custom Dictionaries...** button:

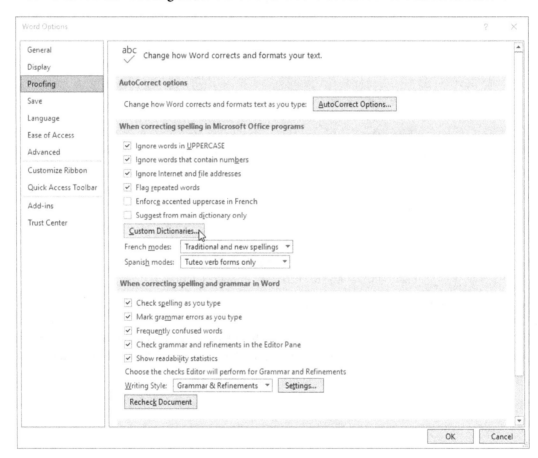

Figure 13.18 – The Custom Dictionaries... button

This will open up your **Custom Dictionaries** window and display all of the dictionaries that you have available in Office:

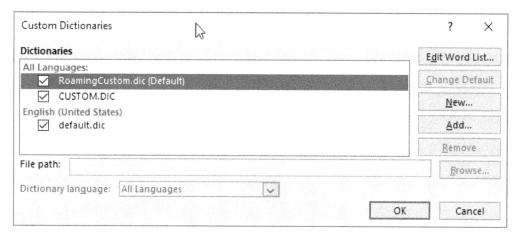

Figure 13.19 – Custom Dictionaries

In my copy of Office, I have three dictionaries listed, as follows:

- **RoamingCustom.dic (Default)**

- **CUSTOM.DIC**

- **default.dic**

RoamingCustom.dic is not an editable file that is saved on your computer but a cloud-based file that is associated with a Microsoft account. In other words, when you sign in with a Microsoft account, this is a roaming dictionary that is associated with your profile and travels with you across computers. Words added to this dictionary (which is why it is the default option) will travel with you automatically, as long as you sign in with the same Microsoft account. Likewise, any mistaken words added will also show up on and across all computers.

3. To edit **RoamingCustom.dic**, click on the dictionary to select it, and then click on the **Edit Word List...** button.

4. Scroll down until you find the word you accidentally added, select the word, and then click on the **Delete** button:

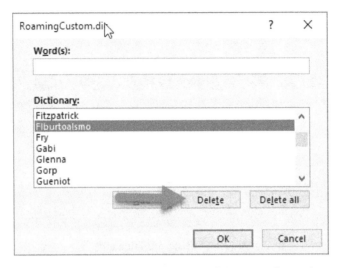

Figure 13.20 – The RoamingCustom.dic dictionary edit window

5. Click on **OK** and return to your document.

Your accidentally added word should now be removed from your roaming dictionary. If you were to type that word as you had typed it again in your Word document, Word would once again mark it as misspelled.

In addition to the previous example of removing accidentally added words from a custom dictionary, custom dictionaries are great for creating lists of specialized and hard-to-spell words or for remembering product names, employee or CEO names (think "Satya Nadella"), acronyms, and jargon. Rather than relying on **Autoformat As You Type**, sharing a company-wide custom dictionary might be an option to consider.

Summary

In this chapter, we highlighted a few common problem scenarios where several mostly automatic features that were designed to be helpful are, sometimes, unintentionally problematic. Most of these issues had to do with Word's AutoCorrect feature. However, the last issue we explored centered around one of Word's proofing tools. The **Add to Dictionary** button, though convenient, invites users to add words accidentally to the roaming dictionary but doesn't offer a way for them to easily undo the action—not without knowing exactly where to go and which dictionary in Word to edit. In this humble author's opinion, that's a design flaw.

So, this chapter demonstrated several methods and tips regarding how to work around these potential frustrations. We examined where to go to quickly edit our author name and initials in the case that our user profile was what Word was inserting incorrectly. We also discussed how to turn on and off certain **AutoFormat** controls and how to write exceptions to popular AutoCorrect rules. And for those times when you just want to go old- school, we discussed how to work around Word's automation features and insert symbols using keyboard shortcuts. We even discussed how to change some keyboard shortcuts if some were difficult to use or remember.

In the next chapter, we will discuss some other common points of frustration for new and veteran users of Word alike—Word's deceptively simple copy and paste options and how, sometimes, they just don't seem to do what we expect them to do.

14

Fixing Frustrating Numbers and Bullet Lists

We have already learned a great deal about lists earlier in this book. In this chapter, we aim to examine how lists can become problematic by looking at a few examples of common problems and how to resolve them.

We will start by looking at what can happen when copying a list from another source, such as Google Docs. Often, the source document may contain formatting that is not contained in the receiving document. This can cause issues with formatting, and we will explore some possible solutions to this.

Styles in Word documents may also be a cause of formatting issues. In this chapter, we will look at how formatting and styles can clash to cause issues with lists. We will also discuss how user error can be a contributing factor.

List styles can provide the solution to most list formatting problems. We will learn how to define a new list style. We will explore the formatting options and create a new list style that we can apply to any list in our document. Lastly, we will learn how to copy that list style into a new document so that it can be applied wherever we need it.

This chapter will cover the following main topics:

- Examining problems when copying lists
- The number or bullet looks different than the line text
- Defining a new list style
- Copying a list style to another document

Examining problems when copying lists

Today, it's not uncommon that you could receive business documents created with programs other than Microsoft Office. You may work with multiple programs. Sometimes, copying from one program to another can be problematic. Copying from one document to another of the same format does not always go well. Anytime you copy from another source, you can have issues with the formatting. Formatting can vary from document to document and in Word, formatting is often based on styles. As we have talked about in *Chapter 8, Saving Time and Ensuring Consistency with Styles*, styles are the best way to work in Word and lists are no exception.

In this section, we will look at the problems with trying to copy a list from Google Docs into a Microsoft Word document and ways we can avoid those problems. Generally, Word and Google docs are very compatible and most formatting can be successfully copied back and forth. However, lists can be difficult because Google Docs and Word use different bullet styles and formatting, as well as the underlying code. Let's take a look.

The following screenshot shows a bullet list that has been created in Google Docs:

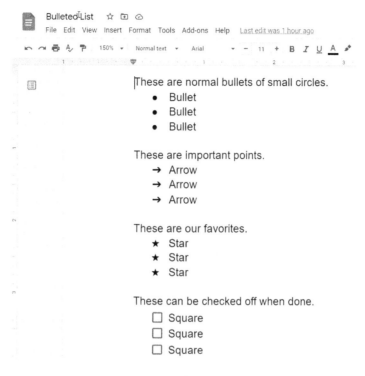

Figure 14.1 – Several lists in a Google Doc

Here is that same list, copied and pasted into a Word document:

Figure 14.2 – The same list copied into Word

As you can see, three of the bullet styles did not copy over. This is not because Word does not have these bullet styles – it does.

Google Docs does an excellent job of saving documents in the `.docx` format that's used by Word. One of the best ways to maintain the formatting of a Google Doc in Word is to save and download the Google Doc as a Word document and then open it in Word. I have downloaded the Google Doc I used in the previous example as a Word document; the following screenshot shows the result when I open it Word:

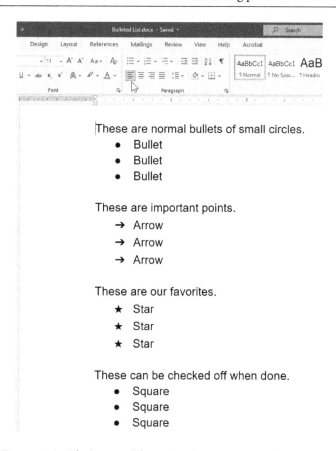

Figure 14.3 – The list saved from Google Docs as a Word document

As you can see, the results are much better than when we copied and pasted them, but it is still not perfect. The open squares in the last list weren't saved correctly. Why did this happen? Honestly, it could be for any number of reasons. I showed this to you so that you understand that when you copy from one format to another, you should not be surprised when you encounter some problems. The best way to resolve issues like these is to create and use styles in Word. If we encountered this problem, we could simply apply the list style we wanted quickly and easily to solve the issue. We discussed styles in detail in *Chapter 8, Saving Time and Ensuring Consistency with Styles* and will be looking specifically at list styles later in this chapter.

Occasionally, you might have encountered a situation where the bullets or numbers in a list appear different from the text in the rest of the line. This is another common problem with lists in Word. In this next section, we will look at why that can happen and how to resolve it.

The number or bullet looks different than the line text

Have you ever noticed that if you begin a line of text with the number 1 followed by a period, then it will create a numbered list? Or if you begin a line with an asterisk, it will create a bullet list? This happens because of a feature called **Auto Format As You Type** as you type. This same feature accounts for other things that may cause your lists to apply some formatting you're not expecting.

The following screenshot is an example of the number list appearing differently from the line text:

The Corporation's internal control over financial reporting includes those policies and procedures that:

1. Pertain to the maintenance of records that accurately and fairly reflect the transactions and dispositions of the assets of the Corporation.
2. Provide the reasonable assurance that transactions are recorded as necessary to permit preparation of financial statements in accordance with generally accepted accounting principles, and that receipts and expenditures of the Corporation are being made only in accordance with authorizations of management and directors of the Corporation.
3. Provide reasonable assurance regarding prevention or timely detection of unauthorized acquisition, use, or disposition of the Corporation's assets that could have a material effect on the financial statements.

Figure 14.4 – A numbered list

This could have been caused by the list being copied from another source incorrectly, or several other reasons. If we show the hidden formatting, we can tell exactly what is happening:

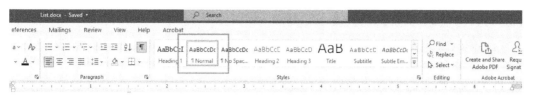

Figure 14.5 – The list with the hidden formatting marks revealed

Our insertion point is in the first line of text, so when we look at **Quick Styles Gallery**, we can see that a style has not been applied here – it's simply **Normal** text. This indicates that the user simply changed the font color. The user most likely hit *Enter* to create a new paragraph and began to type the list. If you look at the end of the first numbered list item, you will notice that the paragraph mark is the same blue as the first line, as are the next two.

What this seems to imply is that the user typed the first list item, and then attempted to change the font color to black – something I must admit I have done myself. Unfortunately, this only changed the selected text and not the paragraph mark. This would then continue with each list item, because of the **AutoFormat As You Type** feature. One way to correct this is to make sure that you have selected the paragraph marks when you change the font color. However, this entire situation could have been easily avoided if a list style had been applied to the list.

In these last two sections, we have seen examples of common problems with lists in Word, and doubtless, others occur. In the next section, we will learn how to define a new list style that we can apply whenever we need. This will help us resolve issues with troublesome lists quickly and easily.

Defining a new list style

Lists can be difficult to work with, and if you work with lists often, you should create list styles. This becomes even more important if you want to have a consistent list style for all your business documents. In this section, we will learn how to define a new list style.

If you want your lists to be anything other than the defaults, you should always use the **Multilevel List** option and create a custom list style. To define a list style, begin by clicking on the **Multilevel List** button. You will find it on the **Home** tab, in the **Paragraph** section of the Ribbon:

Figure 14.6 – The Multilevel List button

Once you click this button, the **List Gallery** area will appear. At the bottom, you will see **Define New List Style…**:

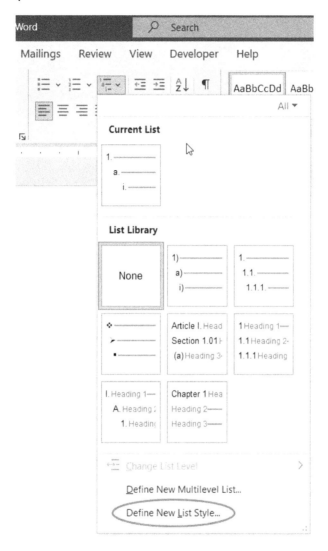

Figure 14.7 – The Define New List Style… option

Click on this and you will get the **Define New List Style** window:

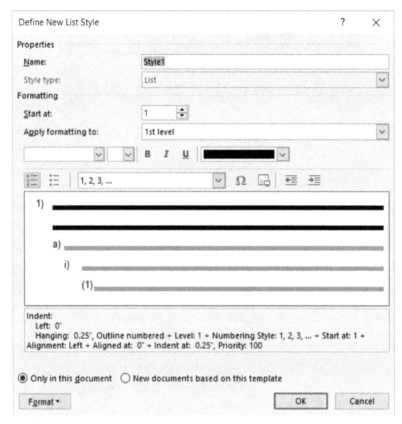

Figure 14.8 – The Define New List Style window

At this point, you will want to name your style. At the top of this window is a name box where you can add an appropriate name. Now, you can start to define your list style. However, I recommend clicking on the **Format** button in the lower-left corner. This will give you more options and more control over your new list style. When you click the **Format** button, you will see a menu of options that you can choose from to format your list style:

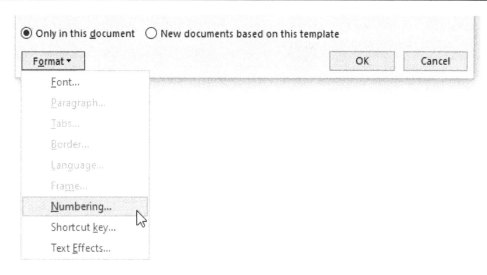

Figure 14.9 – The Format list

The **Format** list contains four options for list formatting.

- **Font**: This option controls the font, font style, size, color, underline, and other text effects.

- **Numbering**: This option gives us the tools to change bullet and number style, alignment, and indentation.

- **Shortcut Key**: This option will allow you to create a shortcut key for this style.

- **Text Effects**: This option gives you the ability to add text effects such as outline, fill, shadow, reflection, glow, and others to the text in your style.

For our example, we will limit ourselves to the numbering option. This is where you are likely to select most of the options for your list style:

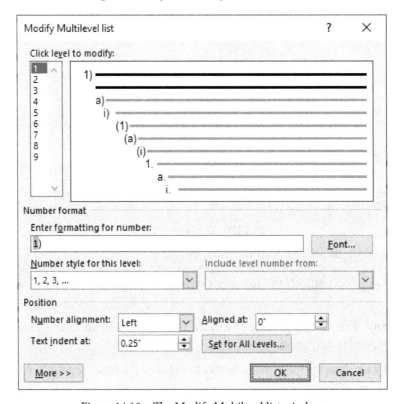

Figure 14.10 – The Modify Multilevel list window

You now have options to change the bullet or number style for all nine list levels. You can also change the number formatting, font, alignment, and indentation. Let's take a look at how to define a new list style and explore some of these options.

The top section is where you will select the list level you want to modify. On the left, you can see a column of numbers from 1 to 9. You can either click on a number from the column, or a level from the window on the right, to select the list level you want to modify. The list level will be highlighted in blue on the left, and a bold black line will be shown on the right. Now, whatever changes you make will be applied to that list level:

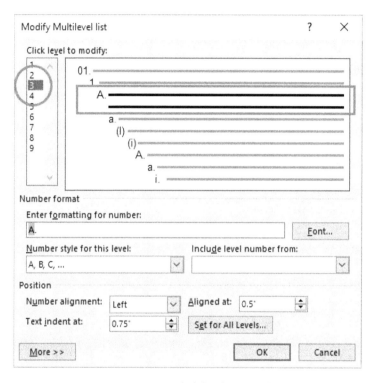

Figure 14.11 – Click level to modify

Below the **Click level to modify** section, you will see the **Number format** section. The first option is **Enter formatting for number**. This is a text box where you can add whatever punctuation or formatting you want around a number, such as a parenthesis or a period:

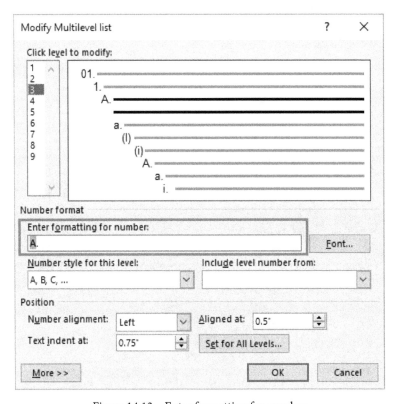

Figure 14.12 – Enter formatting for number

The next option is **Number style for this level**. This provides a drop-down list of styles that you can choose from, including **New Bullet** at the end of the list, so that you can select whatever you want from the fonts on your device:

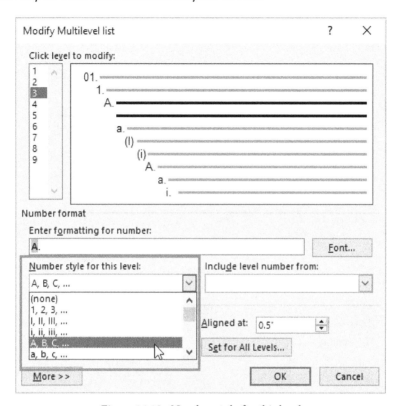

Figure 14.13 –Number style for this level

This style will be applied to the list level you have selected.

To the right of **Number style for this level**, you will find another drop-down menu called **Include level number from**. If you have any level selected other than level one, this will be available. This will let you add a level number to a list level, along with the number style for that level:

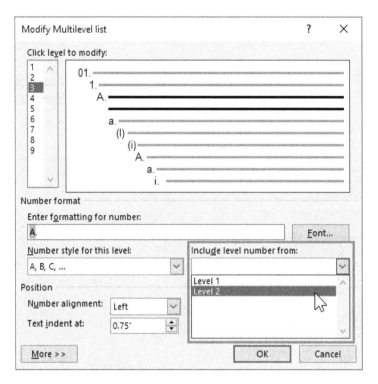

Figure 14.14 – The Include level number from dropdown

I have selected to include the level number from **Level 2**. The following screenshot shows an example of this applied to level three in my sample list:

01. Level 1
    1.   Level 2
    2.   Level 2
02. Level 1
    1.   Level 2
       1A. Level 3
       1B. Level 3
03. Level 1

Figure 14.15 – List with the level number included

Here, you can see that the level number from **Level 2** has been included in the **Level 3** number style. This is an excellent option for outlining.

The final section we are going to look at is the **Position** section, which can be found at the bottom of the window. This section deals with the position of each level of the list number and the text. Here, you will find options to set the alignment of the list level number and the distance the number is aligned at. You will also be able to set the distance the text indent will be from the list level number:

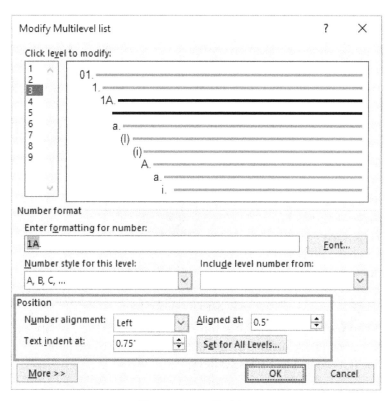

Figure 14.16 – Position

You can set the values for each list level separately. Alternatively, if you click the **Set for All Levels** button, you can set the options for the entire list:

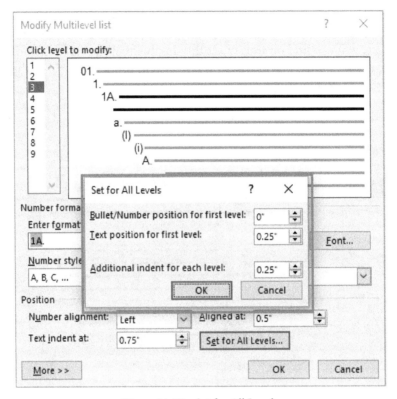

Figure 14.17 – Set for All Levels

Once you've defined your style, it will be automatically added to the **List Styles** section of the **List Gallery** area. I have defined a new multilevel list style and named it `Bill's List`; you can see it listed in **List Styles Gallery**:

Figure 14.18 – The new list style

This new list style is now saved to this document and can be applied whenever necessary. To modify this list style, right-click on it:

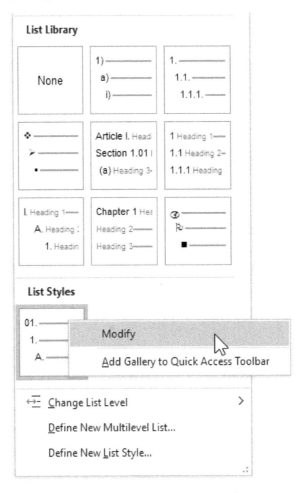

Figure 14.19 – Modifying a list style

The **Define List Style** window will now open, and you can make any changes to your list style. Once you have defined a list style, you may want to use it in another document. In the next section, we will discuss how to copy your list style and use it in another document.

Copying a list style to another document

If you are familiar with **Styles** in Word, you may already know how to import and export styles to other documents and templates. However, the list style that we previously defined is not the same type of style. If you look again at the **Define New List Style** window, you will not see the **Import/Export** button that you would see in the **Manage Styles** window. We can, however, copy a list style for use in another document.

To begin, we must have a list in the source document that has the style applied to it. Then, you need to copy at least the top level of that list. If you only want the list style and not the list, this is a great way to accomplish that. You will now need to go to the document you want to copy the list style to and prepare to paste the list. Place your insertion point where you want the list. From the **Home** tab of the document, in the **Clipboard** section, click on the bottom portion of the **Paste** button. You will see the **Paste Options** menu. The first option is **Keep Source Formatting (K)**. This is the option you want to click:

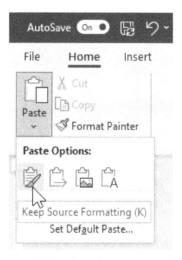

Figure 14.20 – Keep Source Formatting

You mustn't skip this step. Selecting the **Keep Source Formatting** option will ensure that all of your list formatting's will remain intact, and **List Style** will be added to **List Styles Gallery**. If you look at **List Styles Gallery** in the new document, you will see your list style. At this point, you can delete the list you pasted if you don't need it, and the list style will remain for you to use whenever you want it.

To apply a list style to list, you simply need to select the list and click on the list style in **List Style Gallery**. In the following screenshot, I have created a list and will apply the list style that I copied into this document:

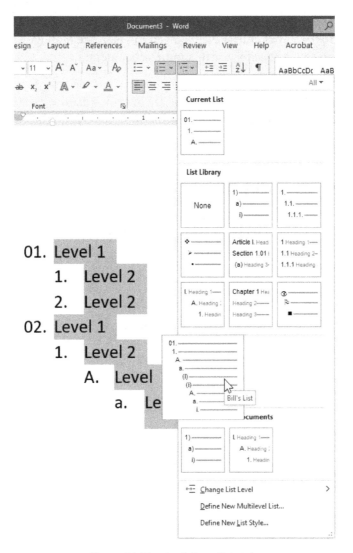

Figure 14.21 – Applying a list style

Applying a list style like this will change the current formatting of the list to the applied list style, giving you the formatting and list style that you desire.

Summary

We began this chapter by looking at some common problems with lists. We saw how a list copied from another format, such as Google Docs, might behave differently than we desire. We learned that downloading the document and saving it as a Word document was better, but still not a perfect solution. We also saw a list with formatting that was inconsistent because a previous style had been carried over to the list because of user error. Next, we explored how to define a list style, which can then be applied to a list and resolve those formatting issues. We also learned how to copy a list style to another document so that it can be used again. List styles are very powerful and can be the best way to resolve formatting issues with all types of lists. Once you've created a list style, you can use it whenever and wherever you need it.

In the last section, we learned about using the **Keep Source Formatting** option when copying a list style. In the next chapter, we will discuss the various paste options and what they do, depending on your document's theme and styles.

15
Stuck Like Glue – Word's Deceptively Simple Paste Options

Copying and pasting in a word processing program is one of the first things beginner students do in class—not only is it a seemingly simple thing to learn and to practice, but it is so darn useful. We reuse content all the time, and for quick on-the-spot decisions, copying and pasting chunks of content is an easy solution.

It's so popular that these commands get the most prime real estate in the **Microsoft Word** user interface—that is, they are in the very first group on the very first tab on the ribbon:

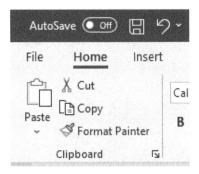

Figure 15.1 – Word's Clipboard group

This group, named the **Clipboard** group, does a bit more than simply copy and paste what you've selected though. In fact, the vast majority of users I've talked to don't at all realize what Word or other **Microsoft Office** programs can do when copying and pasting information. So, when problems do arise when pasting text or tables or pictures or information from some other place (and they sometimes will), users just don't know what to do. All they know is that something that seems so simple isn't working as they expect it should, and it's frustrating.

In many ways, this chapter is about discussing how a topic that seems simple on the surface is actually far more complex than it appears. In this chapter, you will learn more than you ever wanted to know about copying and pasting. We will cover the following topics in this chapter:

- Paste options
- The Word Clipboard
- Changing default paste options

This chapter won't cover every single problem you may encounter, or even all the paste options that you will find in Word (just those that seem simple but still trip up many users). However, it will give you the tools necessary to know where to go within Word when problems arise. But first, let's cover the common paste options that most users will see when pasting text into a Word document.

Paste options

To begin, whenever you paste something into Word, you may have already noticed this little button appear just below the text you pasted:

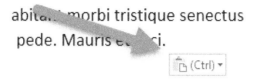

Figure 15.2 – Paste Options button

Then, after you continue typing, that button will disappear, never to appear again. If you happened to click on that button, however, you will notice a series of options related to how your text or whatever object you have copied is pasted:

Figure 15.3 – Paste Options icons

The problem for many users is that the options displayed are icons that are hard to decipher at first. To figure out what each icon means, users must hover their mouse over each icon, wait, and then read the tip text that appears briefly above their mouse.

> **Important Note**
>
> If these **Paste Options** buttons do not appear when you paste text into Word, go to your **File** menu, click on **Options**, and click on the **Advanced** tab. In the **Cut, Copy, and Paste** section, make sure the checkbox for **Show paste options button when content is pasted** is checked.

Not all paste options will appear for every copy action—only options that apply to content that has been copied will appear. In other words, depending on what content you copy, these options may change or have the potential to change every time you copy and paste, making the position of these icons different every time you see this menu.

The four most common options you will see are as follows:

- **Keep Source Formatting (K)**
- **Merge Formatting (M)**
- **Picture (U)**
- **Keep Text Only (T)**

With the **Paste Options** menu open or selected, you can choose any of these options by typing one of the keyboard shortcuts listed in parenthesis. As for what each of those options does, usually, it's the first two that people find the most confusing: Keep Source Formatting and Merge Formatting. If you don't use features like styles or themes, or even stick with Word's default themes and fonts, then you may not see any difference between these first two options. But if you do use your own custom themes and styles or are copying text from other sources outside of Word, then you may see strange formatting being brought into Word and some big differences between these various options, but not exactly what you want. Let's look into these paste options in more detail in the following sections.

Keep Source Formatting

This is the most confusing option for most people. I sometimes have to stop and think hard about it. You are copying information from a source, and that source looks a certain way. Maybe it has a special font or style, or a theme applied to the text.

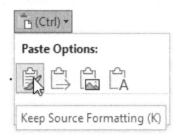

Figure 15.4 – Keep Source Formatting (K) option

This option tells Word that you want to keep that formatting and bring it over into your current document. Usually, this is the option that is selected by default. However, this is also usually the option that most companies do not want to be selected by default.

Most companies will have templates (or multiple templates, a lot of the time) that they will use across documents, and if you are anything like me, you are copying and pasting text from a variety of locations, including **Slack**, **Microsoft Teams**, **Google Docs**—wherever it is your team members and contractors are. If that's the case, you won't want your text to look like all these different platforms. You'll want your text to look the same and be consistent with the document you are pasting into.

That is not what this option does. This option will take the formatting from the copied text and bring it over into your new document alongside whatever you have in there, creating what I call a *frankindocument*. If you don't want a bizarrely formatted, cobbled-together *frankindocument*, then you might try the next option: Merge Formatting.

Merge Formatting

Merge Formatting uses the theme from the paste destination, as well as most options you'll see on Word's **Design** tab.

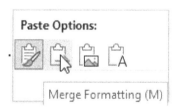

Figure 15.5 – Merge Formatting (M) option

It will also adopt any paragraph and line settings, and direct formatting and properties that immediately surround where you've pasted the text. The difference is, the copied text will keep any emphasis formatting. If there was bold or italics text, for example, that will stay the same. So, the Merge Formatting option is almost the best of both worlds. The document you are creating will still look like your document, in that your theme and fonts will remain untouched. However, any emphasis applied to your copied text will not be lost.

Picture

If you do not see this option on your copy of Word, this may be because you either do not have a subscription to **Microsoft 365** or you are not signed in with your subscription account. This option is currently only available with a Microsoft 365 subscription.

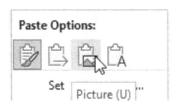

Figure 15.6 – Picture (U) option

As the name suggests, this option takes any text that you have copied and converts it to an image. When you paste that image, you will no longer be able to edit the text, but you can edit the picture as you do with any picture in Word. Just keep in mind that if you choose to go this route for whatever reason, you will need to add alt text, as users with visual impairments will not be able to read the image with their screen readers without this, and the **Paste Options** button does not automatically add alt text for you during the conversion process.

Keep Text Only

If you want to make a lot of changes to how your copied text is formatted, or if you are seeing a lot of garbage formatting in what you have copied, choosing this option strips all formatting from the copied text.

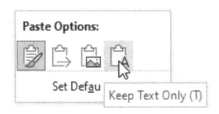

Figure 15.7 – Keep Text Only (T) option

It's like starting from scratch. Sometimes, you just need to start over. I use this option the most when copying content from my website or from other web portals or older programs that just don't seem to play nicely. This isn't as much of a problem as it used to be many years ago, but occasionally, it still pops up every once in a while.

Other options

Other paste options will appear from time to time depending on where and what you are copying and pasting. For example, there is an Office template you can download called **Career change checklist**, as shown in the following figure:

Figure 15.8 – Career change checklist template

When you copy and paste the checklist items, you will see a couple more paste options appear than the usual four options.

If you would like to follow along, you can download this template from Word. This template uses a lot of different styles, fonts, themes, and elements, which makes for an interesting copy/paste example to demonstrate. Here's one example for you:

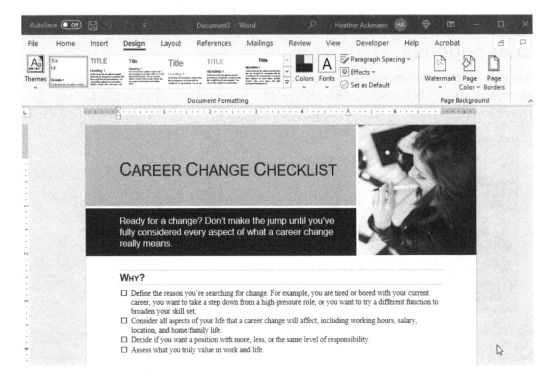

Figure 15.9 – Career change checklist template

In the next section, we're going to be using this template to practice pasting the content under the **Why?** section into another document and see what paste options appear.

Using destination styles

When we open the **Career change checklist** template, we can see at a glance that this template does not use the usual Office theme:

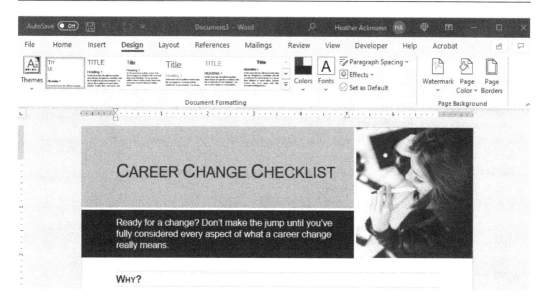

Figure 15.10 – Different theme

By clicking on the **Design** tab, you can see that the colors and fonts are clearly very different. To start, let's begin by copying the first checklist in this document:

1. Move your insertion point to just before the **Why?** heading, then, click and drag your mouse to select all four bullets in this section:

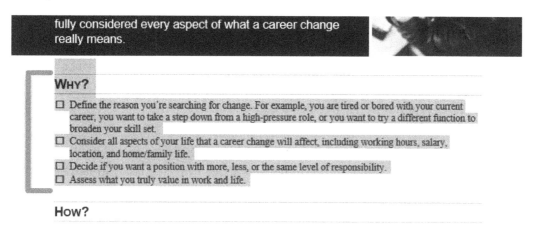

Figure 15.11 – Selecting the Why? bullets

2. Click the **Copy** button on your **Home** tab, or press *Ctrl + C* to copy your selection.

3. Open a new blank Word document.

4. Click the **Paste** button on the **Home** tab, or press *Ctrl + V* to paste your copied text:

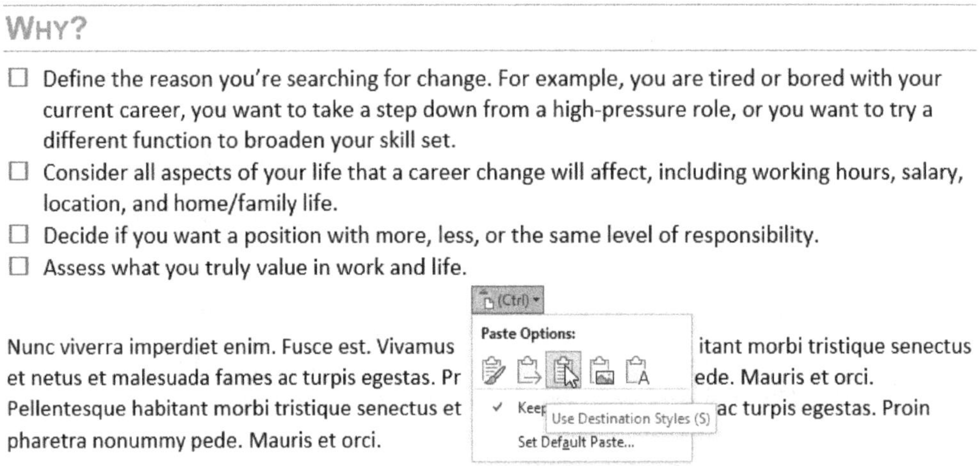

Nunc viverra imperdiet enim. Fusce est. Vivamus et netus et malesuada fames ac turpis egestas. Pr Pellentesque habitant morbi tristique senectus et pharetra nonummy pede. Mauris et orci.

itant morbi tristique senectus ede. Mauris et orci.
ac turpis egestas. Proin

Paste Options:

✓ Kee   Use Destination Styles (S)
Set Default Paste...

Figure 15.12 – New paste options

5. Click on the **Paste Options** button and hover your mouse over the **Use Destination Styles (S)** option.

    Notice how the copied text changes in appearance. Before, the headings were styled in a dark maroon color and the checkboxes were in a dark blue navy color. Now, the headings are bright orange and the checkboxes and bright blue. With the **Use Destination Styles (S)** option selected, the pasted text is matching our current document's styles. Since the copied text uses styles, those styles are not being stripped out. Rather, they are being updated to match the current document's style sheet.

6. Now, hover your mouse over the **Paste Options** menu's **Merge Formatting (M)** icon.

    Choosing the **Merge Formatting** option removes any headings that were with the copied text. But, if the headings were styled with emphasis formatting, such as bold or italics, those formatting options will remain:

Why?

☐   Define the reason you're searching for change. For example, you are tired or bored with your current career, you want to take a step down from a high-pressure role, or you want to try a different function to broaden your skill set.

☐   Consider all aspects of your life that a career change will affect, including working hours, salary, location, and home/family life.

☐   Decide if you want a position with more, less, or the same level of responsibility.

☐   Assess what you truly value in work and life.

Nunc viverra imperdiet enim. Fusce est. Vivamus   itant morbi tristique senectus et netus et malesuada fames ac turpis egestas. Pr   ede. Mauris et orci. Pellentesque habitant morbi tristique senectus et   es ac turpis egestas. Proin pharetra nonummy pede. Mauris et orci.

Figure 15.13 – Merge Formatting (M) option

7.   Click on one of the checkboxes:

Figure 15.14 – Content control

This template uses content controls for its checkboxes, and when we pasted this list over, we also received an additional option in our **Paste Options** menu regarding these content controls:

Figure 15.15 – Keep Content Controls

Underneath our **Paste Options** menu's icons, we have a **Keep Content Controls** toggle that we can turn on and off for whether or not we want to keep our content controls.

8.   Click on the checkbox next to the **Keep Content Controls** toggle to toggle this feature off.

Now, if you click the checkboxes, they are no longer checkable content controls. They have been converted to simple symbols.

So, that is a quick demonstration of how copying and pasting different kinds of text can give you different paste options. In the next section, we will discuss faster ways to paste, including pasting things you've copied not so recently.

The Word Clipboard

Many users who are new to Word have no idea that once they've copied something in Word, Word tracks and remembers what was copied for a short while. In fact, if you want to reuse something you've copied recently, you can do so from a feature within Word called the Clipboard.

You can open the Clipboard from your **Home** tab by clicking on the tiny arrow in the lower right-hand corner of the **Clipboard** group:

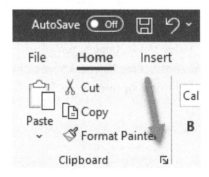

Figure 15.16 – Clipboard button

Clicking that button will open the **Clipboard** pane to the left of your screen:

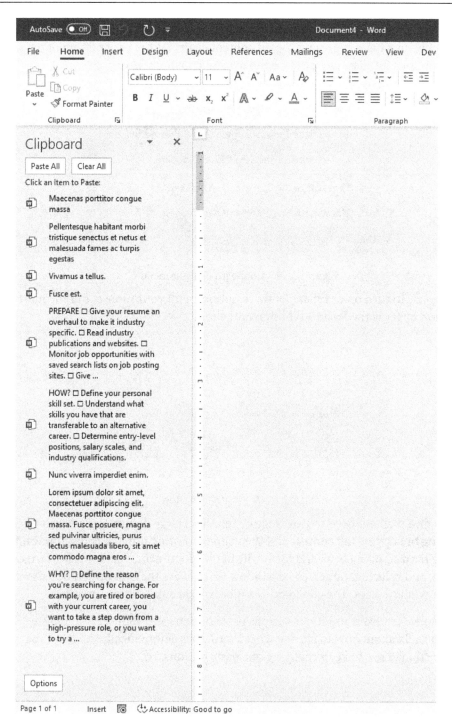

Figure 15.17 – Clipboard pane

This pane will display everything you have copied, including text and pictures, and allow you to quickly insert and reuse any copied content again. At the very bottom of the pane, you'll find options for displaying the Clipboard and copying status:

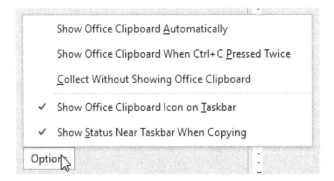

Figure 15.18 – Clipboard Options menu

You can choose to turn on or off any of these options with your mouse. But the most useful option by far is the **Paste All** button at the top:

Figure 15.19 – Paste All button

If you ever find that you need to rearrange or reorder a large document, you can easily do so by cutting or copying the content and then simply pasting it in the order you want it in. If you have tried scrolling back and forth within one document, you know how frustrating that can be, and splitting the screen or window isn't always the best option because it limits both window sizes. The clipboard is a nice workaround in this situation.

So, now that we've talked about our various paste options and some easy and faster ways to paste, let's talk about how to change what Word does automatically the first time we paste, so we don't have to keep changing our paste options.

Changing default paste options

If you collaborate with others and have strict formatting guidelines you must follow, then the chances are you won't want to keep destination formatting too often. In fact, it will probably be very rare. Most of the time, you will more than likely want to merge formatting or use destination styles. For that, you will want to change what Word uses as its default paste options.

To change the default paste options, follow these steps:

1. Go up to your **File** menu, click on **Options**, and click on the **Advanced** tab.

2. Scroll down to the **Cut, copy, and paste** section:

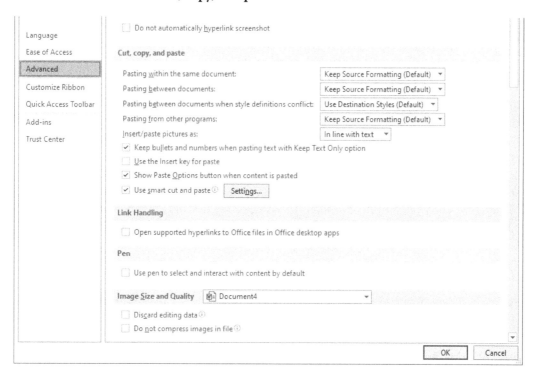

Figure 15.20 – Cut, Copy, and Paste section

3.   Update your paste options and click **OK**.

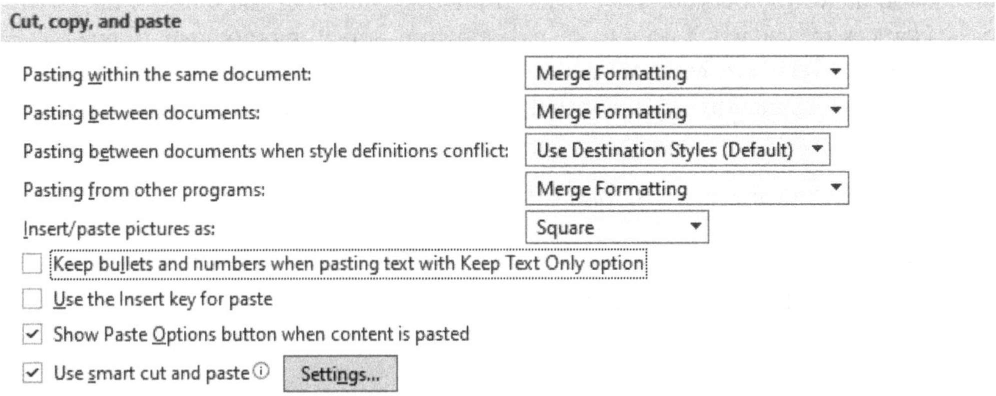

Cut, copy, and paste

Pasting <u>w</u>ithin the same document:	Merge Formatting ▼
Pasting <u>b</u>etween documents:	Merge Formatting ▼
Pasting b<u>e</u>tween documents when style definitions conflict:	Use Destination Styles (Default) ▼
Pasting <u>f</u>rom other programs:	Merge Formatting ▼
<u>I</u>nsert/paste pictures as:	Square ▼

☐ Keep bu<u>l</u>lets and numbers when pasting text with Keep Text Only option

☐ <u>U</u>se the Insert key for paste

☑ Show Paste <u>O</u>ptions button when content is pasted

☑ Use <u>s</u>mart cut and paste ⓘ   Settin<u>g</u>s...

Figure 15.21 – Updated options

Not all paste options will be available. In the preceding screenshot, you will notice that I've changed my options to **Merge Formatting** for the **Pasting within the same document**, **Pasting between documents**, and **Pasting from other programs** drop-down menus. I've kept the default use destination styles option for the **Pasting between documents when style definitions conflict** drop-down menu (that is the only time when that option is available). I've also cleared the **Keep bullets and numbers when pasting text with Keep Text Only option** checkbox. If you have ever copied and pasted a bulleted list and chosen the **Keep Text Only (T)** option and been surprised to see this ugly bullet character left behind (that isn't a real bullet), unchecking this option will remove that ugliness.

Summary

Despite all that we covered in this chapter, shockingly, we didn't cover everything there is to know about copying and pasting in Word. But for most business professionals, the information covered in this chapter will suffice. For most users, figuring out which paste options to use and when is the most difficult task. That is, assuming they see those options appear in the first place. Other tools such as the Word Clipboard and changing default paste options are really more for power and pro Word users.

If you ever get stuck with anything in Word (not just with copying and pasting), there is an entire community of fellow Office users like you—business professionals, academics, teachers, students, and retirees—who would love to help answer any questions you may have.

One great place to go on the web for help is the **Microsoft Community** forums:

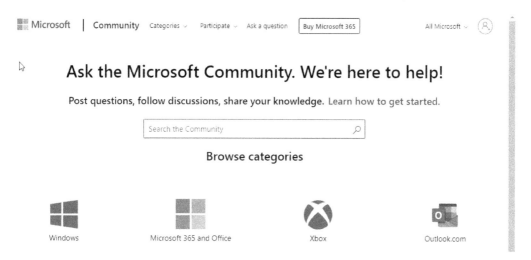

Figure 15.22 – Microsoft Community forums

Many of the people who answer questions on these forums are volunteer moderators, not paid Microsoft employees. You will occasionally find Microsoft staff on this site, but the heartfelt and empathetic answers normally come from real people in the community like you.

Here is the Microsoft Community page:

```
https://answers.microsoft.com/
```

You can post questions and answers by logging in with your Microsoft account. I highly recommend this site for when you get stuck.

Thank you so much for reading this book, and we'll see you on the forums!

Other Books You May Enjoy

If you enjoyed this book, you may be interested in these other books by Packt:

LaTeX Beginner's Guide

Stefan Kottwitz

ISBN: 978-1-80107-865-8

- Make the most of LaTeX's powerful features to produce professionally designed texts
- Download, install, and set up LaTeX and use additional styles, templates, and tools
- Typeset math formulas and scientific expressions to the highest standards
- Understand how to include graphics and work with figures and tables
- Discover professional fonts and modern PDF features
- Work with book elements such as bibliographies, glossaries, and indexes
- Typeset documents containing tables, figures, and formulas

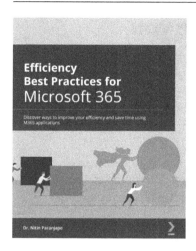

Efficiency Best Practices for Microsoft 365

Dr. Nitin Paranjape

ISBN: 978-1-80107-226-7

- Use different MS 365 tools such as Office desktop, Teams, Power BI, Lists, and OneDrive to increase work efficiency
- Identify time-consuming processes and understand how to make them more efficient
- Create professional documents quickly with minimal effort
- Work across multiple teams, meetings, and projects without email overload
- Automate mundane, repetitive, and time-consuming manual work
- Manage work, delegation, execution, and project management

Packt is searching for authors like you

If you're interested in becoming an author for Packt, please visit `authors.packtpub.com` and apply today. We have worked with thousands of developers and tech professionals, just like you, to help them share their insight with the global tech community. You can make a general application, apply for a specific hot topic that we are recruiting an author for, or submit your own idea.

Hi!

We are Heather Ackmann and Bill Kulterman, authors of *Microsoft 365 Word Tips and Tricks*. We really hope you enjoyed reading this book and found it useful for increasing your productivity and efficiency in Microsoft Word.

It would really help us (and other potential readers!) if you could leave a review on Amazon sharing your thoughts on *Microsoft 365 Word Tips and Tricks*.

Go to the link below or scan the QR code to leave your review:

`https://packt.link/r/1800565437`

Your review will help us to understand what's worked well in this book, and what could be improved upon for future editions, so it really is appreciated.

Best Wishes,

Heather Ackmann   Bill Kulterman

Index

O

object anchors
  working with 285-291
OneDrive
  about 22
  used, for accessing Word documents 33
  Word documents, saving to 23, 24

P

page break
  creating 172
Page break before option 370
page numbers
  adding, to footer 181
  formatting 183, 184
page orientations
  creating 174
  modifying 174-178
pages
  numbering 178, 179
pagination
  about 366
  Keep lines together option 369
  Keep with next option 367, 368
  Page break before option 370
  Widow/Orphan control 366, 367
paragraph return mark 159, 160
Paragraph settings window
  Set As Default button 362-364
paragraph style
  about 190
  applying 190, 191
  headings, for screen readers 191, 192
  heading styles, managing 192-198
  Normal style 190
  Outline view 192, 193

paste options
  about 423, 424
  Keep Source Formatting 424, 425
  Keep Text Only 426
  Merge Formatting 425
  other options 427, 428
  Picture 426
pictures
  inserting 263-266
Print Layout 89

Q

Quick Parts gallery
  about 117
  exploring 117-121
  text, saving to 122-124
Quick Styles
  about 186
  applying 188-190

R

Reading View
  about 89
  Print Layout view, obtaining 92
  switching to 89-92
resume cover letter 106
review mode
  using 301

S

scan mode 301
section break
  creating 173
  inserting 175

CPSIA information can be obtained
at www.ICGtesting.com
Printed in the USA
LVHW051056190222
711543LV00012B/729

9 781800 565432